TOTEMS AND TEACHERS

SOAS LIBRARY
WITHDRAWN

D1427729

18 0930006 X

TOTEMS AND TEACHERS

Key Figures in the History of Anthropology

Second Edition

Edited by
SYDEL SILVERMAN

ALTAMIRA
PRESS

ROWMAN & LITTLEFIELD PUBLISHERS, INC.

Walnut Creek • Lanham • New York • Toronto • Oxford

ALTAMIRA PRESS
A Division of Rowman & Littlefield Publishers, Inc.
1630 North Main Street, #367
Walnut Creek, CA 94596
www.altamirapress.com

Rowman & Littlefield Publishers, Inc.
A wholly owned subsidiary of The Rowman & Littlefield Publishing Group, Inc.
4501 Forbes Boulevard, Suite 200
Lanham, MD 20706

PO Box 317
Oxford
OX2 9RU, UK

Copyright © 2004 by ALTAMIRA Press

All rights reserved. No part of this publication may be reproduced,
stored in a retrieval system, or transmitted in any form or by any
means, electronic, mechanical, photocopying, recording, or otherwise,
without the prior permission of the publisher.

British Library Cataloguing in Publication Information Available

Library of Congress Cataloging-in-Publication Data

Totems and teachers: Key figures in the history of anthropology/
edited by Sydel Silverman. Second edition.
     p. cm.
Includes bibliographical references and index.
  ISBN 0-7591-0459-X (hardcover : alk. paper) — ISBN 0-7591-0460-3
(pbk. : alk. paper)
  1. Anthropology—History. 2. Anthropologists. I. Silverman, Sydel.

  GN17.T69 2003
  301'.092'2—dc21
                    2003012186

Printed in the United States of America

∞™ The paper used in this publication meets the minimum requirements of
American National Standard for Information Sciences—Permanence of Paper
for Printed Library Materials, ANSI/NISO Z39.48-1992.

SOAS LIBRARY

For our students

CONTENTS

PREFACE

Over twenty years have passed since this book first appeared. Its republication seemed merited because, although it had gone out of print in 1995, it was still widely consulted, and it remains one of a very limited number of works that attempt to link biography, social context, and theoretical development in the lives of major figures in the history of anthropology.

The selection of figures included in the book was not an attempt to fully represent the field in the twentieth century, nor did the choice mean that these individuals were deemed to be of greater importance than all of their contemporaries. The book was an outgrowth of a lecture series held at the City University of New York Graduate Center in 1976, at a time of financial crisis in the university and the city. The subjects of the lectures were determined by the availability of anthropologists, mainly in the New York area, who were willing to participate (without payment) and the people they were prepared to talk about, given the series' theme that each lecture would be presented by someone who knew the subject personally. Had the figures been chosen more deliberately, others would certainly have been included, and the selections would have gone much further beyond American anthropology than the sole chapter on Bronislaw Malinowski. Even within the American sphere there are glaring omissions, among them Edward Sapir, Robert Lowie, and A. R. Radcliffe-Brown (placed here in the American sphere because of his influential sojourn at the University of Chicago). Moreover, the decision had been made to limit the lecture subjects to those no longer living—hence, the absence of several noted anthropologists of the period who would have been likely choices. One of those omissions, that of Margaret Mead (who died in 1978), is rectified in the current edition.

Since the original publication, five of the eight contributors have themselves died: Alexander Lesser in 1982, Robert Murphy in 1990, Stanley Diamond in 1991, Eric Wolf in 1999, and Raymond Firth in 2002 (at the venerable age of 101). Of those still alive, all except Robert Carneiro have retired. The contributors to the volume thus represent a generation of anthropologists of the latter twentieth century that is now taking its own place in the history of the discipline. If one of the purposes of the book was to offer a two-layered perspective on anthropology's history, that purpose is better fulfilled in the present edition, which carries forward the biographical sketches of the contributors up to the present or to the time of their deaths. Perhaps a succeeding volume will be written about the contributors by anthropologists of the third generation who knew them.

In the past twenty years there has been a significant growth of interest in the history of anthropology, as seen, for example, in the History of Anthropology thematic volumes edited since 1983 by George W. Stocking Jr. (who has been succeeded by Richard Handler); a book series, Critical Studies in the History of Anthropology, initiated recently by Regna Darnell; and one or two newsletters on the history of the field. Some important new biographies of key figures have appeared or are forthcoming, among them Douglas Cole's on Franz Boas (1999), Darnell's on Edward Sapir (1990) and on several other of the Americanists (2001), Judith Modell's on Ruth Benedict (1983), Stocking's on Sol Tax (2000) and Clyde Kluckhohn (only a sample of Stocking's continuing prodigious output), Sally Cole's on Ruth Landes, Virginia Kerns's on Julian Steward, William Peace's on Leslie White, and others no doubt in preparation. A collection of papers on anthropologists who pioneered the study of education, modeled after the present book, is being edited by Jill Cherneff and Eve Hochwald. Interviews with senior figures have become standard features of several journals, and the recording of oral histories has advanced apace, both as part of systematic projects such as that of the Wenner-Gren Foundation and opportunistically by interested individuals. Moreover, anthropologists have become more conscious of the potential historical significance of the documents of their own professional lives, and an institutional structure—the Council for the Preservation of Anthropological Records, or CoPAR—has been created to encourage and coordinate the archiving of unpublished papers and other materials (see Parezo, Fowler, and Silverman 2003).

Despite this growing interest, we have not yet achieved the promise of an anthropological history of anthropology. We have seen only the beginnings of analytical treatments of the social networks within which anthropologists have worked, of the histories of significant institutions, or of the larger contexts that have shaped anthropological practice and ideas. Nor have we gone very far toward answering the vexing question of the extent to which the personal and the professional are linked in the lives and works of our leading figures. This book came in for some criticism for seeming too ready to attribute facets of the work to the biographies. In my judgment, however, the effort to draw such connections is legitimate, indeed important. If anything, the book failed more by hesitancy to do so than by overreaching.

In this edition, most of the original contributions have been retained intact, as have the edited discussions that followed six of the lectures. However, the chapter on Robert Redfield was revised to include a paper by Eric Wolf, and the Nathaniel Tarn contribution was abridged to allow for this double perspective on the subject. The paper on White was also shortened for consistency with the other chapters. A new chapter was added on Margaret Mead, this one as a double perspective too: a biographical sketch by her close colleague and friend Rhoda Metraux (previously published in the *American Anthropologist*) and a paper by the editor of this book, who was a student and New York acquaintance of Mead. In addition, all of the biographical notes on the contributors were updated.

My major debt of gratitude is to the authors, who contributed to the lecture series with generosity and verve and who edited their lectures for publication. The participants in the discussions did much to bring the ancestral figures to life, and I thank them again for agreeing to have their comments extracted for the book. Sidney Mintz, Robert Carneiro, and Nathaniel Tarn kindly consented to the republication and provided me with current biographical information. Mitch Allen of AltaMira Press saw enough value in the book to sponsor a new edition. Several people helped in the process of obtaining new photographs for this edition and permissions for reprinting those previously used; they are acknowledged in the photo credits.

By the consensus of the contributors, the original edition was dedicated to "our students." They were the inspiration for the lectures and the source of our zeal for expanding, rethinking, and conveying our knowledge of our disciplinary history. Many of them are now teachers and researchers themselves, and another generation has succeeded them as students. Those contributors who will not see the reissue of their writings would surely endorse our dedication of this edition, as well, to our students, both those whom we taught directly and others who may learn from the recounting of our experience of the history of anthropology.

INTRODUCTION TO
THE FIRST EDITION (1981)

That the development of theory is a social process, a product of life histories embedded in time and place, is a principle that most anthropologists take as axiomatic. Yet the rapid expansion of anthropology over the past thirty years and the necessity of simplifying its ideas for teaching purposes have produced a standardized treatment of the history of anthropological theory—as seriated "isms," concepts, and names of notables divorced from the social and personal contexts out of which they emerged. As anthropological theory becomes codified in this manner and as each generation of anthropologists and students becomes further removed from the seminal figures of the field, an understanding of their work as part of a life, a career, a personality, and a social and cultural setting becomes more and more elusive.

The process of theory making in anthropology has not received the scrutiny that has been given to fieldwork, which has been examined in a now-long series of personal accounts aimed at demystification of "the field." But if we understand little of the theory-making process itself, to recover it in the figures of the past is a task bedeviled by traps. The reader of today sees order and consistency in a life's work but misses the contradiction and serendipity, sees "forerunners" of trends that come to light only in retrospect, overemphasizes influences that are credited in print and neglects others that are not. For some figures biographies are written, but rarely are these read or taught as an integral part of the theories themselves.

It was out of a discussion among some anthropologists at the City University of New York (CUNY), early in 1976, of this growing separation of anthropological theory from its own human background that this volume originated. A few

years before, in 1971, Raymond Firth had given a lecture on Bronislaw Malinowski to an audience of anthropologists at the New York Academy of Sciences.
Firth presented the talk as a personal recollection, not intended as a serious
theoretical treatment (and he declined to have it published in the Academy's
annals). Yet the audience was electrified, and many remembered that lecture as
the most useful means they had encountered for understanding Malinowski's
anthropology. Firth's talk became the inspiration for a lecture series, "Recon-
sidering the Ancestors," that was held at the CUNY Graduate Center between
February and December 1976.

Seven anthropologists were invited to discuss the life and work of a major
figure whom they had studied under, worked with, or otherwise known. Since
no one could be paid honoraria or travel expenses—the city and the university
were then in the depths of fiscal crisis—friends and associates in the New York
area were called on. The only guideline given was the purpose of the series: to
convey a sense of how ideas grow out of personal biographies. Inevitably, however, each speaker also reassessed the contribution of his "ancestor" in the light
of the present state of anthropology, and in the process each underlined his own
views and some of the themes of his own work. The papers thus presented a
picture of the development of anthropology at two levels: the formative figures
of professional anthropology, and those of the next generation who have recast
their predecessors' influence into the concerns of contemporary anthropology.

Each lecture was followed by a discussion. The audience always included
other anthropologists who had known the "ancestor" and who as often as not
held views quite different from those of the speaker. The living, and sometimes
combative, quality of theoretical development came out vividly in these discussions, providing some corrective to tendencies toward excessive praise of an admired teacher or overemphasis on the themes selected to organize a lecture.

Attendance at and enthusiasm for the lectures exceeded all expectations.
Ironically, the backdrop to this demonstration of the vigor of anthropology was
an attempt on the part of the senior administration of CUNY to eliminate the
subject from most of the undergraduate curricula. On the day of the opening
lecture, the university chancellor announced a plan for reorganizing the liberal
arts, in which anthropology (along with geology, foreign languages, and several
other subjects) was declared "nonessential." Anthropology was the only field to
respond to this assessment with a unified opposition that enlisted the profession nationwide and across institutional lines of all kinds. On the day of the final lecture of the series, the chancellor's plan was laid to rest.

This collection presents, obviously, only a partial and highly selective view of
the history of anthropology. Several eminent anthropologists, who would immediately spring to mind in any listing of "ancestral" figures, are not represented. The explanation for this is historical, not evaluative. The persons who
appear in the book—as subjects, authors, and discussants—are linked primarily
through the institutional structure of anthropology in New York City.

Institutional anthropology in New York City began with the American Museum of Natural History. Soon after its founding in 1869, the museum created archaeological and ethnological divisions to gather and care for collections, but it was in 1894 under the impetus of president Morris K. Jesup (organizer of the Jesup Expedition of 1897) that the anthropology department became established. Frederick Ward Putnam of Harvard was brought in to head it. In 1895 Franz Boas joined the museum as an assistant curator. After he began teaching at Columbia the following year, Boas formed a close association between the Columbia department and the museum; that association was continued by Clark Wissler, his student and successor as curator. The museum provided the only available research funds and fieldwork opportunities at the time, and most of Boas's students of the first generation gained some of their training there. The museum was also the home institution of the most famous of New York anthropologists, Margaret Mead (who taught at Columbia in an adjunct status). Among the present members of the museum staff is a contributor to this volume, Robert Carneiro.

The Columbia department is the primary connection among the anthropologists who appear in this book. Several got their Ph.D.s under Boas in the first decade of the century, including Alfred Kroeber, Robert Lowie, Paul Radin, and Alexander Goldenweiser. After World War I and until his retirement in 1936, Boas trained another group of students, among them Ruth Benedict, Alexander Lesser, Margaret Mead, Ruth Bunzel, and Gene Weltfish. With Boas's retirement, the one-man dominance of the department gave way to a pattern of polarities between the most influential faculty members. The first of these polarities was that between Ruth Benedict and Ralph Linton. Benedict, still an assistant professor without tenure, was acting chairman at the time of Linton's appointment to Boas's professorship in 1937, and for the rest of their association in the department they maintained a hostile competition. The appointment of Linton, a Harvard Ph.D., was a break in the Boasian tradition at Columbia; president Nicholas Murray Butler, determined that Boas not name his successor, designated a university committee to recommend a candidate, and students of Boas were excluded (see Linton and Wagley 1971: 47–48). Despite their disagreements, both Benedict and Linton fostered the interest in personality-and-culture that dominated the department during this period. Linton's most notable contribution was the establishment with Abram Kardiner of an influential, ongoing seminar on anthropology and psychoanalysis, while Benedict moved toward a wartime focus on "national character."

In the years following World War II, the department saw a much larger and quite different cohort of students: predominantly male, veterans, with materialist predilections and theoretical as well as personal interests in politics. This period at Columbia is described in the paper by Robert Murphy. After Linton left for Yale in 1946 he was replaced by Julian Steward, who immediately became a focus for these interests, although Benedict continued to teach and to

attract a following of her own. When Benedict died in 1948, Kroeber arrived
for a four-year stay as visiting professor, leaving Columbia the same year as
Steward. Among the students of this period was a group who met regularly to
discuss their developing research and who in 1950 dubbed themselves (ironically, but not entirely so) the Mundial Upheaval Society (MUS). Three members of the group are represented in this volume—Stanley Diamond, Sidney
Mintz, and Eric Wolf. Other members were Morton Fried, Elman Service, Ru-
fus Mathewson (a student of Russian literature), and John Murra, who took his
degree at the University of Chicago but was in the Columbia orbit through his
participation, along with Mintz and Wolf, in Steward's Puerto Rico project. A
few years later than this group, Marvin Harris, Robert Murphy, and Marshall
Sahlins received their degrees.

   Leslie White taught at Columbia for a summer session in 1948 (with Stanley
Diamond assigned to him as a research assistant), and there continued to be a
good deal of interest in his theories among the Columbia students. In the 1950s
White brought Service and then Sahlins to Michigan (followed later by Wolf),
creating the so-called Columbia–Michigan axis.

   Several other institutions in New York City, dating mainly from the years be-
tween the world wars, trace further links among the anthropologists who are
part of this book. At the New School for Social Research, created in 1919,
Goldenweiser's courses provided the first introduction to anthropology for
Benedict and White. (The New School's current professors of anthropology are
Diamond and Michael Harner, a participant in some of the discussions.) The
municipal college system (whose oldest component, City College, granted a
B.A. to Paul Radin in 1902) expanded during this period from two to four senior colleges, and anthropology began to be taught in all of them. Brooklyn College, founded in 1930, appointed Alexander Lesser to the faculty in 1939, the
year that Sidney Mintz entered as a freshman. When Queens College was established in 1937, the original faculty included Hortense Powdermaker, who
had taken her degree under Malinowski. One of the early students at Queens
was Eric Wolf, who eventually returned to the city system as a professor at
Lehman College. The series organizer, Sydel Silverman (who married Wolf in
1972), has been on the Queens College faculty since completing her Ph.D. at
Columbia in 1963.

   Three institutions outside of New York City are prominent in this volume:
the University of California at Berkeley, whose anthropology department Kroeber founded, Steward was trained in, and Murphy taught in; the London School
of Economics, where Firth and Powdermaker were among Malinowski's first
students; and the University of Chicago, where White studied long before he
became an evolutionist, where Robert Redfield spent his life, and where
Nathaniel Tarn was launched by Redfield onto fieldwork, which he wrote up
under Firth. That Redfield is, in this book, reconsidered by an anthropologist-
turned-poet, now a professor of comparative literature at Rutgers University,

reflects not only geography but also the social history of New York anthropology.

In preparing their papers for publication, some of the contributors have retained them essentially as they were originally given (Lesser, Wolf, Diamond, Tarn), while others have expanded their lectures (Mintz, Murphy, Carneiro). The editor has also selected portions of the discussions for inclusion in the book, with minor revisions in the interest of clarity. In addition, Firth agreed to revise and enlarge his Malinowski lecture for publication as part of this collection.

Each chapter takes a different approach to its subject. Editorial introductions have been provided to fill in biographical information in those instances where it is not included in the paper and to indicate the generally acknowledged significance of each figure for anthropology. No claim is made, however, that this book offers balanced assessments. Some of the intellectual ancestors of contemporary anthropology are reconsidered here with varying mixtures of objectivity and passion.

Franz Boas demonstrating Eskimo harpooning at the American Museum of Natural History (c. 1900).
American Museum of Natural History Library

I

FRANZ BOAS

Alexander Lesser

In 1883 Franz Boas, then a twenty-five-year-old geographer, left his native Germany on an expedition to Baffin Island in the Arctic, which was to turn him toward a life's work in anthropology. A little over twenty years had passed since the publication of Charles Darwin's *Origin of Species* and the almost concurrent publication of several major works setting forth theories of the evolution of culture—works by Henry Maine, J. F. McLennan, and E. B. Tylor in Britain, J. J. Bachofen in Switzerland, and Lewis Henry Morgan in America. A later work of Morgan's had influenced Karl Marx and Friedrich Engels, and Engels's book based on Morgan was about to appear. These writers of ethnology were lawyers, classicists, or gentleman-scholars; anthropology was not yet a subject taught in universities. The year of Boas's Arctic trip, Tylor (who himself had no university education) received one of the first university appointments in anthropology—at Oxford—subsequently becoming Oxford's first professor of anthropology. In the United States at this time, a number of people were pursuing scholarly interests in American Indians, which encompassed ethnological, archaeological, and linguistic studies. Societies devoted to such interests were founded, among them the American Ethnological Society in New York and the Anthropological Society of Washington, whose members included men employed by the U.S. Geological Survey and (later) the Bureau of American Ethnology to carry out reconnaissance work among the Indians. An institutional organization of anthropology was just beginning to develop, as some of the major natural history museums began to expand their function from that of housing material objects to include research and education in ethnology and archaeology.

Franz Boas was born in 1858 in Minden, Westphalia, of German–Jewish parents; his father was a businessman. He went to school and gymnasium in Minden and then attended universities in Heidelberg, Bonn, and Kiel. After studying a variety of subjects, he was awarded a doctorate in geography at Kiel in 1881. Boas planned the Arctic expedition of 1883–1884 primarily as a geographical study. However, he had long nourished an interest in cultural history and primitive peoples, and he combined his geographical work with ethnological research among the Eskimo. In 1885, while writing his Eskimo monograph, Boas decided to make anthropology his primary field, and he accepted an appointment as an assistant at the Royal Ethnological Museum in Berlin, serving under Adolf Bastian. His work with the British Columbia collections at the museum led to an expedition in 1886, which was the beginning of his lifelong research on the Indians of the Northwest Coast.

At the end of this field trip, Boas made the decision to settle in the United States. His first American position was as an assistant editor of *Science*, where he worked primarily on geographical material. In 1888 he was offered an appointment in anthropology at Clark University. He remained there until 1892, when he became chief assistant in anthropology at the World's Columbian Exposition in Chicago and then curator of the new museum that later was called the Field Museum of Natural History. He left the museum in 1894; after eighteen months without a regular position, he came to the American Museum of Natural History for what was to be a ten-year association. Boas joined Columbia University in 1896 as a lecturer in physical anthropology. He became professor of anthropology there in 1899, a post he held until his retirement in 1936.

The American anthropological landscape into which Boas inserted himself was neither vacant, awaiting his influence, nor without competitors. In the late nineteenth century both armchair theorists and field-workers underwritten by the Bureau of American Ethnology were studying (or speculating about) American Indians and interpreting them in terms of evolutionary schemes, a framework that also guided museum exhibits of the time. In addition, a tradition of typological/racialist physical anthropology held sway and did not give way until the eve of World War II. After Boas embarked on his project to build American anthropology from his base at Columbia, these forces, which had their center of gravity in the institutions of Washington, D.C., and at Harvard—hence the common reference to the Washington/Cambridge axis—remained staunchly opposed to him. The fault line was a theoretical division, counterposing evolutionary and historicist models, racialist and cultural determinism, fixed types and plasticity; it was cultural (predominantly old-American WASP as against the immigrant, often Jewish, early Boasians) and to some extent it was political, with alignments on such issues as immigration, race, nationalism, and policies regarding American Indians.

Boas's anthropology emphasized empirical study, especially through field-work and the collection of texts, toward the goal of recording the rapidly disappearing native cultures. It shifted the concept of culture from a synonym for "civilization" to a plural sense, which stressed the diversity of "cultures"; saw cultures as contexts of learned human behavior; and insisted upon a stance of cultural relativism, which meant it was necessary to understand cultures in their own terms and contexts before attempting generalizations.[1] Boas's strategy of historical particularism was the alternative to orthogenetic evolutionism; while diffusion and contact among cultures were the primary historical mechanisms, increasingly the strategy made room for an interest in how cultures were internally patterned and for a concern with the individual in culture.

Boas's approach combined and alternated between two threads: the historical (emphasizing processes that could be traced through the distribution of culture traits) and the psychological (including both mentalist interests—what makes individual minds different in different cultures—and integrationist concerns with how traits fit together). These two threads reflect two epistemological sides of Boas as well, the historical and the scientific. In general, the first generation of Boas's students, up to World War I, emphasized the first thread; the second generation, in the 1920s, the second. A third generation, which came of age in the 1930s, drew on the historical thread but transformed it.

In the course of his career, Boas fostered the development of American anthropology as an academic discipline and as a profession. He established systematic graduate training, and his students went on to build departments at other major institutions: Alfred Kroeber and Robert Lowie at Berkeley, Frank Speck at Pennsylvania, Fay-Cooper Cole and Edward Sapir at Chicago (and later Sapir at Yale), Melville Herskovits at Northwestern, and others. Boas contributed to the professionalization of museums, played a leading role in founding anthropological journals and professional societies (such as the American Anthropological Association [AAA] in 1902), and organized and promoted a vast amount of research.

Boas's own indefatigable scholarly work spanned ethnology, physical anthropology, linguistics, and (with only one published work but that one a breakthrough) archaeology. Under his influence these were established as components of the four-field approach in the training of American anthropologists. A relentless critic of the incautious theorizing of his day, Boas established new canons of empirical research. His distinction among race, language, and culture; his transformation of the culture concept; and his insistence upon understanding cultures in their own contexts, apart from the observer's ethnocentric standards of evaluation, became premises of modern anthropology. Through his work on a wide range of problems, and through his institutional achievements, he redefined the scope and methods of American anthropology. Franz Boas died in 1942.

In retrospect, Franz Boas was the builder and architect of modern anthropology.[2] This has come to be a general consensus, despite certain controversies. I propose to focus on four themes in his life and work:

1. The way in which Boas filled the role of architect of modern anthropology.
2. What Boas brought with him into anthropology that was the effective factor of factors in modernizing it.
3. How Boas, anthropologist and scientist, was a *citizen-scientist* all his life, whose ethics and ideals for the study of man were far-reaching, humane, and still hold true in our own day.
4. How Boas, far from being antitheory, was himself *the* great theorist of modern anthropology, who established the core of anthropological theory on which the science is based.

Modern anthropology begins with Franz Boas. It begins in the scientific skepticism with which he examined the traditional orthodoxies of the study of man, exposing and rejecting the false and unproven, calling for a return to empirical observation, establishing the truth of elementary fundamentals, opening new pathways, and creating new methods. It begins in Boas's ways of thinking about man and his history, in his use of rigorous scientific requirements for data and for proof, in his rejection of old myths, old stereotypes, old emotionally charged assumptions.

Boas's contribution to the transformation of anthropology was therefore not a simple, single event, a formal statement of principles, or a generalized theory at a certain point in time. Boas worked from problem to problem, consolidating the truth gained and asking the next question. The framework and principles of the modern subject matter are emergents from this ongoing process, in part the residue of truth left after traditional materials and ideas were reevaluated, in part the positive discovery of empirical principles by fresh and original observation.

Boas was aware of this critical character of his method from his early professional years. In 1907, responding at Columbia to a Festschrift which was given him on the twenty-fifth anniversary of his Ph.D., he described himself as "one whose work rests essentially in an unfeeling criticism of his own work and that of others."[3] He wrote a defense of the cephalic index (head form) and its traditional importance as a hereditary trait only a few years before his own research proved it was not strictly genetically determined but was affected significantly by environmental change (1899, 1911a). He condemned his early Kwakiutl and other Northwest Coast research as questionable, superseded by later work (1897, 1901). He came to "disparage his early work on the Kwakiutl language," pointing out its shortcomings (cited in Codere 1966: xiv). He was continually self-critical. "Flawless perfection, then, must not be sought in Boas," as Lowie has put it (Lowie 1944: 64).

But in the end he restructured anthropology and its branches, leading physical anthropology from taxonomic race classification into human biology, breaking through the limitations of traditional philology into the problems of modern linguistics and cognitive anthropology, establishing the modern anthropological meaning and study of human culture.

Along his way, as Boas worked at problems in all fields of anthropology, he came to discoveries and understandings that, through his writing and teaching, became the convictions and effected the consensus from which the modern science of anthropology was born. Many of his writings were summations of plateaus of understanding he had reached in one area of anthropology or another. *The Mind of Primitive Man* in 1911 was his first great general consolidation in book form, a seminal book in modern social thought for technical readers and the lay public alike. In it, Boas reorganized and integrated studies of 1894 to 1911 into closely argued theses that became baselines of anthropology thereafter and fundamental conceptions in social science and social philosophy.

The book provided general anthropology and three of its branches—physical anthropology, linguistics, and ethnology—with a structural framework. Establishing the relative autonomy of cultural phenomena, it gave to the concept of culture its modern meaning and usage. Boas proved that cultures are diverse historical developments, each the outcome of a prior history in which many factors and events, cultural and noncultural, have played a part. He made the plurality of cultures fundamental to the study of man (see Stocking 1968a: 203). He showed how languages, both semantically and morphologically, are each a context of perception that affects human thought and action. Analogously, he showed how cultural environments, especially as contexts of traditional materials, shape and structure human behavior—actions and reactions—in each generation. In so doing he ended the traditional ambiguity in the term "culture" understood interchangeably as both humanistic and behavioral—an ambiguity perpetuated by endless quoting of Tylor's "culture or civilization"—and started the modern era of the concept of "cultures," viewed as contexts of learned human behavior.

A much earlier paper shows that the same essential conception was in his mind more than twenty years before. In "The Aims of Ethnology" (written in 1888), Boas stated, "The data of ethnology prove that not only our language, but also our emotions are the result of the form of our social life and of the history of the people to whom we belong" (1940:636). The concept of social heritage was basic to Boas's thinking all his life.

Several of the theses of *The Mind of Primitive Man* (1911b), taken together, establish the relative autonomy of cultural phenomena, showing that there are no *independent variables* on which the cultural is dependent. First, establishing that race (physical type), language, and culture have relatively independent histories and are not interchangeable terms in classifying man, Boas showed that inner inborn traits ("race" or heredity) are not causal determinants of similarities or differences of cultures. Second, showing that geographical or natural environments are not neatly correlated with cultures as adaptations but always involve preexisting cultures, Boas proved that outer environmental conditions are not *the* causal determinants of similarities or differences of cultures. Finally, establishing that ideas of *orthogenetic* cultural evolution do not fit the facts of actual cultural sequences and history, Boas showed that no necessary, predetermining process of change makes similarities or differences of cultures expressions of unfolding stages of development. These theses became principles of modern anthropology.

It is, I think, important to understand what it was in Boas's training and point of view that led him into the critical reconstruction of anthropology that he accomplished. This is especially important because of further implications for the understanding of Boas's thinking on theory and scientific method. It has been widely held that Boas's training in physics and mathematics was responsible for his scientific reconstruction of the field of anthropology, which was largely preprofessional and somewhat amateurish at the time. Actually, I am convinced that an entirely different phase of his education and scientific experience led to his future work, and I believe he tried to make that clear in his own statements.

Central to Boas's education in science and scientific thinking was the study of natural history, in which he indulged the "intense interest in nature" that he later recalled as characteristic of his youth (1938a: 201–4). Boas attended the Froebel kindergarten in Minden (founded by his mother and where she taught), which provided special nature studies. This experience was unusual for Boas's time, for kindergartens were rare then. Periods of recuperation after illness, spent in the countryside of Clus or at the seaside at Helgoland, acquainted him with the plant life of the woods and the wealth of animals and plants of the sea. He collected his own herbarium and for years "treasured"—his own word—the sea life specimens he gathered at Helgoland. He had a mineral collection and began to study mineralogy early in his gymnasium years. In midgymnasium he studied some zoology (including study on his own of the comparative bone structure of geese, ducks, and hares); astronomy and geology; and more botany—physiology, plant anatomy, and the geographical distribution of plants. His interest in this last subject almost stifled other hobbies, but the study of cryptogams (plants such as ferns, moss, and algae, which reproduce by spores), begun in his own early herbarium collecting, became with a special teacher a subject that fascinated him ever after.

In his later gymnasium years, drawn to all the natural sciences, he studied plant anatomy and physiology, used microscopes in plant study and in work on crystal forms and systems in mineralogy, and made his own map of the distribution of plants in the Minden region. In the universities, the special professors he sought included two biologists (one also a marine biologist), a botanist, and two mineralogists (one also a geologist). He found his studies of plant distributions among his most exciting work, and was elated when, by midgymnasium years—for the most part through study on his own—he could follow fairly well "the evolution of the animal and plant world" and "its transient geographical distribution" (APS, 1).

Natural history, with its empirical approach, involved Boas in observation, description, comparison, and classification; in inductive generalization; and in *an acceptance of the external world*, which became a habit of thinking for Boas. In attempting to understand Boas and what he contributed to modern thought, his statements about his "intellectual interest" in physics and mathematics have been overemphasized, while other statements about his "intensive emotional interest in the phenomena of the world"—along with his long concentration on natural-history studies—have been given too little attention. Boas's background before he became an anthropologist included training in physics and mathematics as well as geography. But to understand what he made of anthropology, it is far more important to know that he came to the study of man as a naturalist, as a student of natural history, and tried to understand man and peoples as part of the natural phenomena of the world.

Among anthropologists, Marian W. Smith is virtually alone in emphasizing this mode of understanding Boas. In a paper on Boas's approach to field method, Smith draws a sharp contrast between Boas's "natural history approach to the social sciences" and the "social philosophy approach of British social anthropology," and she shows that the contrast affected both the methods and content of fieldwork done by the two schools (Smith 1959: 46).[4] The American approach includes all of culture, considers data inviolable, and seeks in data only generalizations or theories that can be reached inductively. The British school, in contrast, begins with assumptions and theories and uses field data and the field situation to test hypotheses that have been deductively derived.

Smith's paper limits the scope of her interpretation, but one suspects from some of her comments that she would have gone on to a conception of Boas and his thinking similar to my own. For example, she says: "Boas, more than any other person, first brought the very mind of man into the natural world. . . . Conceptualization and philosophy no longer breathed a finer air. They could be studied by the same techniques and approaches, by the same attitudes as other human characteristics and consequently lost much of their aura of revealed truth" (Smith 1959: 46).

Smith's paper had a singular impact on some anthropologists. For example, Kroeber, in his discussion "Franz Boas: The Man," had emphasized the mathematical and physical character of Boas's education, training, and lifelong modes of thought (Kroeber 1943: 5–7). Even earlier, in 1935, in a famous exchange with Boas on history, Kroeber had written:

> To begin with, it is of indubitable significance that Boas' educational training was in the physical laboratory sciences, in physics in fact. This led him into psychophysics and physical geography. His doctoral dissertation was on the color of sea water. This in turn led to a one-man, two-year geographical expedition to Baffinland, which brought with it intimate contacts with natives. The result was *The Central Eskimo* and a career of anthropology since. From physics Boas brought into anthropology a sense of definiteness of problem, of exact rigor of method, and of highly critical objectivity. These qualities have remained with him unimpaired, and his imparting them to anthropology remains his fundamental and unshakeable contribution to our discipline. (Kroeber 1935: 539–40)

This attitude of Kroeber's is completely contrary to Boas's own explanation of his manner of thinking. In a paper called "The Study of Geography," in 1887, Boas specifically contrasts the methods of physics with the methods of history (1940: 639–47). He uses "physics" and "history" as conceptual terms for two general types of approaches, the former seeking laws and subordinating particular events to abstract generalizations, the latter seeking the thorough understanding of phenomena—even individual events—and making laws or generalizations merely instrumental to that end. Boas identifies himself with the historical approach, in temperament, in interests, and in methods, and he is unsympathetic to that of physics.

In contrast to his earlier statements, Kroeber wrote in his 1959 preface to *The Anthropology of Franz Boas*, the volume containing Marian Smith's paper, that "natural scientists have never questioned the status of Boas and the importance of his massive contribution," that Boas's anthropological activity at first stemmed largely from both natural history and humanist interests, and that Boas dealt so extensively with non-European and nonclassical languages because they are a part of the total world of nature. "Given the combination of Boas' natural science adhesion and his predilection for human materials, it was almost inevitable that he should concern himself with culture, for culture, including its semiautonomous province of language, is precisely the phenomenal regularities of human behavior" (Kroeber 1959: vi). This is fundamentally different from Kroeber's statements of a few years earlier.

Solon Kimball has made a special point of relating the "natural history" approach to anthropology itself. In a paper presented at an AAA meeting some years ago, he offered the thesis that anthropology had developed historically from the approach of natural history, while sociology had developed from the approach of physics and the formal deductive sciences. Kimball has consistently taken the position—especially in studies of the relation of anthropology to methods and principles of modern education—that anthropology is rooted in the method of natural history (as exemplified by Darwin) and involves "inductive empiricism based upon methods of classification and interdependencies of components" (Kimball, personal communication).

Empirical methods to Boas meant firsthand experience where data were lacking. It meant an end to brilliantly constructed speculations as a substitute for observation. In ethnology, of course, this meant fieldwork, and Boas's own work on the Eskimo is generally recognized as one early example that stimulated the development of fieldwork as the basis of ethnology and cultural anthropology. In discussions of the historical development of ethnology, attention is often drawn (as by E. E. Evans-Pritchard) to the Torres Straits Expedition of the English, in which W. H. R. Rivers and A. C. Haddon participated. Yet much of the work of that expedition was peripheral to ethnology, as, for example, the effort of Rivers to settle psychological questions of the sensibilities of indigenous peoples. Somewhat overlooked in this historical view are the monumental field researches of the Jesup North Pacific Expedition, which was mounted under Boas's inspiration, direction, and editorship while he was at the American Museum of Natural History and at Columbia. This project, which was contemporary with the Torres Straits Expedition, resulted in seventeen massive volumes on Siberia and Northwest Coast North America by various people (with an eighteenth still to be published) and far outweighs Torres Straits in its significance for the development of modern ethnological research.

There is another side to Boas as a scientist—the fact that he was a *citizen-scientist*. His careers as citizen and scientist are interwoven. He accepted a moral obligation to spread scientific knowledge as widely as possible, and he himself applied anthropological findings to human problems in education, race relations, nationalism and internationalism, war and peace, and the struggle for democracy and intellectual freedom.

In his first general book, *The Mind of Primitive Man*, the first words of the first edition are: "Proud of his wonderful achievements, civilized man looks down upon the humbler members of mankind." The last words on the last page read:

> I hope the discussions outlined in these pages have shown that the data of anthropology teach us a greater tolerance of forms of civilization different from our own, that we should learn to look on foreign races with greater sympathy and with a conviction that, as all races have contributed in the past to cultural progress in one way or another, so they will be capable of advancing the interests of mankind if we are only willing to give them a fair opportunity. (1911b: 278)

Later, in *Anthropology and Modern Life* (1928), he applied anthropological knowledge to racism, nationalism, eugenics, crime, and education. Still later, in

Race and Democratic Society, published posthumously by his son in 1945, some of his hundreds of contributions to widely read magazines and newspapers were brought together.

Boas's commitment to active citizenship and social, liberal ideals began in his childhood home, enriched by the liberalism and free thought of his father and mother. Both had given up all formal religious activity and affiliation, and as Boas later recalled, he and his sisters were "spared the struggle against religious dogma that besets the lives of so many young people." With "an intense interest in nature," Boas was able to approach the world around him with an open mind, without religious preconceptions or inhibitions (1938a: 201–4).

Politically, Boas found "the ideals of the revolution of 1848 a living force in [his] home." Relatives and friends of the family had been in the 1848 struggle in Germany and had left for the United States after its failure, some after getting out of jail. Drawn to the liberalism of his time, Boas was deeply troubled about Bismarck's Germany and the limitations and restrictions it could place upon his scientific career (1938a: 201–4).

At twenty-five, while on his expedition to Baffinland, he wrote in a diary of letters that he sent to his fiancée, "Science alone is not the greatest good" (June 27, 1883). "I believe one can be really happy only as a member of humanity as a whole, if one works with all one's energy together with the masses toward high goals" (December 13, 1883). "And what I want, for what I want to live and die, is equal rights for all, equal possibilities to learn and work for rich and poor alike. Don't you believe that to have done even the smallest bit for this is more than all science taken together?" (January 22, 1884). He added, "I do not think I would be allowed to do this in Germany" and "I do not wish for a German professorship because I would be restricted to my science and to teaching, for which I have no inclination. I should much prefer to live in America and to further these ideas."[5]

A combination of circumstances in 1887 made it possible for him to remain in the United States when he returned to New York after a Northwest Coast trip—to marry, to apply for American citizenship (which he obtained five years later), and to begin his American career with the same "American dream" he shared with so many other immigrants to the United States.

Boas's active citizenship did not end with his effort to make his scientific work relevant to human affairs. He was active in matters of principles and in specific situations involving injustice and violations of academic freedom. He resigned from his first teaching position—at Clark University—in a joint protest with other faculty members against continuing infringement of academic freedom by the president, G. Stanley Hall. In Boas's view, a college or university consisted of its faculty and students; trustees and nonacademic administrators were not inherent in it.

A first major test of his principles came in 1914, with the outbreak of World War I. Boas, a pacifist, opposed the war from the beginning. He saw it as fundamentally an imperialist war. In a series of letters to newspapers, he urged that the United States and Woodrow Wilson take the lead in forming a coalition of neutral countries to bring about a cease-fire, and he argued against actions by President Wilson that he charged were leading the United States into the war. In 1917, after the United States declared war, he denounced the action and Wilson in the press.

Boas was not pro-German, as of course was charged. I will support this with a single letter, a letter he wrote to his son Ernst from the field in British Columbia, a few days after the outbreak of war. It is a personal letter, from father to son; it was handwritten and clearly was never intended to get the public hearing I am giving it now.

August 6, 1914

Dear Ernst:

. . . You can imagine that I can think of nothing else than the unfortunate war and the danger to which our aunts and grandmother are exposed. To me it seems like a terrible dream. I cannot visualize how reasonable people and nations which are "leaders of civilization" can conjure up such a terrible war. If Germany loses, such hatred will be created that it will stir up her nationalism for years to come; if she is victorious, such arrogance, that it will lead to the same consequence. If people would only realize what a source of hatred and misfortune the highly praised patriotism represents! That one cherishes one's own way of life is a natural thing. But does one need to nourish the thought that it is the best of all, that everything that is different is not good but useless, that it is right to despise the people of other nations? In our private lives we would not follow such an unethical rule. Why should it prevail in our national life? If one could only exclude this "patriotismus" from our schools and teach our children the good in our culture, and appreciation of the good in other cultures. Instead they artificially cultivate envy and rivalry. (APS, 3)

During the war, Boas took public leadership of an effort to counteract wartime hysteria against German culture. Officially, all things German were condemned. The German language ceased to be taught in American schools. Orchestras eliminated German music from their programs. Boas once made a particular request of a conductor to include a certain Beethoven opus in his next concert; the conductor replied that he felt as Boas did about the quality of that opus but regretted that it was impossible for him to perform it. Boas took the position that as an anthropologist he could not accept the identification of the art and literature of a people with its political administration at a particular time. Heine, Schiller, Bach, and other German artists represented cultural achievements and values that had nothing to do with the Kaiser. It was this position that he took with his students. When Columbia's president, Nicholas Murray Butler, ardently prowar and anti-German, instituted student spying on what professors did and said, Boas responded by writing a full statement of his views and distributing it in mimeograph to all who came to his classes or requested it.

Boas was not alone at Columbia in his pacifism and antiwar ideas. After the 1917 U.S. declaration of war, when a draft to mobilize an army was being readied, J. McKeen Cattell, a professor of psychology, sent copies of a letter he had written to every member of the U.S. House and Senate. The letter urged that a military draft act provide exemption for those who objected to military service outside the continental borders of the United States. The letter was written on Columbia University stationery. President Butler terminated Cattell on twenty-four hours' notice, making forfeit his right to tenure and his accumulations toward retirement. Faculty support for Cattell was immediate. Boas and John Dewey were members of a Cattell Committee, which worked in his support for years. Two other faculty members, James Harvey Robinson and Charles Beard, resigned and joined in the establishment of the New School for Social Research. In the end, Cattell took his case against Columbia to court and won a complete victory; Columbia settled out of court to avoid publicity. It was so quiet an ending to the case that many did not know and do not know that Columbia had lost its first case on academic rights.

Perhaps the most critical controversy involving Boas and World War I came in 1919, after the war, when he published the following letter in the *Nation*:

Scientists as Spies

To the Editor of *The Nation*

Sir: In his war address to Congress, President Wilson dwelt at great length on the theory that only autocracies maintain spies, that these are not needed in democracies. At the time that the President made this statement, the government of the United States had in its employ spies of unknown number. I am not concerned here with the familiar discrepancies between the President's words and the actual facts, although we may perhaps have to accept his statement as meaning correctly that we live under an autocracy, that our democracy is a fiction. The point against which I wish to enter a vigorous protest is that a number of men who follow science as their profession, men whom I refuse to designate any longer as scientists, have prostituted science by using it as a cover for their activities as spies.

A soldier whose business is murder as a fine art, a diplomat whose calling is based on deception and secretiveness, a politician whose very life consists in compromises with his conscience, a business man whose aim is personal profit within the limits allowed by a lenient law—such may be excused if they set patriotic devotion above common everyday decency and perform services as spies. They merely accept the code of morality to which modern society still conforms. Not so the scientist. The very essence of his life is the service of truth. We all know scientists who in private life do not come up to the standard of truthfulness, but who nevertheless would not consciously falsify the results of their researches. It is bad enough if we have to put up with these, because they reveal a lack of strength of character that is liable to distort the results of their work. A person, however, who uses science as a cover for political spying, who demeans himself to pose before a foreign government as an investigator and asks for assistance in his alleged researches in order to carry on, under this cloak, his political machinations, prostitutes science in an unpardonable way and forfeits the right to be classed as a scientist.

By accident, incontrovertible proof has come to my hands that at least four men who carry on anthropological work, while employed as government agents, introduced themselves to foreign governments as representatives of scientific researches. They have not only shaken the belief in the truthfulness of science, but they have also done the greatest possible disservice to scientific inquiry. In consequence of their acts, every nation will look with distrust upon the visiting foreign investigator who wants to do honest work, suspecting sinister designs. Such action has raised a new barrier against the development of international friendly cooperation.

New York, October 16   Franz Boas

In the light of controversies over ethics within the AAA in recent years, this letter seems a direct and simple plea for scientific integrity. Its anti-Wilson innuendos were not new. Boas had opposed World War I openly and had criticized Wilson's policies in letter after letter in the *New York Times*.

However, Boas's letter in the *Nation* was denounced by the Anthropological Society of Washington in a lengthy statement to the AAA at its meeting in December 1919. The Harvard–Cambridge anthropology group sided with the Washington society. The statement of the Washington group read as follows:

Resolutions of the Anthropological Society of Washington

The attention of the Anthropological Society of Washington having been called to an open letter published in *The Nation* of December 20th by Dr. Franz Boas under the title, "Scientists as Spies," and after said article was read and duly considered, the following resolution was adopted and ordered to be submitted to the American Anthropological Association at its meeting in Boston; to Section H of the American Association for the Advancement of Science meeting in St. Louis; and to the Archeological Institute of America meeting in Pittsburgh, with the request that suitable action be taken by these associations. Also that a copy of this resolution be sent to *The Nation* and *Science* with a request for its publication.

Resolved: That the article in question unjustly criticizes the President of the United States and attacks the fundamental principles of American democracy; that the reflections contained in the article fall on all American anthropologists who have been anywhere outside the limits of the United States during the last five years; that the information thus given is liable to have future serious effects on the work of all anthropologists outside the boundaries of the United States; and that the accusation, given such prominent publicity and issuing from such a source, will doubtless receive wide attention and is liable to prejudice foreign governments against all scientific men coming from this country to their respective territories, particularly if under government auspices; therefore *Be it resolved*, that in the opinion of the Council of the Anthropological Society of Washington, the publication of the article in question was unwarranted and will prove decidedly injurious to the interests of American scientists in general; that the author has shown himself inconsiderate to the best interests of his American colleagues who may be obliged to carry on research in foreign countries, and that his action therefore deserves our emphatic disapproval.

At the meeting, after a great deal of discussion, the following resolution was moved instead of the long statement from the Washington Anthropological Society.

Resolved: That the expression of opinion by Dr. Franz Boas contained in an open letter to the editor of *The Nation* on the date of October 16, 1919, and published in the issue of that weekly for December 20, 1919, is unjustified and does not represent the opinion of the American Anthropological Association. *Be it further resolved*: That a copy of this resolution be forwarded to the Executive Board of the National Research Council and such other scientific associations as may have taken action on this matter.

I have presented the text of Boas's letter and if anyone can find a word in it that says it represents anybody's views but his own, I would like to know it. It was a personal statement of his convictions, and it involved no one else. He did not name the persons he was referring to. Nevertheless, Boas was censured, by a vote of about two to one.

The Washington Anthropological Society distributed its original statement widely, in spite of the fact that it had not been passed by the AAA. A great deal of the rancor aroused was allegedly due to Boas's publication of a professional statement in a public, nonprofessional magazine. Yet Boas had sent it earlier to *Science*, which was then edited by J. McKeen Cattell, the same Cattell who had been kicked out of Columbia for his pacifist letter to Congress on Columbia stationery. Cattell replied: "I fear I must decide that it would not be advisable to print the letter entitled "Scientists as Spies" in *Science*. I of course concur in all that you say, but it seems to me desirable for *Science* to avoid, especially at the present time, all questions of a political character, even though they do relate to scientific matters." I don't know how Boas felt about that letter, but he sent his statement right off to Henry Raymond Mussey, a friend who was editor of the *Nation*. Mussey immediately accepted it for publication and wrote to Boas: "Thank you very much for your disturbing letter on 'Scientists as Spies' sent us for publication. It is indeed a distressing thing that scientific men should stoop to such dishonorable practices, and I am very glad indeed to have the opportunity of giving publicity to your protest." That is how Boas's letter happened to appear in the *Nation* rather than in *Science*.

There is a final note to this early controversy over professional ethics. The next month (on January 9, 1920) Cattell published in *Science* the full text of the communication from the Washington Anthropological Society, in the form that had been *rejected* by the AAA meeting.

I close this page of history by noting that one scientist wrote the Washington Anthropological Society to ask, in view of the statement it had circulated and had asked everybody to act upon, whether Boas's charges in the *Nation* letter were true. He noted that the Washington group had made no reference to that question at all.

Following his censure, Boas resigned as representative of the AAA to the National Research Council, who accepted the resignation regretfully. Apart from this, I have no evidence that his participation in the AAA was ever terminated, even transiently. Annual reports of the Association in succeeding years show him still to be a member of various committees that he had been on previously.

Stocking has treated this incident in "The Scientific Reaction Against Cultural Anthropology, 1917–1920" (1968b). He focuses on the manner in which opposition to the development of Boas's cultural anthropology, fortified by jealousy of his achievements, caused the *Nation* letter to be used as an excuse for violent anti-Boas action. I think the letter also stands as an example of Boas in action on issues of scientific ethics.

Over the years, as Boas became known through his work and public statements as a strong liberal on academic and political issues and on race relations, he accepted board memberships on and allowed the use of his name by many public-service citizens' organizations and ad hoc committees. He also organized some of his own. His main means of action was to make public statements to the press or write letters to the press, or to form a committee that then took public or private action as the matter required. It was in this way that Boas initiated two large-scale national actions in relation to the rise of Hitler and Nazism. The first followed a Nazi denunciation of Jewish science. Boas responded with a public statement signed by over 8,000 American scientists, affirming that there was only one science, to which religion and race were irrelevant. Later, after Hitler came to power in 1933 and Boas's books (among others) were burned, Boas organized a group at Columbia called the Committee for Democracy and Intellectual Freedom. The idea spread rapidly to other universities, where chapters were formed, until the committee had more than 11,000 members.

Boas also joined other American scientists in organizing committees to help refugee scientists from Hitler's Germany and other countries overrun by the Nazis. The primary effort was to find the scientists positions in the United States or elsewhere in the free world. Boas was engaged in this activity at the moment he died in December 1942. Along with Claude Lévi-Strauss, Boas had arranged a luncheon at Columbia in honor of Paul Rivet, a refugee linguist from Vichy France. Boas suddenly collapsed, in Lévi-Strauss's arms, and died even as he was in the middle of a sentence about a new idea on race.

A major part of Boas's scientific work and its application concerned race and race relations, especially the problems of the American Negro. He was probably the first scientist to publish that Negro and white were fundamentally equal, as were all so-called races. He embodied this view in the title of one paper, "The Genetic Basis for Democracy." American Negro leaders, organizations, and universities were quick to recognize in Boas a source of strength. For W. E. B. Du Bois, a founder of the National Association for the Advancement of Colored People (NAACP) and editor of its publication *Crisis*, Boas wrote a paper for the first issue of that magazine, on the Negro and the race problem in America (1910). He gave a commencement address at Atlanta University in 1906. He participated in the organization and work of the Association for the Study of Negro Life and History and its publication the *Journal of Negro History*, and later of the Council on African Affairs, of which Paul Robeson was chairman and Max Yergan director.

As an indication of what such African American leaders thought of Boas, I have a message that Max Yergan sent to Boas's daughter, Helene Yampolsky, after Boas died: "On behalf of the Council on African Affairs, I express deepest regrets over the death of your father. He was a guide and inspiration to us in our deliberation and activities for the welfare of African peoples. The work of organizations like ours is possible because Franz Boas has lived" (APS, 4).

I began this discussion by selecting four principal points for emphasis. I have touched on three: (1) that Boas was the architect of modern anthropology; (2) that the element in his training and experience that made him the modernizer of the study of man was the empirical way of thinking of natural history; and (3) that Boas was a *citizen*-scientist who applied the work of anthropology to problems of society and was an activist on academic and political issues—in both ways serving as a model for anthropology as a humanitarian science.

I come now to my final theme, Boas as theorist. Far from being antitheory, Boas was himself, I would argue, *the* great theorist of modern anthropology, who established the core of anthropological theory on which the science is based.

Inescapably, discussions of Boas on theory must begin with his handling of the theory of evolution. Here are his words on that subject in 1888:

> The development of ethnology is largely due to the general recognition of the principle of biological evolution. It is a common feature of all forms of evolutionary theory that every living being is considered as the result of an historical development. The fate of an individual does not influence himself alone, but also all suc-

ceeding generations. . . . This point of view introduced an historical perspective into the natural sciences and revolutionized their methods. The development of ethnology is largely due to the adoption of the evolutionary standpoint, because it impressed the conviction upon us that no event in the life of a people passes without leaving its effect upon later generations. The myths told by our ancestors and in which they believed have left their impress upon the ways of thinking of their descendants. (1940: 633)

Clearly, in his early anthropological thinking Boas (1) accepted biological evolution as scientifically valid, (2) understood evolution in *historical* terms, not as orthogenetic, and (3) affirmed evolution as a *first principle* of ethnology and anthropology.

These statements must be emphasized in view of oft-repeated assertions that Boas was antievolutionary. No statement could show more clearly that he not only accepted evolution but accepted it as *basic*. Yet he did reject the so-called evolutionary ideas of some anthropologists. What did he reject, as distinct from the evolution that he affirmed?

In *Primitive Art* he wrote, "Evolution, meaning the continuous change of thought and action, or historic continuity, cannot be accepted unreservedly. It is otherwise when it is conceived as meaning the universally valid continuous development of one cultural form out of a preceding type" (1927: 80). Essentially he was opposing orthogenesis, which is defined as follows by Webster's dictionary:

In biology, variations which in successive generations of an organism, follow some particular line, evolving some new type irrespective of natural selection or other external factor. Determinate variation or evolution. Sociologically, the theory that social evolution always follows the same direction and passes through the same stages in each culture despite differing external conditions.

Orthogenesis, by its very definition, is a contradiction of Darwin's theory of evolution. Darwin based evolutionary change on the principle of natural selection; among the vast number of variations occurring in each new generation, some were "selected" to survive and reproduce, others were not. Natural selection in turn must be understood as historical in character. Forms or species are subject to variation and change. So, too, is the environment in which they occur. The interaction between variations of form and the changing environment is an event of a particular time, not predetermined by either system. In modern biology, orthogenesis is not a fundamental evolutionary process. The point is made in George Gaylord Simpson's *Meaning of Evolution* (1949: 22) and in various other treatments.

It was this distinction between orthogenesis and evolution in its historical, Darwinian sense that Boas had in mind, as has been noted by some. Sherwood Washburn has written about this, referring to "evolution" as the term was used by Tylor, Spencer, Morgan, and their contemporary throwbacks. "There is no evolution in the traditional anthropological sense. What Boas referred to as evolution was orthogenesis, which receives no support from modern genetic theory. What the geneticist sees as evolution is far closer to what Boas called history than to what he called evolution" (Washburn 1963: 522). In an article on Boas I wrote: "Boas' critique was directed not against the principle of evolution as historical development, which he accepted, but against the orthogenesis of dominant English and American theory of the time. He opposed history to orthogenesis" (Lesser 1968: 101).

Boas himself made the distinction in clear terms in several places. In 1920, he wrote in "The Methods of Ethnology":

> the hypothesis [of evolution in traditional anthropology] implies the thought that our modern Western European civilization represents the highest cultural development toward which all other more primitive cultural types tend, and that therefore retrospectively we construct an *orthogenetic* development towards our modern civilization. (1940: 282; italics mine)

In 1919, in a discussion at an American Ethnological Society meeting, Boas is reported by the secretary, Robert H. Lowie, to have spoken as follows: "Professor Boas pointed out that in comparing the doctrines of unilinear evolutionists to those of biologists we are not quite fair to the biologists, since they do not postulate a single line of evolution without any divergences; what the cultural theorists of the earlier period did was to stress the *orthogenetic* character of cultural evolution."[6] In 1938, discussing problems of the laws of historic development, Boas wrote: "When these data are assembled, the question arises whether they present an orderly picture or whether history proceeds haphazardly; in other words, whether an *orthogenetic* development of human forms may be discovered, and whether a regular sequence of stages of historical development may be recognized" (1938b: 3; italics mine).

Several aspects of this view of evolution help explain Boas's view of theory and his work as a scientific theorist. First, he uses the fact of evolution as proof "that every living being is the result of an historical development." He understands evolution as history and as evidence of the historicity of living things. In effect, Boas's view is a major theory, both of culture and of man. It states that every culture is the result of a long history and that every such history involves a great complexity of events, accidents of history, and interrelation of factors.

In relation to Boas's view of evolution as basic to anthropology, note that he is speaking empirically. The empiricism he brought from natural-history studies called for generalizations or scientific theories that are *inductive*—that come out of the data and that serve to bind them together.

As Darwin's theory of evolution expressed in a generalization both the continuity and change of living forms—the idea of *descent with modification*—so a
similar theory of the historical evolution of cultures served to express their continuity through time and their diversification and change—the idea of *continuity with change*.

Additionally, Boas established the modern *theory* of culture. Stocking has
shown that it was Boas who established the modern use and meaning of the
term. But more than that, in doing so he established the central theory of modern anthropology.

When Boas showed that cultures and their diversities could not be explained by differences in outer environment, natural environment, or geography; when he showed that cultural diversity could not be explained by
differences in inner makeup of human groups (the racial argument); and finally, when he showed that cultural diversity was not a matter of stages of predetermined development or orthogenetic evolution, he made cultures and
their histories the primary determinants of diversities or similarities at any
time. Cultures became the basic factor in the understanding of cultural man.
In anthropological thinking and explanation, the concept *cultural* replaced
the concept *natural*. The culture concept did away at one blow with efforts to
explain human nature biologically and physiologically (as with concepts of instinct or inherent drives).

I would suggest, then, that two great theories in anthropology were contributed by Boas: the idea that in culture history, culture is the primary determinant, rather than some noncultural independent variable; and the theory of
culture in its modern sense, as learned behavior. Both of these are inductive
theories, based on the comparison and contrast of human cultures.

The immense influence of this anthropological discovery and development is indicated, for example, by John Dewey in his article, "Human Nature":

> Anthropology, on the other hand, has made it clear that the varieties of cultural and
> institutional forms which have existed are not to be traced to anything which can
> be called unmodified human nature, but are the products of interaction with the
> social environment. They are functions, in the mathematical sense, of institutional
> organization and cultural traditions, as these operate to shape raw biological mate-
> rial into definitively human shape.
>
> If we accept the extreme partisan stand, it may be regarded as now generally ac-
> cepted that the immense diversities of culture which have existed and which still
> exist cannot possibly be derived directly from any stock of original powers and im-
> pulses, that the problem is one of explaining in its own terms the diversification of
> the cultural milieus which act upon original nature.
>
> As this fact gains recognition, the problem of modifiability is being placed upon
> the same level as the persistence of custom or tradition. It is wholly a matter of em-
> pirical determination, not of *a priori* theorizing. (Dewey 1932: 536)

Dewey adds further on:

> The present controversies between those who assert the essential fixity of human
> nature and those who believe in a great measure of modifiability center chiefly
> around the future of war and the future of a competitive economic system moti-
> vated by private profit. It is justifiable to say without dogmatism that both an-
> thropology and history give support to those who wish to change these
> institutions. It is demonstrable that many of the obstacles to change which have
> been attributed to human nature are in fact due to the inertia of institutions and
> to the voluntary desire of powerful classes to maintain the existing status (Dewey
> 1932: 536).

In Boas's own view of theory (in the sense of scientific generalizations or
laws), as he outlined it in his 1887 paper "The Study of Geography," he made
the historical character of human phenomena basic (1940: 639–47). The goal
in such a field of study is "the thorough understanding of phenomena"; in
other places he speaks of "complex phenomena." Regularities or generalizations which are discoverable are viewed pragmatically, not as an end in themselves but as an additional tool in analysis. This, I suggest, is not an
antitheory or antigeneralization position, but a reversal of emphasis. He suggests that in the complex field of human cultural history, theory—read laws
or generalizations—is not the end, but, where discoverable, one means
among others to be used in scientific analysis and for the understanding of
phenomena.

As a generalizer in his own right, Boas is the most generalizing anthropologist I have read. I once wrote a paper called "Research Procedure and
Laws of Culture" (1939), in which I tried to show the nature of laws as working assumptions. I limited myself to selected illustrations from Boas, because he was supposed to be nontheoretical. I found most of the illustrations
in the lengthy article he wrote years ago for the *Encyclopedia of the Social
Sciences* on "Anthropology" (1930). In that article, on every phase of the
subject, he tries to generalize as much as possible as to what the import of
the data is. The article is full of generalizations, some of which even take the
specific form of attempts to state laws. I think it is important to realize that
a generalization for him was arrived at inductively and was an attempt to
sum up, to pull together, the meanings of the many facts so far known. In
practice, it was always subject to further questions, further inquiries, further
verification.

Boas moved onward from problem to problem throughout his active scientific life. He taught his students to attempt to do the same. He left anthropology an open field of inquiry, its methods rooted in empirical observation and
experience, its goal an ever wider and deeper knowledge of man, its ideal—
contributions toward a better world for all men.

DISCUSSION

ERIC WOLF: Kroeber at one point—in fact, in the debate with Boas that you quoted from—accused Boas of not being really historical, of not being interested in history. Boas apparently defended himself—he was amazed that Kroeber would say that. What went into that controversy?

LESSER: From Kroeber's standpoint what went into it was his own concept of history. All Boas meant by history was the kind of history you read in any history book; he wasn't thinking of anything more than that. Kroeber also attacked Boas for publishing a whole book on primitive art and not discussing style. Boas replied that this was beyond his understanding, because there was a chapter called "Style" and also a long chapter on the style of the North Pacific Coast. He didn't know what Kroeber meant by saying he had never discussed style. In the same way, he didn't know what Kroeber meant by saying that he was not historical. Kroeber was willing to grant that *The Central Eskimo* was an historical study, to which Boas demurred, saying that apart from one or two comments it was a descriptive study, and there wasn't one word of reconstruction or a major historical statement in the entire book. Why Kroeber should call a descriptive ethnological study history, he didn't know.

As in his position on theory, on historical reconstruction Boas was very wary of anticipating the facts. He gave a talk once, "The History of the American Race," in which he told his audience—because it was primarily a lay audience—that he was going to let down his hair and speak about whatever he thought about the subject, and it wasn't based upon facts, it was based on his own speculations. He gave a brief talk on the origins and history of American Indians. This paper, because it was so lucid and simple, was immediately adopted by many people as a basic reference on the actual origins and history of American Indians, and it was quoted, almost line by line. So he stopped. He said to himself (as he later told me): If I can't say anything speculative and let people know I am thinking and dreaming about this now, and let it be taken as such, I'm not going to say anything. So he stopped making speculative reconstructions, except where he thought they would be understood as such. He never said they were necessarily accurate, and he used to change them every few years.

He didn't believe in historical reconstruction unless it was based upon sound methods, and for history of peoples without written history, sound methods to him meant that you began with archaeology. On this point he was clear, that if you didn't have archaeology you didn't have anything. He promoted archaeology in the Jesup studies, and at the establishment of the Mexican International Institute he promoted and worked on archaeology, uncovering the stratification of the Valley of Mexico and establishing the existence of the Archaic below the advanced strata. This was the first clear case of stratigraphic results in American archaeology. He wasn't particularly interested in doing archaeology, but he stimulated others to do it. A number of young archaeologists got their Ph.D.s with Boas at Columbia, and he worked closely with archaeologists, at the American Museum of Natural History and elsewhere. For instance, he went with J. Alden Mason to Puerto Rico one time, where Mason did some archaeology.

I think that the whole problem is that Kroeber's meanings and concepts are vague and indecisive. Among the letters of Boas, there are some commenting on his students, and of Kroeber he said one time, "He never thinks anything through." If you are familiar with some of Kroeber's work you may decide what you think of that statement. In contrast to that, he said that Sapir was his great illustration to himself of an anthropologist. He tried all his life to get Sapir to Columbia and never succeeded.

GENE WELTFISH: Dr. Lesser, I think that in some ways you have made anthropologists sound much too logical as personalities. Their shenanigans have been enormous. For one thing, in the 1920s, when the Americanist Congress was held at the American Museum, we—the Boas school—were accused of being too theoretical and not knowing our facts, while the Harvard school really had the facts. So we rose up and spilled the facts. Then, in 1939, at the meeting of the AAA at which Sapir presided, the question of a resolution against the Nazi classification of the races came up. Sapir proposed the resolution. Thereafter the whole meeting split. On one side were most of the people; on the other side was a poor little group which included Boas, you, me, May Edel, and Gladys Reichard. We voted for this resolution. All the rest of the gang rose up and voted against it, on the grounds that the Germans were a friendly power. Afterward Sapir, with his fine sense of humor, said, "This resolution was proposed by A. E. Hooton of Harvard." Everyone thought they were voting against a resolution proposed by Boas. So the shenanigans of anthropologists over time should be made clear. They aren't really logical.

LESSER: I thank you for that statement, but I was not talking about the shenanigans of anthropologists, but about Boas. I don't think he was guilty of many shenanigans. One of the reasons, I think, has been correctly discussed by Stocking in his historical analysis of the reaction against cultural anthropology. He credits the attacks on Boas not only to a disagreement with his concept of culture as basic, but also to the fact that many of these individuals were deeply envious of Boas and his achievements, and also to the fact that he persisted in his concepts and ideas and didn't withdraw them and eclectically accept the opposite because somebody insisted upon it. I think Stocking has a point there. In other words, it took a long time for non-Boasian anthropologists to accept the modern concept of culture, to give up the emphasis upon instinct and to look at learning and culture instead. These things, and the fact that there were no inferior races, came hard. Even in 1919 there were a lot of anthropologists who were still using the idea of inferior races and publishing old-fashioned physical anthropology.

Roland Dixon's book *The Racial History of Man* was for twenty-five years on the shelves of most colleges and universities, as if it were a basic study of the history of races and their spread. It was based upon a simple error, which is shown in the discussion of his method at the beginning of the book; namely, that if you have a normal curve distribution, with extremes and a middle, then the extremes are pure types and the middle is hybrid. He used this idea in his analyses of statistical results from all over the world on three measurements—nose, head, and height of head. On this basis there is a four-hundred-page book of analysis of the racial history of man—not one word of which is science. Dixon, who was a professor at Harvard, never retracted a line. There was a whole series of typological thinkers in physical anthropology at Harvard who refused to recognize the problems of biometrics.

This went on while Boas was teaching the exact opposite. He reviewed these things, he had his say about them, but he couldn't stop people from having their right to free speech. In the long run he won; that's the important point. The reaction against him is another story.

BIOGRAPHICAL NOTE

Courtesy of Sidney Mintz   1976

ALEXANDER LESSER, born in 1902, grew up in New York City. He attended Columbia College from 1919 to 1923, majoring in philosophy under John Dewey. A
course with Boas aroused his interest in anthropology and led him to take evening
courses with Alexander Goldenweiser at the New School for Social Research. After college Lesser spent three years in business, then decided to go on with graduate work in social philosophy. He thought, however, that this required an
empirical base in social science, and he turned to Boas's anthropology, which
seemed to him the most scientific of the social sciences at Columbia. He completed his Ph.D. in 1929 with a dissertation on Siouan kinship, one of a series of
kinship studies in which he attempted to show that general laws exist in social phenomena. In so doing, he was challenging and bridging the divide that had emerged
in the anthropology of the time between historical and functional approaches.

   During the 1930s Lesser did extensive field research among the Plains Indians,
principally on social organization, religion, and linguistics. His two years of intensive fieldwork among the Pawnee, along with his first wife Gene Weltfish, led to
his *Pawnee Ghost Dance Hand Game* (1933), a groundbreaking study of what later
came to be known as a revitalization movement. Taking up the problem of the Indian rejection of assimilation, it combined social history, which for Lesser meant
recognition of the assaults that white contact had inflicted on the Indians, with
analysis of the cultural innovation in the Indian response. In 1935 Lesser served
as field leader for the Laboratory of Anthropology (Santa Fe) Field Training Expedition among the Kiowa Indians. Organized collaboratively, it resulted in a se-

ries of studies that reflected Lesser's emphasis on economic factors in the contact situation. Through his work with students from Columbia on this project, which continued in seminars (some in conjunction with William Duncan Strong) and in his input on dissertations, Lesser created a link to a third Boasian generation during the 1930s, whose approach to culture incorporated a concern with economic and political realities and for whom culture history included the impact of contact.

Lesser presented his views on the compatibility (in fact, the necessary interdependence) of history and functionalism at an AAA meeting in 1935, provoking a heated debate with A. R. Radcliffe-Brown. In 1939 he again caused a sensation at the AAA with a paper on evolution, a subject still taboo at the time (the paper was eventually published in 1952). Attacking the profession's "nihilism as regards problems of cultural sequence and development," Lesser argued that evolution in the Darwinian sense could be joined with culture history, and he advocated an evolutionary research strategy that could avoid both the pitfalls of Social Darwinism and the confusion of "necessary" and "sufficient" causes. In the uproar that followed, Lowie, Malinowski, and others declared that they had never been "antievolution."

After holding a series of temporary teaching positions at Columbia and elsewhere (including a course taught jointly with Boas at New York University in 1934), Lesser joined the Brooklyn College faculty in 1939. From 1947 to 1955 he served as executive director of the Association on American Indian Affairs (AAIA), where he promoted legal action to protect Indian rights and to oppose assimilationist government policies intended to negate the government's treaty obligations and other entitlements of Indian groups. In his role at the AAIA, Lesser encouraged a number of anthropologists to write action-oriented articles for the association's magazine, the *American Indian*. He presented his own views on Indian policy in an influential paper (1961a), reprinted under the title "The Right to Not Assimilate." After his years as a powerfully effective applied anthropologist, Lesser returned to academia to teach at Brandeis University. In 1960 he went to Hofstra University as chairman of the department of anthropology and sociology. He retired in 1974 as a professor emeritus.

Lesser's ideas on social regularities, the role of history in cultural analysis, the dynamics of Indian–European contact, and the concept of "social fields" to replace notions of primitive societies as isolates (1961b) all have proven to be ahead of their time, although they did not receive—then or since—the recognition they deserved. He remained committed to Boasian anthropology all his life and in his last years was a vigorous defender of Boas's legacy; but in fact his work repeatedly departed from Boas and took creative new directions. Lesser himself minimized these advances, regarding them as extensions, not rejections, of the tradition in which he was trained.

Alexander Lesser died in 1982. A collection of his essays, edited by his onetime student Sidney Mintz, was published in 1985.

Alfred Kroeber in 1920. Courtesy of the Bancroft Library, University of California, Berkeley

2

ALFRED L. KROEBER

Eric R. Wolf

In 1901 Franz Boas's fledgling department at Columbia awarded a Ph.D. to
Alfred L. Kroeber. That same year Kroeber was appointed as an instructor
in the anthropology department that had just been created at the University
of California, although Boas thought he was not ready to work independently. Kroeber would pursue a career of prodigious scholarship and training of other scholars for sixty years. He attained an eminence in American
anthropology second only to that of Boas, becoming after Boas's death the
senior figure in the field.

Kroeber's approach was firmly rooted in that of his teacher, although
there were significant differences between them. He took Boas's historicity,
which Boas had introduced as a corrective to theories based on precon-
ceived schemes of cultural development, and made it the central feature of
his anthropology. He inherited from Boas the concept of culture as an autonomous realm, which could not be explained in terms of race or geography or "mentality," and extended it into an explicit statement of cultural
determinism in "The Superorganic" (1917)—which, however, he later re-
canted. Like Boas, he described culture–environment relationships while
denying environment any explanatory power, but went further than Boas in
stressing cultural creativity. Unlike Boas, his view of history excluded any
role of the individual and any interest in personality.

Kroeber's substantive specialty was American Indian (especially Californian) ethnology and languages, but his writings were encyclopedic in scope,
ranging over the subfields of anthropology and over the cultures of all parts of
the world and all periods. He was one of the first anthropologists to undertake

analysis of complex "high" civilizations, endeavoring to show that aesthetic and intellectual achievements followed principles of cultural history. Kroeber's syntheses stand as embodiments of the "grand view" in anthropology.

To reassess Kroeber's work—to reconsider what he said and what he meant—is a difficult undertaking, for he has left more than 700 publications, many extremely weighty and very few that are simply occasional remarks. They range all the way from studies of Romance glottochronology, California Indian basket designs, and Zuni clans to discussions of the novel in Europe and Asia and studies of changes in women's dress over a hundred-year period. In order to truly master this body of material, one would have to be Kroeber and start at the beginning and live as long as he did.

For anthropologists of my generation, Kroeber was the living embodiment of American anthropology. His books and his words accompanied us through graduate school, and he appeared in our professional lives again and again. I knew him only after his retirement, when he gave a course at Columbia, a course entirely dedicated to the Yurok. But his influence at Columbia was strong through his students, especially Julian Steward, whose understandings of anthropology should, I think, be seen as a reaction to Kroeber—in a sense an outcome of a dialectic between Kroeber and himself. When I met Kroeber personally, I found him personable and delightful, a benign, Apollonian, Olympian figure. But at that time he must have been more mellow than he had been earlier in life, because there were many people who lived in terror of him. I saw him last in 1960, shortly before his death, at a conference he had organized, "Horizons of Anthropology," at Burg Wartenstein in Austria. He had brought together the oddest assortment of people I have ever had the pleasure of meeting. The group included Claude Lévi-Strauss, Cristoph von Fürer-Haimendorf, Wilhelm Milke (who will go down in history as the man who included a measurement of the curvature of the earth in his calculations of diffusion rates), and Dell Hymes, among others. I asked him why he had invited us all, and he said that he did so because we were all mavericks. It is as a maverick, then, that I address myself to the task of assessing this ancestor. I am helped in this by several biographies or biographical statements that have come out on Kroeber, especially that by his second wife, Theodora (T. Kroeber 1970); by Steward's short appreciation of him (1973); but especially by Hymes's obituary in *Language* (1961).

Kroeber was born in Hoboken, New Jersey, in 1876; he died in Paris in 1960, on his way back home from that "Horizons" conference. His parents were German Americans. His father had come to the United States at the age of ten. His mother was born in New York, where Kroeber grew up. The parents were Protestants. The language of the home in Kroeber's youth was German; Kroeber said that he spoke English with an accent when he went off to school. Kroeber himself characterized the comfortable world in which he lived—his father imported European clocks—as "Deutsch-amerikanisch." It was a liberal bourgeois world in which German Jews and gentiles still shared the illusions of the bourgeois Enlightenment, a respect for learning, and the literary-philosophical heritage of Kant, Goethe, and the German idealists.

Kroeber and his friends were also raised in the German tradition of natural-historical interests—a tradition that insisted on the preparation of herbaria and on the collection and mounting of butterflies and beetles, and that sent boys and girls to Bronx Park to explore for minerals and fossils. Kroeber retained throughout his life an interest in and gift for the observation of insect and animal existence. Theodora Kroeber tells of him spending most of a day on the shore of northern Peru, sitting on a rock a few yards offshore, observing an octopus and slowly stroking its tentacles with a reed over a long period of time, as if to reassure the wary beast that he meant no harm. One of his unfinished book-length manuscripts is called "Hard and Small"—a whole book on insectivores—where he waxed especially enthusiastic about the aquatic shrew. He similarly retained an active interest in literature. He translated Heine into English and Housman into German, spent hours comparing different versions of Keats, and wrote a comparative study of the novel in Europe and Asia.

Kroeber entered Columbia College at the age of sixteen and got his B.A. in English in 1896. He went on to write on the Romantic drama for the M.A. in 1897. But in 1896 he had by chance taken a course with Boas, who had just arrived at Columbia. It was concerned with the analysis of American Indian languages, and Kroeber felt enormously stimulated by it. "Boas's method," he would write later, "was very similar to that of the zoologist who starts a student with an etherized frog or worm and a dissecting table" (T. Kroeber 1970: 47). He then embarked upon the study of anthropology, with psychology as a minor. In 1901, after two summers among the Arapaho, he wrote his doctoral thesis on decorative symbolism of the Arapaho, receiving the second Ph.D. in anthropology awarded by Columbia. A field trip for the Academy of Sciences in San Francisco took him to California in 1900, and the following year he became the first member of the Department of Anthropology at Berkeley. He was associated with Berkeley until his retirement in 1946. He continued to write and to lecture, holding visiting appointments at various universities, until his death fourteen years later.

Except for one period of disruption, he was an extraordinarily well-attuned man. This period deserves some explication. In 1913 his first wife died of tuberculosis. Shortly afterward, Kroeber himself became seriously ill with what we now know to have been Ménière's syndrome—an affliction of the inner ear—but which was then thought to be due to a case of nerves. The disease left him permanently deaf in the left ear.[1] In 1916 he experienced the death of a friend, the last Yana Indian, Ishi, whom Kroeber had befriended after he was found exhausted and lost outside a California town. I think this death had a considerable impact upon Kroeber. Then in 1917, Kroeber completed the massive *Handbook of the Indians of California* (which was not published, however, until 1925); with this body of work done he didn't quite know where to go next. Finally, the long shadow of war starting for the United States in 1917 must have dimmed that naive liberal faith of the German Americans in their new land. Whatever the reasons, Kroeber went into psychoanalysis in 1917. He became a practicing analyst in 1918, continuing this practice until 1922. This period of uncertainty, to which Kroeber would later refer as his "hegira," ended in 1926 with his second marriage to Theodora Kracaw, a gifted storyteller and writer. He never returned to an interest in psychoanalysis after 1922.

Kroeber wrote a great deal and contributed to all the subfields of anthropology. I will refer to only a few items from his prodigious bibliography. The *Handbook of the Indians of California* was followed by *Anthropology* (1923), which for a long time was the only textbook on the subject available to American students. It was a textbook for students who went into anthropology in the '20s and '30s, was still the basic text at Queens College when I went there in 1940, and was one of the ten books required of all students in the first year at Columbia during the late '40s. In 1931 Kroeber completed *Cultural and Natural Areas of Native North America*, which was not published until 1939 (an example of the long history of publication lag). The dates for *Cultural and Natural Areas* are significant because they show that the element surveys of the '30s—the collection and mapping of thousands of traits in hundreds of tribes—came after Kroeber completed the book that presents an integrated picture of the North American cultural map. A key sentence that explains the idea behind the element surveys appears in *Areas*: "It should be possible to determine an approximately objective measure of cultural intensity by measuring culture content—by counting distinguishable elements, for instance. This is a task which no one is ready to perform for the continent, but theoretically it is feasible and it might be worthwhile" (1939: 222). After finishing *Cultural and Natural Areas*, he began *Configurations of Culture Growth*, which was started in 1931, completed in 1938, and set in type only in 1944. The revised version of *Anthropology* appeared in 1948; chapters 7 to 14 on patterns and configurations were the essential new additions. Several books of essays followed, including *The Nature of Culture* (1952) and *Style and Civilizations* (1957).

Kroeber came to anthropology through linguistics, and he maintained an abiding interest in the study of language throughout his career. His view of the study of language and linguistics affords us the most productive point of entry into this vast corpus of his theoretical writings. It can be argued, without danger of distortion, that his understanding of linguistic data and findings provided a cognitive map for much of his anthropology. He was clearly aware that language was only a part of culture, but he thought that its study—as a part of culture—held lessons for the study of other aspects of culture as well. This approach is best exemplified by his remarks at a Viking Fund talk in 1947, which is included in *The Nature of Culture* as item 12, "The Causes of Culture." We have here the programmatic statement of some of his theoretical understandings. It is true, as Ralph Beals has noted, "that many of his theoretical formulations are embedded more or less incidentally in a profusion of phenomenological data" (1968: 457). It is also true that his varied interests led him in many different directions, some of which he would pursue for awhile and then abandon, at times to the disappointment of students whose dissertations he initiated and then never returned to. Yet I think that his basic theoretical thrust was remarkably of one piece, was set very early, and was highly consistent. In 1947, he wrote:

Now there are actual, established fields of organized study which deal almost exclusively with quasi-cultural forms, and which therefore serve as useful touchstones for the qualities that may be expected to distinguish sciences of the narrow as compared with the broad construction of culture. Of such studies, linguistics is the best known, most reputable, and neatest and most advanced in method. Relatively to other studies of man, linguistics is characterized by several traits: (1) Its data and findings are essentially impersonal, anonymous. (2) Its orientation is spontaneously historical, and potentially historical even for languages whose past has been lost. (3) The emphasis is on pattern, or structural interrelation, and away from so-called "functional" interpretation involving need satisfaction, drives, stimulus-response, and other explanations which "decompose" the phenomena dealt with into something ulterior. (4) Explanation is not in terms of genuine scientific cause, that is, efficient causes in the Aristotelian sense, but of "formal causes," that is, of other forms as being antecedent, similar, contrasting, or related. (5) Indeed, "explanation" in terms of producing cause is largely replaced by "understanding" in terms of historic contexts, relevance, and value significance. (1952: 107)

Kroeber here states the major points of his anthropological approach. I would like to take these points up one by one, because they apply to a vast range of things that he was interested in. The first among the characteristics of linguistics that he sets forth is "impersonality," the stress on language structure and not on how language is spoken; as Ferdinand de Saussure might have said, on "langue" and not on "parole." Transposed to aspects of culture other than language, this criterion emerges as the principle of the superorganic. The term is, of course, Herbert Spencer's; Kroeber borrowed it knowingly and made use of it in his paper, "The Superorganic," first published in the *American Anthropologist* in 1917.

That essay is multifaceted; it covers a very wide agenda. One of its aims was to protest "the blind and bland shuttling back and forth between an equivocal race and an equivocal civilization" (1952: 22), in other words to counteract the confusion between race and culture. Closely related to this was a second intent—and this needs to be underlined—to speak out against the danger of applying Darwinian or post-Darwinian principles of the evolution of life to the evolution of culture. Kroeber admits the reality of cultural evolution: "there is obvious, even to the least learned, a growth or evolution of civilization." It is true, he argues, that culture "exists only in and through living members of the species" and is "outwardly so similar to the evolution of plants and animals" in this regard; but one must guard against "sweeping applications of the principles of organic development to the facts of cultural growth" (1952: 23). To paraphrase him further: The growth of new species of animals takes place through changes in their organic constitutions. Human cultures, however, change through invention and diffusion, without concomitant organic alterations. No amount of reference to biology and heredity will explicate cultural cumulation and variation.

Then Kroeber takes one additional step. Francis Galton, K. Pearson, and others argued that heredity operates in the domain of the mind as well as that of the body, but their supposed corollary "that therefore heredity is the mainspring of civilization, is an entirely different proposition, without necessary connection and without established connection with the former conclusion" (1952: 40). Civilization, Kroeber says, is "not mental action but a stream of products of mental exercise. . . . Mentality relates to the individual. The social or cultural, on the other hand, is in its essence non-individual" (1952: 40). Darwin and Gregor Mendel dealt with populations made up of individuals, "but a thousand individuals do not make a society" (1952: 41), and cultural products and knowledge cannot be explained by reference to the individual whose name is associated historically with their invention or diffusion. Even individual geniuses are but "indicators of coherent pattern growths of cultural value."

> When we cease to look upon invention or discovery as some mysterious faculty of individual minds which are randomly dropped in space and time by fate; when we center our attention on the plainer relation of one such advancing step to the others; when, in short, interest shifts from individually biographic elements and attaches wholeheartedly to the social or civilizational, evidence on this point will be infinite in quantity, and the presence of majestic forces or sequences pervading civilization will be irresistibly evident. (1952: 45)

This, written in 1917, is essentially the program for *Configurations of Culture Growth*, begun in 1931, the book Kroeber regarded as his best and most original contribution. It best demonstrates how he translated the linguistic criterion of impersonality into the anthropological concept of the superorganic.

Take the second characteristic: Linguistics is "spontaneously historical." It is important to recognize that here Kroeber has reference to historical linguistics and not structural linguistics as we now know it. The implication is that cultural forms, like linguistic forms, are connected genetically in time and contextually in space, and if we are to understand cultural phenomena we must always visualize them in their context of time and space. Again, in *The Nature of Culture* there is an essay in which he makes the point that historical understanding tries to maintain the context of time and space, whereas those people interested in general processes, that is, scientists, try to abstract from particular connections in time and space to more abstract analytic propositions. He accuses Boas of being interested much more in process than in history.

> The dealing with time sequences is likely to be the first answer. But this trait seems only an incident. The essential characteristic of the historic approach appears to be the endeavor to achieve a conceptual integration of phenomena while preserving the quality of the phenomena. This quality the strictly scientific approach does not attempt to preserve. On the contrary, it destroys phenomena as phenomena in utilizing them for its own conceptualizations of a different order. Time and space certainly enter into the considerations and results of science proper; but its findings or end-results are timeless and spaceless formulations, in the sense that they are independent of specific or particular time and place. The findings of the historical approach, on the other hand, are necessarily always given in terms of specified time and space—phenomenal time and space, we might say, in contrast to the abstract measure of time and space in science. A dateless and placeless finding in human history, natural history, paleontology, geology, or astronomy would make no sense. If a dateless and placeless block of phenomena is discovered, the first problem of any historical discipline is recognized to be the findings of its date and place. Conversely, where a phenomenal lacuna appears in the date-place frame, the filling of this lacuna with the relevant phenomena is felt to be a need and problem. The historical approach is therefore always reconstructive in its nature—reconstructive as to the phenomena themselves and as to their dates and places. (1952: 70)

This, then, is the source of his intellectual quarrel with Boas, a matter that has been the subject of some misunderstanding. Just as the task of historical linguistics is the reconstruction of the probable linkages between linguistic forms in time and space, so the task of culture history, Kroeber says, is the probabilistic reconstruction of connections between cultural forms both temporally and spatially. Sometimes, probable connections could be discovered through application of the age-area principle, even where other temporal perspectives were missing. Here Boas departed from the argument and refused to have anything to do with it, and Kroeber accused him of being interested in "process," like sociologists and functionalists, and lacking an interest in history. Kroeber held the task of reconstruction to be valid and primary. Only thus would laws of change be discovered, and they would be—to underline another phrasing of Kroeber's—not laws of causality, but laws of formal variation, as in the sound shifts of historical linguistics.

Kroeber's studies of changes in women's fashion reveal his search for laws of formal variation, not of causality. These studies are numerous and have always been perplexing, because he seemingly disregards questions about the fashion designers, the audiences that buy the fashions, how the clothes are produced, and the like. These are studies of formal changes and variations in particular dimensions of women's skirt length and skirt width over time; he is interested in defining the sound shifts, if you like, the cyclical shifts back and forth within a particular pattern that is made up of a series of elements. These studies of fashion seem to me to be some of the exercises most diagnostic of his particular interpretation.

Kroeber's first criterion marking linguistics—and by implication the kind of cultural study he favored—was impersonality; the second was history. The third criterion was "the emphasis . . . on pattern, on structural interrelation, and away from so-called 'functional' interpretation," which Kroeber stigmatizes as essentially psychological and biological in character. The term *pattern* conjures up Ruth Benedict's patterns of culture, but Kroeber had something rather different in mind. Benedict's patterns were essentially psychological; his were not. He says he is not interested in the psychological domain; he is not interested in the socialization of personalities into a culture.

> In the Benedict approach a pattern is a psychic constellation molding the typical personality of a society by imparting a certain warp to that society's culture. The basic patterns referred to [in Kroeber's essay] are the more pervasive and permanent forms assumed by a specific mass of cultural content, and they tend to spread from one society to others. In short, basic patterns are nexuses of culture traits which have assumed a definite and coherent structure, which function successfully, and which acquire major historic weight and persistence. (1952: 92)

Elsewhere he uses the imagery of culture as a stream. In looking at the overall stream of culture and the jostling of the culture elements or traits that make up that stream, one can notice eddies or whirlpools in time and space. These are particular cultures, exhibiting eddylike or whirlpool-like patterns of greater or lesser duration. There are also other patterns—flows or waves, he says—that crosscut these eddies and whirlpools. They are what he called "systemic patterns" in his 1948 *Anthropology*. Examples of such systemic patterns are the alphabet, the calendar, the universal religions, and plow agriculture. Once again, writing in 1951, he drew a parallel from historical linguistics, likening these patterns to groups of

> historically related languages such as the Indo-European ones or the Semito-Hamitic. These share a pervasive pattern of structure. This may be considered a grand system, to which the smaller correspondent would be any particular language with its tendency to maintain much of its particular plan of structure through successive periods of alteration. (1952: 94)

I think the image of language was never very far below his consciousness. He compared style to grammar on numerous occasions. One such is in *Style and Civilizations*:

That the members of our civilization and of others are very little aware of total style need not discourage us much. Every human language has such a patterned style— we call it its grammar—of which the speakers are unaware while speaking, but which can be discovered by analysis and can be formulated. The coherence of a grammar is never total or ideal, but is always considerable; it certainly much exceeds a catalogue of random items. Cultures are larger, more varied and complicated sets of phenomena than languages as well as more substantive and less autonomous. But the two are interrelated—in fact, language is obviously a part of culture, and probably its precondition. So the structure of cultures, like that of languages, also seems potentially describable in terms of an overall patterning. (1957: 106)

Although he doesn't say it, I would then add: "—in terms of a grammar."

Thus, there is an interest in the recognition, delimitation, and characterization of "patterns"—small and large, temporary and enduring, localized and widespread—in occurrences of phenomena and their co-occurrences, but not in causality. This is the fourth criterion. "Explanation is not in terms of genuine scientific causes, . . . but of 'formal causes,' that is, of other forms as being antecedent, similar, contrasting, or related" (1952: 107). His *Configurations of Culture Growth* deals with the appearance and disappearance of clusters of inventions. In his conclusions to the book, he notes that some have held that there might be a correlation of such clustering with wealth or population, but he postpones discussion. "No serious long-range and comparative studies appear, however, to have been undertaken on this problem, and it seems wise to defer opinion until they shall have been made" (1944: 839). *Cultural and Natural Areas of Native North America* (1939) is full of suggested correlations between aspects of the environment and aspects of culture. This work, in fact, led him to studies of native populations and their clustering. But the purpose of the study was not the analytic study of processes. Kroeber reiterates that

while it is true that cultures are rooted in nature, and can therefore never be completely understood except with reference to that piece of nature in which they occur, they are no more produced by that nature than a plant is produced or caused by the soil in which it is rooted. The immediate cause of cultural phenomena are other cultural phenomena. (1939: 1)

It is not adequate, he felt, to explain the process of cultural production by reference to general analytic processes. Once again he accuses Boas of being interested in process, to the detriment of history—"the purpose of history is genetic." Culture must not be explained in terms of analytic reference back to psychology or biology. It must also not be referred back to "behavior." For example, kin

terms—contrary to Lewis Henry Morgan and W. H. R. Rivers—are only indirectly and not directly shaped by social life. They "reflect unconscious logic and
conceptual patterning" (1952: 172). Kroeber criticized "the injection into anthropology of the concept of behavior, first developed as a corrective in the internal
emancipation or purification of psychology" (1952: 8). He always hated the idea
that anthropology might someday come to be ranked among the behavioral sciences, and he detested sociology as ameliorative do-gooding that mixed sloppy
values with science. In the end, however, he made his peace with Talcott Parsons
by dividing up the world between sociology and anthropology, much as the kings
of Spain and Portugal divided up the world between the Spanish empire and the
Portuguese empire in the Treaty of Tordesillas of 1494.

The distrust of sociology and behavioral references seems to me to be strongly
influenced by his particular liberal German bourgeois background, which dis-
trusted politics to the utmost and stayed away from involvement in it. In this milieu, people believed in peace among men, universal understanding, the increase
of enlightenment, the happy coexistence of German gentiles and Jews in the midst
of ever-increasing prosperity. They believed in progress: The world would grow
more civilized, and people would come to understand one another. Politics, however, was dirty business. Kroeber lived in the environment of the New York Ethical Culture Society that was, and still is, an embodiment of those values. I suspect
that much of Kroeber's view of the world came filtered through this set of values.[2]

Thus, Kroeber was grimly determined not to mix science and politics. He
played a leading part in the organization of language programs for the U.S.
Army in World War II (the ASTP, or Army Specialized Training Program), but
he saw this as nonpolitical. He took part in the Indian Claims cases of the
1950s, but the involvement made him deeply uneasy. He unleashed a veritable
bolt of lightning against Dorothy Gregg and Elgin Williams (1948), who
launched a kind of premature New Leftist attack on anthropology, criticizing it
as the "the dismal science of functionalism." Kroeber lashed into them as ad-
vocating "an authoritarian panacea" and stated his belief that "the method of
science is to begin with questions not with answers, least of all with value judge-
ments," and "Science is dispassionate inquiry" (1949: 320).[3] He was enraged
when Morris Swadesh—with whom he entertained close collegial relations—
protested his ouster from City College for radical activities and tried to address
a session of an international congress then meeting in New York City. Kroeber
opposed the reorganization of the American Anthropological Association into a
larger professional organization, wanting to keep it a collection of scholars without applied or public interests. One can find throughout his writings a strong
sense of distaste for anything that had to do with politics, with involvement in
nonscience, and I think also with sociology—all those enterprises that had to
do, he thought, with trying to improve the world.

The fifth criterion in Kroeber's list is "value significance." In linguistics,
Kroeber says approvingly, "'explanation' in terms of producing cause is largely

replaced by 'understanding' in terms of historic contexts, relevance, and value significance" (1952:107). Kroeber came to think of culture as having two ingredients (so he calls them), one of which he calls *reality culture*, the other *value culture*. Oddly, Kroeber rarely defined values; he preferred instead to list exemplifications of the concept in terms of concepts put forth by others, such as ethos, eidos, patterns, and postulates. Yet there are passages in his posthumous *Roster of Civilizations and Culture* (1962) that come closer to a definition of his own than I have been able to find elsewhere. He wrote, apparently in 1957, that value culture was to be so called

> on the ground of having value, or being an end in itself, and not merely means to practical ends. It includes all purely aesthetic and intellectual activity; but without being rigorously delimited to such activity. It certainly includes an element in every religion, though religion usually also contains organization and institutionalization; and it includes some part of morals, though morality is directed also to personal conduct and action. What is called "creativity" coincides pretty closely with a concern for value culture as just defined. (1962: 9–10)

Values are thus culturally produced ends in themselves. Culturally produced, they are superorganic. They may not be explained with reference to physiology, biochemistry, or psychology. Such an explanation, he said on an earlier occasion, disregards the essential specific properties of values. These are retainable only as long as the phenomena of value continue to be "inspected" on the cultural level (1952: 138). The inspector of values must make no value judgments of his own. He must focus his interest on "values as they éxist in human societies at given times and places . . . as they make their appearance in the history of our species; in short, . . . values as natural phenomena occurring in nature—much like the characteristic forms, qualities, and abilities of animals are defined in comparative zoology" (1952: 137).

What, then, is the role of the anthropologist who wishes to understand culture as a stream of forms sui generis, without reference to human biology, psychology, ecology, or sociability—the anthropologist who turns away from science with its apparatus of cause and effect, and seeks instead to discover the laws of motion of constellations of forms without an appeal to movers; who wishes to note the gamut of human values without reference to human creators but as ingredients located in the arrays of cultural forms? His task is to classify the cultural eddies and whirlpools, to delimit and contrast such patterns as are discernible in the stream of culture; classification, above all. Kroeber said on many occasions that classification is what the anthropologist is supposed to do: "I feel that the study of both culture and language is in crying need, in its own right, of far more systematic classification of their multifarious phenomena. Perhaps we have a surplus of bright ideas and a shortage of consistent ordering and comparison of our data" (1960a: 17). And elsewhere: "Anthropologists . . . do not yet clearly recognize the fundamental value of the humble but indispensable task of classifying—that is, structuring—our body of knowledge, as biologists did begin to recognize it two hundred years ago" (1960b: 14). Again: "Culture area classifications were somewhat comparable to the pre-Darwinian taxonomies of the plant and animal kingdoms; and like them they contained an implicit developmental theory. . . . I regard such a formulation as one of the things that the world of learning has the right to expect from anthropology" (1962: 15–16).

To order and classify, Kroeber relied heavily on counting, that is, on statistics. I will cite only a few examples out of many. In 1919, in order to discover the relationships between sixty-seven dialects of twenty-one California linguistic stocks, he sorted 225 cognates into tables, thus inventing an early form of lexicostatistics. In 1916 he carried out a seriation of surface sherds of sites near Zuni, unaware of the fact that A. Kidder had already introduced this method a year earlier (an instance of parallel invention). In 1919 he began his plotting of variations in women's fashions—an interest carried forward with Jane Richardson in a quantitative analysis (Kroeber and Richardson 1940)—in order to show that a constellation of forms obeyed an inherent rhythm of variation and stability. In the years between 1934 and 1938 the culture-element survey of native western North America went forward, in which thirteen field investigators collected data from 254 tribes or bands. In the 1950s he wholeheartedly embraced glottochronology, applying the method to Romance and Athabascan languages. In 1960 he added "Comparative Notes on the Yurok Culture" to W. W. Elmendorf's *The Structure of Twana Culture*, showing that the two cultures differed in only 4 elements out of about 2,000 but that these 4 elements were decisive in imparting to Yurok culture its distinctive patterned difference from the other (Elmendorf and Kroeber 1960).

I undertook to write about Kroeber to try to understand this body of work that accompanied many of us through so much of our lifetimes. In pondering the corpus of his work, I found there were themes in it that continue to have resonance for us. I would summarize them as follows:

1. The emphasis on societies and cultures as open sets or systems, existing in mutual interchanges with one another.
2. The emphasis on cultural form and the possible implications of cultural forms, a problem that still remains with us, though often muted in the search for function.
3. The interest in style or pattern cohesion, a phenomenon that still defies explanation in its own terms in anthropology.
4. The suggestion that some aspects of culture may be generated without specific utility or cause, which provides a salutary antidote to the sour utilitarianism of adaptationists.

Yet what is most striking now is that totally absent from Kroeber's work is any sense of the relevance of the concept of adaptation.[4] This was, above all, the contribution to American anthropology of Julian Steward, and it was something that Kroeber never understood, cared about, or paid any attention to. There were any number of occasions when Steward tried to explain to Kroeber what he was about, and Kroeber would continue to talk about theories of pottery on the Peruvian coast or about the importance of knowing the connectedness of cultural elements in time and context. Steward's concern with cultural causality and his attempt to plot parallels in culture types and sequences of culture types were simply of no interest to him.

What did Kroeber think he was doing? He thought of his anthropology as a variant of natural history. He returned to this definition many times, but nowhere more clearly than in 1955 when he said:

> The phenomena are given as directly as possible and in their contextual relation of occurrence. This context is preserved: if explanations are made, they are marginal, as it were, and do not fundamentally disturb the context. This is the method of what in the earth and life sciences is widely known as natural history. The use of this very term natural history for a branch of knowing that deals with phenomena far more by description than by narration is indication that the difference between these two techniques of narration and description is incidental to the more fundamental quality of organized presentation of knowledge with all possible preservation of the data in themselves and in their relations of occurrence. *In short, it is phenomenal presentation.* (1963: 110–11)

Taking this view as a definition of his own efforts and as a portrayal of his discipline allows us to unravel some of the theoretical threads that run through the body of the man's work.

As a natural historian he is in the tradition of Alexander von Humboldt, who called himself a cosmographer (a geographer, we would say nowadays) and defined the task of cosmography as follows: (1) to seek "a knowledge of the chain of connections, by which all natural forces are linked together, and made mutually dependent upon each other"; and (2) "to analyze the individual paths of natural phenomena without succumbing beneath the weight of the whole" (von Humboldt, quoted in Kluckhohn and Prufer 1959: 12). Classification and taxonomy were the tasks through which these connections would emerge, by noting similarity or difference of form and following out a logic of forms. Here we may recall that Kroeber often referred to his interest in cultural taxonomy and classification as being Linnean and pre-Darwinian—noting the multitude of organisms (cultural phenomena) in their total array and variation, but without any theory of natural selection (or cultural selection).

But Kroeber at the same time aimed at being a natural historian of the superorganic. In his article on the superorganic he speaks of the emergence of culture as a saltation, a jump, a change from quantity into quality, but occurring in *nature*. "Nature is not set aside." This is fundamental, for it distinguishes him from culture historians like Wilhelm Windelband and especially Heinrich

Rickert (1863–1936), with whom he carried on a running debate in numerous publications. Rickert, a neo-Kantian, held that science was applicable to the study of matter but that the phenomena of value (mind) could not be reduced to matter and required a method of their own: the famous "understanding" or *Verstehen* of phenomena in their space and time continuity (a concept that also crops up in Max Weber). Kroeber's solution to the problem posed by these German idealists is surprising. Rickert's contraposition of science as adequate to the study of matter, and history as adequate to the study of culture, is false, Kroeber says, because there are genuinely historical components to the sciences of astronomy, geology, and biology. Moreover, if the superorganic occurs in nature, if nature is not set aside, then values—quintessential ingredients of culture—must be "natural phenomena occurring in nature—much like the characteristic forms, qualities, and abilities of animals as defined by comparative zoology" (1952: 137). While in organic species values are inherent in their genetic equipment, in culture they are superorganic: inherent in cultural patterns. But in the search for cultural connections, for the connection of elements and patterns in time and space, Kroeber was a cosmographer like Humboldt, a seeker after the chain of connections by which all natural forces are linked together; one could paraphrase this, for Kroeber, as the chain of connections by which all cultural forms are linked together. This is the concept of The Great Chain of Being, which Arthur Lovejoy has so lovingly analyzed. It is the pre-Darwinian idea that all things manifest in nature are connected in some way ultimately in the mind of God.

Finally, Kroeber thought of himself as a *natural* historian of culture, and he argued at length against those like Georg W. F. Hegel, Arnold Toynbee, N. Danilewski, Oswald Spengler, P. A. Sorokin, and many others who would endow history with a teleological meaning. Yet beneath the scrupulous historian of culture there lurks ultimately a natural philosopher, a *Naturphilosoph* of the German Romantic tradition. There may be no causality in Kroeber, but there is a principle—a prime mover—that appears in disguise wherever a pattern climax enters its ascendant phase and reaches toward its culmination. It is the prime mover of "cultural productivity" or "creativity," the active concern with value culture. There is one reference in Kroeber's *Nature of Culture* that shows that he was himself aware of an inconsistency in his demand for impersonality and noncausality. "My own theory of 'deterministic' pattern realization and exhaustion contains a concealed factor of striving and will, in the individuals through whom the realization is achieved. A creative urge and spark must be accorded them, and potentialities of the same to all men" (1952: 9). He goes on to say that if he once compared culture to a coral reef, reflection should have caused him to note that the reef consists of living polyps. "The free will of the polyp may be minute, and his individuation somewhat limited, but his activity is definite." Behold, beneath the array of culture moving like a coral reef or iceberg—another metaphor of Kroeber's—there is *creativity*. It is, however, not the creativity of determinate men, in determinate relationships with and against one another, but an abstract flicker of creativity present in all organisms. When he was once asked why mollusks had produced no Newtons or Alexander the Greats, he answered, half in jest but half seriously, that maybe they had, but perhaps no one had noticed. Thus in the movement of the coral reef, the mollusc biota, and human culture, creativity is the abstract prime mover.

With this, we have returned to the fold of German idealist philosophy from which the cosmography of Alexander von Humboldt took its departure. What is this creativity but Hegel's *Geist*, becoming manifest in world history, or Friedrich Schelling's universal Spirit ever bent on individualizing, particularizing itself? At the bottom of the iceberg stands—God; and it is perhaps in this sense that Kroeber once said—it was at the conference just before his death— that anthropology was his religion. Where, after all, does the Great Chain of Being of pre-Darwinian naturalism derive its unity, if it is not from the mind of God?

DISCUSSION

STANLEY DIAMOND: You stimulated me to think of the period at Columbia when Kroeber was there. With reference to the culture–language analogy, it's also true that Kroeber was strong on the distinction between race, language, and culture which Boas had formulated, and also very strong on the fact that grammar did not express meaning. I wonder how you would handle that.

WOLF: I think that Kroeber had no interest in meaning. His linguistic analogy is somewhat similar to Lévi-Strauss's, that is, an interest in the externality of form—that people eat with chopsticks, that sitting on chairs involves a certain arrangement of the furniture, that the European novel is written in a certain style and pace and pattern, and the like. Questions of meaning are, as far as I know, rarely discussed. What comes to mind is a discussion of Yurok narrative and poetry, which is a splendid wording of the quality of the Yurok style of delivery. It talks about how the Yurok recite and talk, but it never touches on what they're talking about. It describes the outward manifestation of the style, but doesn't get to meaning. Values in themselves are also highly disembodied things; concern with the body, concern with afterlife, asceticism—these are abstract labels for meaning. But I think that meaning is not there.

DIAMOND: I meant that Kroeber insisted that grammar was merely formal and in that sense did not express meaning, which was the general view of the Boas "school." The second thing: With reference to Kroeber's belief in progress, he listed a number of factors as criteria of progress—the quantitative accumulation of cultural traits; the diminution of the focus on the body (and he was prone to reduce ritual performances among primitive peoples to physiological performances, a curiously reductionist formulation despite—or perhaps because of—his superorganic); his insistence that there had been an improvement in such things as the treatment of prisoners of war; and so on. These criteria went parallel with Boas's, and they antedated Robert Redfield, who apparently lifted them from Kroeber in his *Primitive World and Its Transformations* (1953). Kroeber also made an interesting formulation in his textbook, either prior to Redfield or at about the same time, on the folk–sophisticate polarity, which I always thought was better, if less elaborate, than Redfield's.

WOLF: I do think that Kroeber had a belief in progress, and he expressed it that way. I find that somewhat inconsistent with the view of culture as a coral reef or iceberg; it doesn't quite fit. There are various points where he waxes biological or psychological without any kind of mea culpa. I found that discussion of what is "primitive"—having to do with the focus on the body—terribly revealing. Kroeber's views in this matter are perhaps a reflex of the subculture from which he stems: that anything to do with blood and body fluids must be primitive. This view is also strangely at odds with his reified picture of culture as an iceberg. Suddenly, we shift from culture to biology. Yet to get away from biology, you need progress, which means doing away with all these body fluids.

I agree that his formulation of the sophisticated element in contrast to the folk is useful, but contrary to Redfield he was never interested in the carriers of culture. Redfield worried about who the people were who were communicating with one another—the sweet-voiced singer on the temple steps who transmits a particular myth to other people who listen, the difference between sacred figures and lay preachers, the audiences and publics. Kroeber had no interest in who was talking to whom, and there is nothing in his polarity of folk/ sophisticate about communication interchange relationships, which Redfield did have an interest in.

DIAMOND: But Kroeber does mention the greater density of communication.

WOLF: Yes, he talks of *more* culture content and *more* people. But there is nothing of the communication process, the transfer of meaning and information, or the relationship between sender and receiver. There are, in fact, no people. His program in *The Configurations of Culture Growth* is to note these cumulations of cultural growth or their disruption, never asking who the people are, the elites or the specialists or the people who produced the culture content. His Florence is a set of blips on a curve—there are so many people painting in particular styles who happen to be living in Florence, for reasons unexplained. There is no concern with the Italian city-state, for example, or with the kind of organization of the libido that made these things possible, or with any other of the possible ways of going about an explanation. He's not interested in that. It all remains very abstract, very Olympian—frightening, ultimately.

DIAMOND: I agree. But I was referring to Kroeber's expression of the greater density of communication in *primitive* societies. He recognized that, even if he failed to understand or empathize with it. It is a paradoxical footnote to his overriding progressivism.

MICHAEL HARNER: I think Kroeber would have enjoyed your presentation. There are two points I want to make. First, I think that Kroeber, being located in northern California, was faced—to a degree that no other major university anthropologist was—with the responsibility of salvage anthropology. This may have reinforced his natural-history bent. He had the great responsibility to utilize his own talents and those of his students in salvaging for posterity what was left of the Californian and western North American Indian cultures—and of course there was near unanimity about the value and priority of such activity at that time among anthropologists working in the western United States.

Another point: Kroeber had a tremendous capacity for recall. He could remember the comment of a particular informant, and say "On the twelfth of August in 1923, Mary So-and-so told me such-and-such." I often wondered whether this remarkable ability for recall and retention of data might have been related to his tendency not to go the route of causally oriented reductionistic analysis.

WOLF: Your second comment makes sense to me. I didn't say much about his various Indian friends, from whom he learned a great deal and recorded a great deal. At the same time, I'm not so sure about the salvage ethnography, because there were a lot of salvage ethnographers—in a way, we were all salvage ethnographers. Yet many people working with North American Indians had the sense that ethnography was a record of *people*, not just abstract museum traits but people who had once lived, had problems, used their culture, and behaved in certain ways. While it is intellectually permissible to abstract at any given point, I think that you have to remain aware that you are abstracting, and at some point the abstraction has to come back to the point of origin if it is to be fruitful. In Kroeber, this tendency to take the culture element out of the behavioral matrix, or the societal matrix, or the adaptational matrix—the real life of people—was quite complete. He was insistent on it.

SALLY McLENDON: Kroeber found in California an astounding number of distinct social groups—a far greater number than the chapter headings in the handbook of California Indians suggest—in the midst of rapid culture change and devastation by depopulation. California seems to have been, in fact, one of the areas of greatest ethnographic and linguistic diversity in native North

America, and Kroeber must have found a research situation best approximated in recent times by the New Guinea highlands in the early '50s. Harner is right about the pressure of salvage anthropology in shaping Kroeber's California research, and yet Kroeber and his interests seem to have largely shaped the nature of salvage anthropology in California. California offered a research situation which could have occupied dozens of anthropologists productively during several years of intensive research. However, Kroeber chose to attempt to handle this research opportunity almost single-handedly, except for the assistance of his own early students, S. A. Barrett, T. T. Waterman, P. Goddard, and R. Dixon, who were already involved in California ethnography, and later his colleague at the museum, E. W. Gifford, who had joined the museum as an ornithologist. Able professional peers like Sapir were not encouraged or supported, and less well-trained but experienced field-workers like C. H. Merriam and J. P. Harrington felt themselves to be positively excluded.

Many of the ethnographic sketches in the handbook of California Indians were written on the basis of two or three weeks of fieldwork. Such short periods of fieldwork meant that little participant-observation was possible, and in fact the fieldwork seems to have been intended primarily to sample a certain range of ethnographic and linguistic phenomena in California. Once surveyed, however, there was surprisingly little subsequent in-depth research on individual cultures, social groups, or languages. Rather, the focus seems to have been on increasingly detailed surveys, culminating in the Culture Element Distribution studies in the '30s. One wonders how much Kroeber's interest in pattern and generalization was triggered by his attempt to deal single-handedly with the ethnographic and linguistic diversity of California and by his own propensities for fieldwork, as well as how much our present conception of California ethnography and ethnology was excessively shaped by Kroeber's research strategy.

GENE WELTFISH: I think we shouldn't gloss over lightly the culture element studies. For almost ten years an enormous amount of work was done, and a great many people invested their whole careers in it. Then one terrible day at a meeting of the AAA, Kroeber stood up and announced that it wouldn't work, that he had hoped that by accumulating all the traits he would be able to get at which cultures were related, but not one single insight had come to him. You can't imagine what—after ten years and an enormous amount of material— happened at that meeting.

WOLF: I think that is very characteristic of Kroeber. He set a lot of people onto work on problems, and when after they came up with something and showed it to him, Kroeber had lost interest in it.

ROBERT CARNEIRO: I think there is some connection between Dr. Weltfish's observation and Kroeber's attitude toward evolution. He stood between the two poles of history and evolution. He did not want to do history, in the particular and narrow sense. What he wanted to do he called "descriptive integration"—a step or two away from history—in which you begin to isolate patterns from their particularistic matrix. At the same time, he was loath to go much beyond this, and he was very unhappy with Leslie White's cultural evolutionism. He was afraid, I think, of finding really broad patterns, general trends that went beyond the data as he saw them. This is reflected in the conclusion of *Configurations of Culture Growth*. He expressed there a disappointment that after all the years he had invested in this work, there wasn't more in the way of obvious trends and general direction. There was cyclicity—things peaked and then went down again—but what he had hoped to find wasn't there. I think this can be explained partially by the fact that the very things in which he chose to look for order and pattern were things that would show only a limited amount, that would show cyclicity but not the broad directional changes that one sees in, say, economics, technology, or political organization.

WOLF: I think you are absolutely correct. All the problems that Steward and the Whiteans began to think about Kroeber simply had no interest in, and was probably afraid of. His kind of interest in narrow patterns, their variability, and their formal implications is by no means dead. I recently received a letter from a colleague expounding on the history of the form of chairs in China. If Kroeber were alive he would say that that's the kind of anthropology he understands, and the fact that the Chinese have had a revolution he would probably not find very interesting.

PAUL TOLSTOY: I wonder whether you are not criticizing Kroeber for something that he didn't do. One of the things that he did not do, of course, was to look for causes. But would you not allow his reticence in that regard as a legitimate stage in the search for knowledge? Perhaps he did not feel at that time that the kind of information was available or the kind of conceptual tools were available that made a search for causes appropriate.

WOLF: It's true that you ought not to criticize somebody for what he doesn't set out to do. At the same time, in such work as *Configurations of Culture Growth*, there is no pointing out a program that other people—economic historians, art historians, sociologists of the Renaissance—could pick up or in some way make use of his material. The work is not organized so as to invite comment from people like Joseph Needham working on Chinese science or Marvin Becker working on the social organization of Florentine artists. It is totally self-contained and, as such, has a kind of elegance. It gives form to an incredible quantity of material. But there is no invitation to others to connect it with anything outside, and the world in 1930 was not devoid of people who might have addressed themselves to the problem. He liked ordering phenomena, and I suppose I think that ordering phenomena is not really sufficient.

WARREN DEBOER: Do you have any comments on the circumstances by which Kroeber spawned Julian Steward?

WOLF: I don't know the facts that would provide an adequate answer to your question. Steward himself often talked about the North Berkeley gang to which he belonged, which included Jaime De Angulo, now known to most people by his delightful little book called *Indian Tales*. Those were Prohibition days, and they used to make gin in the bathtub. Lowie would occasionally come around, but Kroeber would not. Kroeber warned them about the iniquities of their conduct, professional and otherwise. That's one kind of light on their relationship. Another one is that Steward worked on that elements survey—in which he had to go out and collect thousands of elements. He hated it but he did it, and Kroeber forced him to do it. Steward was always falling sick, sometimes with the imaginary illness that he developed at just the right point. He tells of being sent out to the Hopi to collect endless elements while he was running a 104-degree fever. Kroeber said, "You get out there and you collect them"—more or less in those terms. I think their relationship was essentially that of tyrant to student. It was very productive. This was a person who had written, after all, *Cultural and Natural Areas of Native North America*, and he pointed Steward in that direction. Steward's interest was in trying to see how those relationships actually worked out in the case of the Paiute and Shoshoni band, and it must have fueled Steward's energy quotient considerably. I suspect a lot of it was addressed to Kroeber, who then never read it.

TOLSTOY: Wouldn't you call that an invitation?

WOLF: Yes, of a kind. I don't know what would have happened to Steward without Kroeber. Steward always maintained a very respectful attitude toward Kroeber. The one thing that comes out in the introduction he wrote to Kroeber's writings, which are fundamentally at odds with everything that Steward himself stood for, is a highly respectful attitude. There is a wish to recognize Kroeber for who he was. Kroeber, for his part, saw in Steward a promising but not very interesting student. At the meeting where Steward presented his paper on "Cultural Causality and Law" (1949), Kroeber reacted to it by not paying attention. That is a form of invitation, but of opposites.

DIAMOND: Kroeber's antagonism and opposition to Leslie White has been brought up here, but I have never really seen that except in a trivial methodological sense, not in terms of outcomes. That is to say, Kroeber is a superorganicist, an idealist ultimately, and White is a mechanical materialist; but they have in common that they lack dialectics, and at critical points you can exchange one method for the other and even one set of findings for the other. So that Kroeber is surprisingly reductive all of a sudden, and then you find White doing the same kind of thing, despite his emphasis upon the symbol and upon what he calls "culturology." There are parallels of an inverted kind with Kroeber, but what they lacked was dialectics.

WOLF: I think that Carneiro put his finger on the essential difference: White was interested in explanation—in terms of economic, political, demographic, and other factors—mechanical though they may be on occasion. For instance, White's review of *Configuration of Culture Growth* (1946) says essentially: Here we've got this book with all these curves and all these geniuses popping into existence at various points, and the book *never* really poses the question of why this should be so and never refers to the economics of the time, never refers to the politics of the time. So they could have had a good argument going. I do think that neither of them is dialectical; in fact, both are extraordinarily positivistic. Kroeber is, to my mind, natural-scientific positivism in anthropology driven to the end.

DIAMOND: My candidate for that award is White.

MERVYN MEGGITT: You made a point parenthetically that I think is revealing: the references to those aquatic metaphors—the river, the whirlpools, the eddies, the drops of water that can't be distinguished in the stream. Here we see in Kroeber what is essentially a vacuous hydrography. When you referred in passing to Lévi-Strauss, it seemed to me that there was a fairly good fit: Kroeber with his novels that write themselves, Lévi-Strauss with his myths that think themselves. It's true that Lévi-Strauss attempts to avoid vacuousness with a kind of Cartesian bearing of structures in the pineal gland. Nevertheless, I think that the analogy here is more than an analogy. I believe you are seeing here homologous products of a similar kind of cultural background.

WOLF: I have a feeling that the business about streams has a historical connection, and your comment then applies to that whole historical school. The German nature philosophers are continuously streaming and eddying. The ultimate referent is probably Mother Nature with her milk and effluvia, but they would hardly admit this.

BIOGRAPHICAL NOTE

Photo by June Finfer   1980

ERIC R. WOLF was born in Vienna in 1923. As the only child of an Austrian father and Russian mother, as a Jew in the decaying Habsburg state, and as a youth living from the age of ten in the contested Sudetenland in Czechoslovakia (where his father was the manager of a textile factory), he grew up with the experience of cultural differences and ethnic conflicts. Sent to England in 1938, his first discovery of social science came two years later in an alien detention camp, where another internee, Norbert Elias, gave some lectures on sociology. Later that year Wolf came to the United States. He spent three years at Queens College, where he learned through an accidental choice of a course that the discipline he had already read in had a name. The war then intervened, and he joined the U.S. Army's Tenth Mountain Division, serving in northern Italy.

After the war, Wolf returned to Queens College, where he studied with Hortense Powdermaker, Joseph Bram, and Kimball Young. Upon his graduation in 1946, he used his G.I. Bill benefits to enroll in the anthropology department at Columbia. His main teachers were Ruth Benedict and Julian Steward, the books of Karl Wittfogel and V. Gordon Childe, and several of his fellow students. Steward's Puerto Rico project gave him the opportunity for his first fieldwork (1948–1949), but his analysis, along with that of Sidney Mintz, departed from Steward's cultural ecology, marking the beginning of both Wolf's and Mintz's political-economy approach. After receiving his Ph.D. in 1951, Wolf went to the Bajío region of Mexico to study nation formation.

From 1952 to 1955 Wolf was a research associate of Steward's at the University of Illinois. His academic appointments thereafter took him to the University of Virginia (1955–1958), Yale (1958–1959), and the University of Chicago (1959–1961). In 1960 he returned to interests formed early in his life—peasants of the Alps and problems of ethnicity—and carried out field-work in two ethnically contrastive villages in the South Tyrol region of Italy (a study that he continued jointly with his student John W. Cole). Returning from the field, he accepted an appointment at the University of Michigan (a telegram transcribed by the Italian post office offered him "penure"). He remained at Michigan until 1971, when he joined the City University of New York as a Distinguished Professor at Herbert H. Lehman College and the Graduate Center.

Beginning in the 1950s, Wolf wrote extensively about peasants, communities, and informal social relations, always treating them as embedded in processes at the level of state and nation. In this work and in his comparative analysis of peasantries (1966), he defined peasants in terms of their relationship to groups that held liens over their production and to the state that guaranteed those liens, thus differing from the dominant anthropological view of peasants as "subcultures" with distinct value orientations. The political upheavals of the 1960s turned his concern with peasants toward rebellions and political movements, and in *Peasant Wars of the Twentieth Century* (1969a) he compared the involvement of rural peoples in the revolutions of Mexico, Russia, China, Vietnam, Algeria, and Cuba.

During the 1970s Wolf embarked on a major project to trace the effects of European expansion on the peoples who make up the anthropologist's ethnographic record; the project culminated in *Europe and the People Without History* (1982). He drew on Marxian concepts, using them as analytical tools to grasp the impact of the successive European searches for commodities and then the spread of capitalism around the world over five centuries. The unfinished issues in that effort subsequently led him to investigate the role of ideology in political systems and, more generally, the relationship between ideas and power. He developed these concerns through case studies of the Kwakiutl, the Aztecs, and Nazi Germany in *Envisioning Power: Ideologies of Dominance and Crisis* (1999).

Wolf was interested in the full range of cultures from the ethnographic classics to peasantries to nation-states, in an approach that combined history, political economy, and a view of social and cultural forms as rooted in larger contexts. He played an important part in the development of the anthropology of complex societies, especially in anthropology's shift from a focus on face-to-face groups toward an engagement with processes of state formation and colonial and capitalist expansion. Eric Wolf died in 1999, shortly after completing a retrospective collection of his major papers, *Pathways of Power: Building an Anthropology of the Modern World* (2001).

Paul Radin (c. 1958). Photo by Ralph Norman; Robert D. Farber University Archives & Special Collections Department, Brandeis University Libraries

3

PAUL RADIN

Stanley Diamond

The term "Boasians" conceals the substantial differences that existed among Franz Boas's students and the divergences that many of them took from Boas's own views. Paul Radin, who received his doctorate under Boas in 1911, is a case in point. Putting into practice Boas's prescription to record aboriginal cultures through intensive work with informants in the native language, he produced one of the most exhaustive investigations of a tribe ever achieved, but his concentration on a single tribe differed from the ways that most of his contemporaries carried out the Boasian program. Devoted, like Boas, to careful documentation of cultural facts, he was at the same time highly critical of the statistical methods and distributional studies of culture traits that Boas developed. Like Boas and Alfred Kroeber he defined his task as history, but he disagreed with both of them on what that meant. Above all, he stands out among anthropologists of his time for his concern with the individual. Like Boas and Edward Sapir, but more than either, he saw a central task of ethnology as understanding the relationship of individuals—"specific men and women"—to their cultures. He became the first anthropologist to publish an informant's autobiography, popularized as Crashing Thunder.

Radin's main interests were in the religion, mythology, and worldview of primitives. In line with his belief that to do history required "intensive and continuous study of a particular tribe," his ethnographic work was devoted primarily to the study of a single culture, the Winnebago Indians, but he derived from this work a broad, philosophical view of the nature of primitive culture in general.

Understanding Paul Radin, his position in the intellectual life of our time, and his role as an anthropologist in particular requires more than the usual effort at social biography.[1] He was one of the last artisans of modern scholarship, at the threshold of the computer age. He was an immigrant, but more than an immigrant, for he linked two continents. His life expressed two civilizations, European and American, and one aboriginal culture in depth, the Winnebago. He was himself a Jew of the Enlightenment. He was born in Lodz, in Russian Poland, in 1883. He was brought to the United States in infancy, and he died in New York City in February 1959. But he never severed his European roots, and he could never abandon himself to the New World completely, except, ironically, for his association of nearly half a century with the Winnebago Indians of Wisconsin. The Old World solidarity of his family of origin, like that of so many immigrants, had shattered under the impact of the American experience, and neither his siblings, who predeceased him, nor their children could have given or can give us now a coherent recounting of his life. He had no children, though he was married twice, the second time in his late forties. Even formal résumés of his career are sparse. They are usually inaccurate because Radin rarely bothered to put himself on record in international directories of famous men. Since he moved from establishment to establishment, state to state, country to country, and job to job, there was very little institutional continuity to trace. Only his work reflects the inner unity of his life.[2]

The host of friends he left behind, from Sweden to Mexico, knew him only in phases and primarily as a teacher, yet his gift for spontaneous intimacy made each friend feel that he shared a particular secret about Paul that was best left unspoken, and that may have been true. But the notoriety that this Chinese vagabond of a scholar was bound to generate turned him into a figure both widely known and mysterious, even impenetrable in certain ways; that is to say, a legend. If, as Paul Valéry pointed out, no one has ever gotten to the bottom of a word, no one ever sounded the depths of Paul Radin, because he was pre-eminently a man of words in the most involved sense of that term. He was deceptively transparent; he was a kind of a poet in that respect. Almost without exception, his friends and acquaintances, whether celebrated or not, viewed him with the special affection reserved for the pure in heart or for a child or scamp or free spirit, or for the innocent and not-so-innocent trickster. Radin was an authentically distinguished person. He was no mere schoolman, scribe, or high priest of some establishment of learning, and he was more than the sum of the influences that helped to shape him.

The personal and social background against which he constructed his life was complex. He was the offspring of a German-Russian Jewish family that had become secularized in the mode of the *Haskalah*, the Jewish strand in the Western European Enlightenment that had diffused from a German center to the restive youth of ghetto and pale, carrying with it the anticlerical, antifeudal, experimental, and rationalist faith of the French Encyclopedists. The reaction against Orthodox Judaism in the Reform movement, which had among its objectives the replacement of Yiddish—the voice of the ghetto—by Hebrew as a literary and secular tongue, and the adoption of modern European languages, along with modifications of Judaic ritual, was reflected in the life of Radin's father; he was a Reform rabbi, a Hebrew scholar, and a linguist. Herman Radin, who was Paul's oldest brother, became a New York physician, and Max Radin, next in line, was a distinguished legal scholar. These secular professions, which refocused the traditional Jewish concern with ritual learning but did not abandon learning as a ritual, were ideologically correlated with a humane and skeptical liberalism. Such skepticism and rationalism were largely reactive, a protest against the cramping social-intellectual orthodoxy of the patriarchal and theocratic past. Yet the passion for scholarship, the commitment to human realization in the world, and in Paul's case, the fascinated concern with religion and ethics, maintained a distinctively Jewish cast. Moreover, Radin's intellectual cosmopolitanism, his radicalism, his conception of learning as a moral enterprise, and his capacity to live almost exclusively the life of the mind, thereby depending upon a legion of friends for a variety of services, represent further elements that characterize the Jewish scholar *en passage* from the traditional milieu to the modern industrial and urban world.

Radin received an elite education at the College of the City of New York, entering as a subfreshman and pursuing a five-year course. He graduated in 1902, at the age of nineteen, and then began a "flirtation with zoology," as he called it, at Columbia. After completing a thesis on the embryology of sharks, he became restive with the limitations of natural science and was attracted in his second year at Columbia by James Harvey Robinson, who was a skeptical and rationalist historian. But it wasn't until 1907 in Munich, where he had gone to study the zoology of fish and substituted work in physical anthropology under J. Ranke, the noted anthropologist, that Radin began to consider anthropology as a career. The following year he made the decision final. Studies at the University of Berlin under Karl von den Steinen, Eduard Seler, and Paul Ehrenreich (whose acceptance of Andrew Lang's theory of primitive monotheism influenced Radin's later work) helped draw Paul in the direction of anthropology.

Radin had an early excursion into material culture, working for a month or so at the museum in Prague and writing his first paper on the technique of networking among the South American Indians, but the interest was temperamentally alien to him and quickly abandoned. He returned to Columbia under the tutelage of Robinson, and he took a minor in history while majoring in anthropology under Boas, receiving his Ph.D. in 1911. Unlike his contemporaries, then, Radin was not initially drawn to anthropology by Boas but first pursued his subject in Europe; and before he became an ethnologist, he was trained in historiography and had reflected upon the problems of history. Despite the fact that Radin never labored in the Boasian vineyards, going forth early and alone into the world (as Lewis Mumford recalled) and without the master's blessing, it was probably the combined effect of Robinson's skeptical humanism and Boas's empirical insistence upon the indivisible potential of primitive and civilized mentalities that originally led Radin to question all notions of primitive inferiority.

He soon settled into a permanent preoccupation with the Weltanschauung of primitive peoples. His first field trip to the Winnebago was undertaken in 1908. Subsequent monographs and articles on almost every aspect of their lives were to develop into one of the monuments of American anthropology. This work includes ten substantial books, among them a general account of Winnebago culture (1923), the informant's autobiography (1920), and several studies of mythology.

But Radin was also a student of contemporary Western civilization and had been even before he became a professional anthropologist. As Cora DuBois relates, James Harvey Robinson grilled him relentlessly in 1910 during his doctoral orals at Columbia on medieval education and the order of argument in Saint Augustine. Anthropologists then were expected to be grounded in their own culture before being considered fit for the study of another. But this grounding was, in Radin's view, the basis for an understanding of his own alienation from the prevailing values, without which "the task of understanding the primitive could not be accomplished." His alienation, wedded to his self-knowledge and his knowledge of his culture of origin, freed him from any presuppositions governed by ad hoc acceptance of Western values or, equally important, by merely blind and personal disaffection from them. He emerges then as a kind of self-liberated intellect, a shaman who cured himself. He was his own patient throughout his life in that respect, an anthropologist who recognized that he must be engaged in a lifelong dialogue with his own culture. This assumption was more fully appreciated by European than American intellectuals, whether anthropologists or not, who were perhaps less skilled than the Americans in the art of critical accommodation to society. Indeed, Radin is celebrated in Europe as an intellectual *and* an anthropologist. He lectured at Cambridge under W. H. R. Rivers from 1920 to 1925, later at the four major Swedish universities, and at the Eranos Conference at Ascona in 1949. In 1952 he was recalled to Cambridge, and he lectured subsequently at Oxford, Manchester, and finally at C. G. Jung's institute in Zurich.

Radin, who remained a cheerful exile in his own society to the end, found a way of life of studying primitive peoples that precluded opportunistic or unreflective commitment to the major institutions of his own time and place. He migrated from coast to coast—as between the United States and Europe—during his half century as a professional anthropologist. But he was never at a loss for a job. Among other places, he taught at Berkeley, Fisk University, the University of Chicago, Kenyon College, and finally Brandeis. In the words of Julian Steward, "his charm . . . got him about every job in Anthropology in the country." During the early Depression years, when many of his colleagues and students were unemployed, he managed to find support for work in anthropology from government agencies hitherto unconcerned with such efforts. He undertook an exhaustive survey of ethnic minorities, the first of its kind, in the San Francisco Bay area for the W.P.A. in 1935. Bibliophile and bibliographer (and quondam book thief), he compiled a catalogue of over 1,000 pages on Mexican literary and historical materials at the Sutro Library in 1939. Moreover, a variety of foundations over the years pressed modest but sustaining funds into Radin's hands, permitting him a continuum of work. Radin had as lively a talent for attracting personal angels as he did for alienating bureaucrats. Mary Mellon of the Bollingen Foundation, Leonard Althwaite of the Rockefeller Foundation, and Paul Fejos of the Wenner-Gren Foundation were among those who extended material and moral support during critical periods.

Radin was not without administrative pretensions. He organized and served as secretary of the Southwestern Ethnological Society and spent a year in a government agency, the Bureau of American Ethnology. Toward the end of his life, he served as arbiter of grants in anthropology for the Bollingen Foundation. His accomplished friends, as usual, were beneficiaries.

Radin's ability to create associations beyond the limits of the anthropological profession was an index of his cultivation. Anthropology was never really a career for Radin. It was never a specialized discipline; it was a way of life. If he had no permanent home anywhere, he was at home everywhere. His personal and professional lives were of one piece; that is to say, he had style. Friends and antagonists alike never questioned the integrity of his pursuit. Like a hunter after game, he followed the human spirit in its manifold shapes throughout history and across cultures, bent upon discovering the conditions for its most vigorous existence, unappalled by whatever he found, always alert to the universal implications of a particular cultural form. He had no patience with sectarian jargon or other contrivances that had the effect of turning the study of man into an academic mystery, and he never deflected his concern away from the great, recurring troubling themes in human history. Typically, in concluding *Method and Theory of Ethnology*, he called for renewed effort in determining basic human nature. "That the culture pattern hides this knowledge from us forever," he wrote, "is a counsel of despair" (1933a: 267). Radin believed in "the existence of universal dimensions of human psychology which exist outside the framework of history." It was grasping these, he believed, that would then make it possible to distinguish the primitive from the civilized with more sophistication. This was related to Ludwig Feuerbach's—and to a degree Karl Marx's—notion of a species-being or human essence, the normative sense of a human potential; that is what he was getting to.

Although, as his professional history shows, he had a sure instinct for survival, Radin never came to terms with modern techniques. He never learned how to use a typewriter, and he laboriously wrote out his voluminous notes and manuscripts in so medieval and minute a hand that a magnifying glass was sometimes necessary to decipher the script. A contemporary transformation of an eighteenth-century Hasidic rabbi, Radin commanded his environment by the power of his expression, by the variety and immediacy of his insights, by his verve and spiritual generosity. The more practical arrangement of things for his own convenience he left to others. As an intimate from his Berkeley period wrote, he was the least mechanically talented man imaginable. I often wondered how he survived in bachelorhood without a roommate or some other attendant. He could not or would not learn to drive a car and therefore spent hours in streetcars. He could not use a screwdriver or hammer for minor household repairs, and he scarcely knew how to turn on a gas range. Thus, he would rail against leaking faucets in his apartment and other newfangled cultural elements that he could not manage or subdue.

For all of his ceaseless traffic with colleagues and students, with whom he would spontaneously set up his Hasidic court, most memorably outside the classroom, Radin remained—as Mark Van Doren has noted—an essentially lonely person. One is tempted to speculate in this connection on the role of an adored and catered-to youngest son in a transitional Jewish family, and on the isolation that threatens those who have learned to depend upon others for the practical conduct of their lives. Paul did not mind being disliked, but he subtly insisted upon love in return for the gift of his being to the world—and he was usually loved, for as a natural teacher he found himself only in giving himself.

He was a creator and formulator of meaning. Whatever the personal background of his predisposition, he was a thinker, a "poet-thinker," a "thinker-artist," a "priest thinker," designations that he himself used to describe one of his two contrasting historical temperamental types—first in *Primitive Man as Philosopher* (1927), then in *Primitive Religion* (1937) and in subsequent works. He was decidedly not a man of action, not a layman. He could live only in a cerebral blaze of reality. His commitment to the intellectual life drove him to see and perhaps to exaggerate the culture- and class-determined dichotomy between action and thought (which others had also expressed, if not in precisely the same terms) as a universal temperamental division. (I refer to William James, Robert Lowie, Jung, and others, who had made this distinction before Radin had.) At least Radin's background in learning sensitized him to analogous processes elsewhere. Late in life, Radin adopted the position that these two contrasting temperaments can and usually do, in reality, complexly coexist in the same person. Therefore, in retrospect, he seems to have invented ideal types, despite his antipathy to such abstract efforts. Although a student of Greek civilization capable of pursuing research in the classical language, Radin was not attracted to the notion of the Aristotelian mean, either as a description of human temperament or as a guide to behavior.

Yet the intensity of his intellectual commitment never moved him to glorify the position of intellectuals, particularly since the rise of civilization. I have never met a man who was more suspicious of intellectuals and who was himself more of an intellectual. He regarded them as dependent upon the official academy, which was in turn linked to the ruling establishment; along with Boas in this respect, he therefore viewed them as bound by convention and, for the most part, incapable of pursuing interests other than their own—they knew which side their bread was buttered on. He was constantly aware of the linked exploitative and creative roles of intellectuals of the kind he called "priest-thinkers." He regarded them as the inventors of religious systems, thereby reflecting their own profound need to create a coherent universe of meaning, while catering to the intermittent needs of their "layman followers." He imagined that the priest thinkers, or shamans, or medicine men were the original formulators of the primitive monotheistic synthesis—a later social convention in Judeo-Christian-Islamic civilization—but actually as a "pure" faith as common, or uncommon, among primitive peoples as among ourselves. If the drives of the priest-thinkers were "neurotic" and their hunger "economic," this did not for Radin inevitably throw the significance of their insights into question. It is important to understand that; Radin was not a reductive thinker. But the exploitative reality and potential of civilized intellectuals troubled him all his life.

However personal and obscure the origins of this feeling may have been, it gave him good reason to deny identification with any bureaucracy except on his own idiosyncratic terms. It is hard to believe that he ever made a formal reply to a formal memorandum. His informality with students and hostility to administration; his penchant for teaching in experimental environments, such as Black Mountain College and Fisk University (where he collected still unpublished life histories of former slaves and accounts of Black conversion experiences); his flexible arrangements at Kenyon College; and his fruitful and footloose periods of residence and work in Europe attest to his ambivalence about the social role of the intellectual. He was in the Socratic tradition himself, or tried to be. That is, the public aspects of the pursuit of knowledge meant for him extended exchanges in the marketplace, not isolation within the Platonic academy.

This sensitive and refined urban intellectual was at home in the cognitive worlds of primitive peoples, which seemed more real to him in basic respects than our rationalizing civilization. He quotes with approval the words of an old Eskimo to Knut Rasmussen:

> Our narratives deal with the experiences of man, and these experiences are not always pleasant or pretty, but it is not proper to change our stories to make them more acceptable to our ears, that is if we wish to tell the truth. Words must be the echoes of what has happened, and cannot be made to conform to the mood and the taste of the listener.

Or, in Radin's own words, "If one thing can be said to hold true for primitive civilizations everywhere, it is the ruthless realism and objectivity with which man has been analyzed there." But Radin did not believe, any more than Jean Jacques Rousseau (whose work was not a direct influence on him), in a "return to the primitive." Neither one entertained the notion of an idealized or noble savage (Denis Diderot's notion, not Rousseau's). Quite the contrary, Radin's aim was to reveal the whole gamut of human possibilities, expressed in the daily lives of primitive peoples, as the foundation for a more critical evaluation of civilization. The primitive experience was in Radin's view an essential part of our historical consciousness, and it was also an index to the universal psychic character and needs of the species.

In *Primitive Man as Philosopher*, he dismissed theories about the automatism of primitive life as being merely projective of an increasingly routinized modern condition. One concludes from the totality of Radin's work that he found primitive mentality to differ in degree but not in kind from its civilized counterpart. He believed that, despite the variety of cultural forms involved, primitive peoples respond to the major challenges of life in sophisticated, profound, and—to a civilized person endowed with self-knowledge—understandable ways. That is, if we are human, he felt that they were quintessentially human. Therefore, Radin rejected all theoreticians who stigmatized or seemed to stigmatize primitives as being incapable of abstraction (technically defined), as reflexive participants in an inchoate entity, as linguistically inadequate, or as lacking individuality. Above all, Radin never merely analyzed the lives of people called primitives; by some alchemy of insight he transmuted himself, time and again, into their spokesman. In his lifelong work on the trickster, for example, he emphasized the cosmic richness of the imagery, the ambivalence of the human impulse toward creation and destruction symbolized in the dual image of the deity, and the Sisyphean struggle—expressed in trickster mythology—to create and consequently to rescue meaning from the chaos of sensory impressions, biological needs and appetites, from enigmas of personal, social, and cosmic origins, and from death.

Radin's elaboration of the dual conception of the deity, and therefore of humanity and of the cosmos, had descended from Andrew Lang and had been anticipated in the work of Paul Ehrenreich, Boas, Kroeber, and Roland B. Dixon. Indeed, both the Americanists and the German Historical School had been preoccupied with that issue. However, Radin, who was explicitly opposed to Catholic apologetics, was to explore the nature of god (or the nature of the views of god) among primitive peoples more fully than any other American ethnologist. These are universal human issues, but Radin saw them as central to the social and ritual life of primitive peoples. This question of the relative weight given to certain themes among primitive peoples, in comparison with ourselves, led Radin to believe that although basic human nature is indivisible, it is more visible among primitive peoples. In dealing with African folktales, for example, Radin interpreted a Ba'ila story about a woman who went in search of god, which is parallel in theme to the Book of Job but more realistic in its climax. In the end the old woman dies because she is morally unaware, that is, she refuses to accept her existential burdens as part of the common lot of humanity.

Primitive life was then for Radin closer in its structure and ideology to the roots of comedy and tragedy—that is, what we would dichotomize and name as comedy and tragedy. It was precisely this conception of aboriginal society as the arena of a universal human drama, based on the quest for meaning and identity and expressed in primitive rituals, that made his work and friendship memorable to a diverse group of writers, artists, and philosophers. Among them were Mark Van Doren, who wrote the foreword to *The Road of Life and Death* (1945), Lewis Mumford, C. G. Jung (who profited from Radin's knowledge of myths and folktales and who intrigued Radin because of his respect for primitive experience, but with whose theoretical conclusions Radin finally disagreed), Alan Tate, John Crowe Ransom, John Dewey (who in his foreword to *Primitive Man as Philosopher* held that Radin's conception of a temperamental rather than scholastic origin of classic themes in philosophy was of revolutionary importance for the history of ideas), Huntington Cairns, Mabel Dodge Luhan, and others. Radin's anonymous translation of Hans Vaihinger's *Philosophy of As If* and his translation of record of Alfred Adler's *The Practice and Theory of Individual Psychology* in 1925, among other distinguished works, further commended him to a larger circle than that of professional anthropology.

In the broader intellectual current of his time, Radin's work had a dual significance. He made the study of primitive perception intrinsically meaningful and intellectually worthwhile. Therefore, in Van Doren's words, "if we are without pride, we may learn something we had not previously known about the meaning of life on earth" (1945: xiv). Moreover, Radin helped clarify for us the sources of our discontent with our own culture, for he conceived, it has been said, the Western world as a conquest civilization. It appeared to him frequently that the values of social science itself were only reflections of the dominant social and economic currents peculiar to the civilization in which they existed. To the extent that this was the case, he felt that studies of primitive life continually face the risk of reflecting ourselves and the established framework of Western thought more than the dimensions of primitive society.

Radin was both a marginal man and profoundly radical, but his radicalism lay in the general historical meaning of his work, not in elaborated, or even specific, political formulations or tactics. That meaning derives from his general conception of primitive society. This is clearly delineated in *The World of Primitive Man* (1953), which is among the more effective full-length syntheses that have thus far been attempted. There he writes, "If one were asked to state briefly and succinctly the outstanding positive features"—and he emphasized positive features—"of aboriginal civilizations [by which he meant cultures], I for one would have no hesitation in answering that there are three"; he then specifies respect for the person, a remarkable degree of social and political integration, and the existence of an irreducible minimum of socioeconomic survival that all human beings are under ordinary conditions guaranteed and that transcend all other conflicts and group interests. He then goes on to synthesize primitive economic and social structure, philosophy, religion, and psychology. The result is no less than an implicit, inductive, historical, and normative theory of human nature, or species-being.

Radin would have been shy of so sweeping an evaluation of his work, since he was theoretically grounded in the careful explication of specific cultures and persons. Nonetheless, his perspective on the primitive has an obvious forerunner in the Morgan–Marx notion of primitive communism. There is also a link to Robert Redfield and to the folk–urban polarity theorists. But Radin's work is richer, more substantive, and more historically realistic. Redfield, for example, describes primitive society in general terms; he does not succeed in establishing a functional model synthesizing the range of behavior in which actual persons engage. Another of the significant differences from Redfield is worth remarking on. Redfield imagined, along with Kroeber, that moral consciousness has expanded with civilization. This is the confusion of the *is* with the *ought*. Radin, on the other hand, was at great pains to establish a remarkably subtle spectrum of moral insight as a primitive characteristic, generic, in fact, to the structures of primitive societies. In such areas he was skeptical of the idea of progress (although he understood the general dynamics of the evolution of civilization well enough and had outlined this in a very long and as yet unpublished manuscript). This attitude, together with his scrupulousness as a scholar, also accounts for his refusal to politicize his work programmatically. However, as a spokesman for native and minority peoples, he wrote widely for popular journals, and he also dissected the racial myth, in a book by that name (1934) and in a number of articles.

His radicalism, then, was rooted in his respect for the aboriginal human potentiality, which he insisted was already formed even among the most primitive of those societies that he held to be the proper subject of ethnology. He concludes *The World of Primitive Man* by stating, "Perhaps it is fitting that primitive man, here in the guise of an Eskimo hunter, should teach us this: nature is great, but man is greater still" (1953: 360).

Despite the fact that Radin refused to anchor himself to the anthropological establishment, his larger impact on the life of his time is a function of his dedication and accomplishment as an anthropologist. He never stopped writing, and although his range did not match that of Boas, who played the orthodox rabbi of the shul to Radin's rebellious Hasid, his work was more integrated than that of Boas and more extensive than that of any of his contemporaries, with the exception of Kroeber. But Radin achieved more depth in his range than did the latter. A glance at Radin's publications, some 200, reveals—in addition to the interests for which he is best known—formal linguistic, archaeological, and social-structural material (all a primary function of his concern with the Winnebago), and unique and exhaustive bibliographical collections.

Radin's concern with the Winnebago forms the main thread of his life's work. From the time of his initial contact with them, he turned himself into an instrument of historical reportage. For Radin, this was a skilled, highly technical vocation. He always remained skeptical of the more romantic claims of participant observation, which—substituting a cheaply won rapport for the hard work of mastering the native idiom—too often resulted in what he called a pretentious impressionism. He wrote, "These defects could possibly be obviated if the investigator became a member of the tribe. This is generally out of the question." It would mean spending a good portion of one's life in a primitive community, and that no well-qualified ethnologist that he knew of was prepared to do, even were funds available for the purpose. (Frank Cushing was a man of whom he spoke with affection, because Cushing in fact became a Zuni priest and never wrote as much as he could have about these people. He chose a silence that spoke louder than words, as Radin contended.)

For Radin the question was never one of going native, but of understanding the native in oneself while maintaining one's personal and social identity.[3] Learning well from Boas despite their temperamental antinomy, Radin had concluded earlier that only prolonged association with specific primitive persons, intimate work with native informants in their own language, and faithful transcription and analysis of the native texts could produce reliable ethnographic and theoretical results. Thus he was always suspicious, as he states in *The Method and Theory of Ethnology* (1933a), of what he judged to be easily won insights into the most intimate patterns of native behavior, in the absence of familiarity with the language, long-term fieldwork, and grounding in the lives of specific individuals—as distinct from the generalized person fleshed out from an ethnological skeleton whom the ethnologist then endows with uniqueness. He was opposed, in short, to the merely abstract, methodological individual, the typical member of the particular culture that is deduced from the information that the anthropologist gathers.

For Radin, history was experience, and history could be more fully reflected, more complete, among primitive peoples in primitive cultures than among class-divided, occupationally compartmentalized, state-organized societies such as ours, wherein experience is dissociated and fragmented. In primitive societies, he believed, people were more likely to emerge in their natural variety, so to speak. This is one of the reasons that he emphasized basic temperamental distinctions in a nonpejorative way. He didn't think that such distinctions, or the whole variety of distinctions of which we are genetically capable, could emerge in modern society as we know it—modern capitalist or capitalist-patterned, class-divided society—because of the reduction of persons to social roles. He also believed, along with Boas, that only the native person could reflect his culture and that—and here he was unique—only the ensemble of these individual reflections could be defined as history. To understand what he meant by that, one has to appreciate that the primitive person is in a situation in which his own society is largely transparent to him (as Marx might have said), whereas in our situation, our "complex," alienating society is *not* transparent to us but stands over and above us as an impenetrable reification. To Radin the experience of multifunctioning human beings in a primitive society was tantamount to the history of that society. History, in short, was not mere chronology, or an abstracted sequence of technological events, or some other aspect of the social whole, but the totality of human experience in the given culture, a totality that was ever present and could be grasped by each fully engaged participant, although from personally distinctive, if complementary, perspectives. The role of the ethnologist was therefore that of a midwife, and all European interpretations of indigenous cultures were false if they were not inherent in the narratives of native individuals.

The relentless honesty of this view, whether one agrees or not, can hardly be denied, for what Radin meant was that anthropology acting as other than midwife presents a European conception of the past and does so for Europe's sake. The purpose might be comparative, for example, illuminating some aspect of modern civilization, but too often the function—if not the conscious purpose—of anthropology has been the rationalization of the imperial mission in one way or another; of this Radin was convinced, although he did not often use rhetorical language. For the problem, Radin wrote, resolves itself into finding the native. To this search he devoted a lifetime, and by 1920 he had published the autobiography of a Winnebago Indian, thus pioneering the discovery of the primitive as a *person* in American ethnology. Radin did ask questions of the data; he asked abstract questions and came up with answers. He did not depend only upon what informants said about their particular societies. However, the purpose of the kinds of questions he asked was almost always a critique of our civilization—that was his fundamental enterprise.

Radin's command of the Winnebago language and his respect for their unwritten literature have had few parallels in the history of ethnographic investigation. As Dell Hymes has noted, "Boas had no peer in American anthropology and in philological work except his students, Sapir and Radin" (1965: 334). Hymes says that for Radin linguistics was a means to the ends of ethnography and aesthetic appreciation; as to the latter, it is possible to appraise him as a literary historian and exegete on oral literature in the grand tradition. Apart from voluminous Winnebago texts—many of which remain unpublished—and other raw materials in the archives of the American Philosophical Society, Radin authored a series of Wappo (1924), Huave (1929a), and Mixe (1933b) texts; a grammar of Wappo (1929b); notes on Tlappanecan (1933c); and a sketch of Zapotec (1930). He had been a joint Harvard–Columbia fellow at the International School of American Archaeology and Ethnology in Mexico in 1912–1913. He was also concerned with historical linguistics, publishing a classification of the languages of Mexico (1944) and carrying through a decade-long analysis of Patwin, 1930 to 1940. Most importantly, in one of his early works called *The Genetic Relationship of the North American Languages* (1919), he argued for their essential continental unity. Sapir, ironically enough, at that time criticized this opinion, pointing out certain technical errors; yet many years later Sapir's distinguished student Morris Swadesh, in a revolutionary effort, developed conceptions that were parallel to those of Radin's 1919 book. It deserves note that Radin's concern with the languages of primitive peoples was based, as was his inquiry into their cultures, on a thorough knowledge of his own civilization. He was at ease in German, French, Spanish, Latin, and Greek.

By the time Radin matriculated at Columbia, Kroeber and Clark Wissler had graduated. His older colleagues included Lowie and Sapir. His age-mates were Frank Speck, Alexander Goldenweiser, and Ruth Benedict. Lowie and Sapir remained his closest friends in the profession. Lowie's and Radin's families had been intimate in the youth of both men, and Radin had spent four years (1913 to 1917) with Sapir in the geological survey of Canada, studying the Ojibwa (1913). But his deep respect for Lowie and Sapir and for Boas, whom he regarded as one of the seminal personalities of the century, did not restrain him from a cogent attack on the Boas circle along its entire circumference. In *Method and Theory of Ethnology* in 1933 (which apart from Lowie's conventional *History of Ethnological Theory* [1937], published four years later, was the only systematic excursus into ethnological theory written by an American until more than a generation later), Radin assimilated ethnology to history and rejected the presuppositions of most of the Boasians. Partly as a result of his early training with Robinson and Ranke, he chastised Boas's quantitative and distributional approach to culture data as the fundamental error of the American school, an error which in Radin's view led to overgeneralized, external, and patchwork histories of traits, in abstractly deduced time perspectives, rather than to specific histories of societies as experienced and created by their members. As Father Wilhelm Schmidt claimed, despite the demurrers of the Americanists, the general *methods* of the Boas group—as distinct from its premises and its conclusions—were not so different from those of the German Historical School. Radin always felt rather wistfully that there was a contradiction between this overall character of the Americanists and Boas's insistence on prolonged fieldwork and textual efforts in particular societies. After all, Boas as a grand—if necessarily, and thankfully, inconsistent—mentor, had stated as early as 1888 "that ethnology deals with the history of primitive societies."

Radin's reciprocated antipathy to Kroeber is symbolic of his alienation from the major trends of his time. The Kroeber–Radin polarity was evident in the total career of each scholar. Kroeber entered the institutional world early at the University of California. He was perhaps the single most powerful administrator in the history of anthropology. He labored to build a school and worked with teams of graduate students. He was a compiler and classifier of endless facts and quotes, and a power on the job market. He was a man of formal probity and bearing, a sort of Confucius to Radin's Lao Tzu, and the two personalities struck sparks against each other. Intellectually, Kroeber's notion of the superorganic and his consequent lack of interest in the person in history, his sweeping efforts to classify whole civilizations by configurations of traits and qualities, and the eclectic mix of the intuitive and the quantitative in his methods were opposed to Radin's approach to anthropology. Moreover, Kroeber's insistence—in agreement with Boas, despite other disagreements—that ethnology was a natural science whose subject matter was composed of discrete, isolable, and objectively determinable elements that could be traced and categorized on their own terms did violence to Radin's focus on the person as the index and measure of culture. Kroeber's approach violated Radin's perception that to probe deeply enough into particular forms was to reveal universal meanings. Kroeber's view also abused Radin's sense of history as the human agent, as the agency for revealing the nature of humanity (including those aspects that he believed existed outside the framework of history) and the necessary conditions for human fulfillment. In short, Radin believed that in the deepest ethnological sense (not in the ethical sense), Kroeber's work lacked historical integrity. That summarized his critique of American ethnology in general.

As an original, Radin fostered no formal genealogy of students. He affected the lives of countless friends and colleagues, but he never intruded on personalities. When in the last years of his life contributions were invited to his Festschrift, *Culture in History* (Diamond 1960), fifty-two papers were submitted and published. The authors ranged from Leslie White—who, astonishingly, wrote a very sympathetic paper on the (of course, inevitably irrelevant) worldview of the Keresan pueblo—to ten European scholars. Paul died several months before the appearance of the book. Fortunately, he was aware that it was being prepared, and characteristically, he tried to take an active part in its preparation. His final academic position was as professor of anthropology and then, at the age of seventy-five, chairman of the graduate department at Brandeis University, to which we called him from four years of residence and work at Lugano. At Brandeis, he was to join, besides myself, Robert Manners and Alexander Lesser (who was appointed at about the same time). Coming to Brandeis, a relative stranger to the new, emerging American scene, Paul felt and was led to feel that he had found a permanent home, but that more recent version of the bureaucratization of American learning was even less compatible than earlier ones and proved more than he could bear. His heart had faltered for many years, and he finally died, full of plans and laughter, several days after a seizure that overtook him during a professional lecture in New York City. It was my misfortune that I was engaged in fieldwork in Nigeria at the time of his death.

There are those of us who believe that the passage of time will establish Paul Radin as possessed of one of the finest sensibilities among that small band of distinguished intellectuals who defined the classic period of American anthropology.

DISCUSSION

ALEXANDER LESSER: If I followed you, at one point you said that Radin was committed to textual studies and the analysis of peoples by way of their own languages, and at another point you said that he was critical of that approach and of the long time required to accomplish it. On the one hand, you emphasized that he *was* committed to it; on the other hand, you emphasized that he was *against* it. For myself, I find that typical of Radin, the taking of positions both ways.

DIAMOND: I don't think it is inconsistent in the pejorative sense. He spent fifty years working with the Winnebago. Almost everything that he did, all of his theoretical work, all of his conclusions, came from specific ethnographic work. He was among the first, perhaps *the* first in American ethnology, to publish a substantial autobiography of a Native American. His textual work arose from weeks, months, years with informants. He could not become a Winnebago, but he worked with informants in the Winnebago language over long periods of time, and he spoke Winnebago fluently. He would translate the material and publish it. That was as close as one could humanly get to the necessity, as he viewed it, of representing the people's own history of their own society.

LESSER: When I visited the Winnebago in 1928, which wasn't too long after his work with them, the culture was in the kind of breakdown that was happening among many American Indian groups. Those of Radin's informants that I saw, I saw in the city and not anywhere else. I would say, then, that even at the time he visited them, he was engaged in what used to be called "getting back to the native condition," rather than seeing something that was going on at the time. It seems to me very doubtful that there was a viable Winnebago culture at the time he was there, any more than there were viable cultures for most other American ethnologists.

DIAMOND: That is correct. Yet most other important American ethnologists—Lowie, Kroeber, and Boas among others—also wrote and generalized about *primitive* cultures, trying to reflect the "native condition." They did this without dissimulation of the actual historical circumstances of their fieldwork. The point is that all so-called ethnological descriptions are constitutions of reality, constructions—there is no such thing as an ultimately accurate, final description of the positivistic "truth" of any society.

LESSER: But what Radin found was a nonviable survival of Winnebago—the effects of contact with non-Winnebagos. How he would get from that to some in-depth feeling of primitive life, I am not sure. Yet you make that the crux of his intellectual understanding. From my own experiences of working with some items of his, I know that he was pretty sloppy about what he put down about the Winnebago, for instance about kinship. That may not disturb you. You have created a beautiful picture of all the best things that could be said about Radin. But I don't know any evidence, for instance, that he ever discussed the idea of anthropology as a phase of the conquering West, which is a newly current view. It's a pretty good understanding that we've reached recently, that a great deal of anthropology has to be seen in the light of the imperialist era and the control of all peoples of the world.

DIAMOND: This isn't the place to evaluate Radin's work on Winnebago kinship. But I don't think the idea about anthropology and imperialism is new. It has been latent for about 250 years, in my judgment, from our very origins in Montaigne through Rousseau, Marx and others. And Radin was more aware of these matters than any scholar of his time, including Boas. His whole definition of history runs counter to any Western bias. Only a radical anti-imperialist mind could have conceived *The World of Primitive Man*. At the same time, Radin has got to be seen against the background of his time—and in the light of his choice of language and subject. One might even say that his anti-positivistic struggle with Boas, Kroeber, and others was an aspect of his profound emancipatory consciousness.

In any event, I can hardly fault Radin for not using the precise emancipatory language of my generation. After all, who did in his generation or the one that succeeded it? But his convictions are clear in his work.

LESSER: Latent and current are two different things.

DIAMOND: What you say about the baseline of primitive existence is, of course, true; but it is far more complex than that. You can't go out positivistically and find a case which represents all of the various characteristics that we impute to primitive society. That is a result of the kinds of questions we ask, and a result of our subsequent syntheses. When I say Radin was steeped in Winnebago culture and in the Winnebago language, I do not mean to imply that he was *confined* to the Winnebago, any more than Boas was to the Kwakiutl. He also did work on African cultures, particularly through their literature, their poetry, their mythology, that is, their oral traditions (transmuting, I suppose, his Winnebago experience in this respect). Oral traditions reflect the experiences of people, and working with them was one of the ways in which Radin began to develop a synthetic model, or quintessential notion, of what primitive society was about. We have been doing this in anthropology for a long time, in the absence of any positivistically arrived-at ethnographic present. This is one of the challenges—and at the same time one of the handicaps—of the profession and is also, as I have indicated, a general historiographical problem.

We are all in quest of the same thing; each anthropologist using his or her own set of questions to discover something about the nature of man on earth, with reference to his or her own condition. The most significant results can be shown to converge, or reinforce each other. But there is no such thing as a perfectly objective portrait of a primitive society. Radin did not presume an ethnological present that was simultaneously an ethnological past; he was fully aware of the paradox. But he thought that by looking at these societies and getting a sense of a radically different way of life, he was casting light upon his own. The distinctions which he uncovered were significant and subtle and they justify the primitive–civilized dichotomy. That was all he ever pretended to do. It was, I think, enough.

LESSER: The question you have raised about getting at the primitive is not only sound, but is so sound that I would say that what anthropology was and is trying to do when it does that—and what Radin was trying to do—is impossible. If anthropology rests on the achievement of the impossible, it rests on nothing. There is no such thing, as you say, as the purely primitive, as the pristine primitive. But Radin did what other anthropologists did, which is not correct: to somehow derive what the primitive was all about from his imagination, from his literary and poetic feeling, rather than from any data that he could bring to bear.

DIAMOND: I think that you misconstrue that nature of "data." The myths, legends, oral traditions of primitive peoples represent data; and he spent a lifetime collecting that kind of information. But anthropology doesn't rest there. A merely abstract social science is an impossible enterprise. It is and must be a dialectical enterprise; it involves both what we formulate and what we do in relation to what we formulate, which in turn shapes our formulations. The most conscious, most highly developed dialectic is, in my judgment, revolutionary; its cutting edge is politics.

Now there is a powerful political undercurrent in Radin's work. Radin is always bearing in mind the existence of societies which had exploitative class and state apparatuses; that is the comparative basis of his work on primitive society. He was fully aware of the problems of our own society and he wrote quite a bit about them, particularly with reference to racism.

LESSER: One more thing about Radin. He spoke regularly, repetitively, about the necessity of working from textual materials and understanding the native language. But his *Primitive Man as Philosopher* from beginning to end is based upon translations that he accepted from other people, of languages he knew nothing about. The book opens with translations of Eskimo poems, and he accepts the translated versions as a basis for interpreting the thought of the Eskimo. This is the exact thing that had been done before linguistic anthropology. I don't say that his imagination and his grasp of the potential of primitive thinking were unsound; I do say that he never proved his view.

DIAMOND: I don't know what you would demand of the man. He knew as many languages as anybody I ever met. About the Eskimo: He depended upon sources that were ethnographically "reliable"; he depended upon Knut Rasmussen, for example. It's true he didn't know any African languages, either, and he had to depend upon translations, both in working with informants and in using the ethnographic literature. But who hasn't—in parallel circumstances? And "prove his view" is an empty, positivistic phrase, given the complexity of the anthropological enterprise.

LESSER: But in the case I am talking about, the translation was made by someone, an American poet, who had no real control over the Eskimo language. He went through that book with a group of us at Columbia before it was published, and he discussed it in detail in some lectures. I am saying that to use the words in a translation as the basic proof that certain conceptions and ideas were held by the people is contrary to what he himself said was the only sound approach.

DIAMOND: Again, Radin never thought in terms such as "basic proof." I think I made the point that Radin was not a thoroughly consistent man. I wouldn't like to meet a thoroughly consistent man. I think that the degree of inconsistency in anthropology is due to the nature of the material with which we work; its ambiguity is extreme. Moreover, inconsistency is in the very nature of language to begin with, and it is part of the inherent dialectic of thinking. Fortunately, people like Radin (or like Boas and Marx) were capable of expressing significant ideas and seminal notions in the face of these generic inconsistencies with which we must all deal.

There is a larger point, however. A translation of poetry, or of poetic language, is *always* an invention. That is a well-known literary cliché. But—as Vico, Boas, and many others have pointed out—the languages of primitive peoples themselves are poetic, connotative, highly concrete, and metaphorical. As the contemporary ethnopoets believe, a practicing poet among ourselves, or our poetic faculties as ordinary human beings, are most likely to bring us closest to their meanings. Even Evans-Pritchard said something like that with reference to the understanding of primitive religion—that the grasp of it requires the poetic faculty.

MERVYN MEGGITT: When I read Radin's *Method and Theory* as an undergraduate—when I was far too naive to appreciate how much there was in it—I was delighted by what appeared to be a kind of iconoclasm. But over the years I was more and more taken by the analogies between the approaches of Radin and Géza Roheim, in the attempt to establish a dialectic between an investigator and a people: Radin, long working with Winnebago materials; Roheim, a relatively short period of time spent among aborigines but until the day he died wrestling with the data from Central Australia, within a specific kind of neo-Freudian framework. Both show a pitting of the overcivilized Western European mind—as I think they would see it—trying to come to grips with the mythology, ritual, worldview of one particular society. Roheim, like Radin, never believed for a moment that the people in question were pristine. But I think that he and Radin were doing the same sort of thing, and we benefit from it.

DIAMOND: In a certain broad sense, although Radin would not have agreed with many of Roheim's psychoanalytic formulations.

ERIC WOLF: I wonder if you could say something about this temperamental figure of the shaman who constitutes meaning in Radin's universe.

DIAMOND: What he called the *speculum mentis*. I think there were two seminal figures in Radin's mind. One of them was the trickster, the other was the shaman. The trickster, he believed, was the authentic *speculum mentis*, a universal figure. Radin was fascinated by human ambiguity and social ambivalence. He felt that they were repressed in contemporary society for various reasons (and therefore could not be confronted and transcended); bureaucratic structures obviously do not encourage the expression of ambiguity or the tremendous creative energy that is involved with it. But Radin saw in the trickster myth (and he spent years and years going through all kinds of materials) a different mode of expression of ambiguity—its confrontation, its cultural history, so to speak, its transcendence. Much of his work on religion has to be understood in those terms. The trickster, of course, is giver and destroyer, creator and negator. He is the burlesque of the sacred; at the same time, he *is* sacred. The world is the result of the trickster's energies, almost by accident; at the same time, the trickster can obliterate. He is the messenger of the gods, and he *is* God. Here we have the notion of the tragicomic duality of human life in the universe, a duality which Radin believed was personified and acted out over and over again in primitive society, both in religious projections and in rituals. This confrontation and transcendence is a primary source of art and has bearing on our own time, I think, for we divide tragedy and comedy. It is only among certain fortunately situated persons (like Shakespeare) that there sometimes occurs a dramatic fusion which can be called tragicomic. In the rituals of earlier periods in the West, this fusion is sometimes evident. In the medieval cathedrals, all kinds of people and events converged—prostitutes, merchants selling their wares, religious ritual and the *opposite* of religious ritual. Among the Greeks, during the Dionysian festivals, there was the tragic trilogy and then the satyr play, which was a total reversal of the theme that had gone before— the comic reversal of the tragic. But these "fusions" must be understood as historically relative, for compared to what happens in primitive society, they remain dichotomized.

In primitive societies, Radin thought, the tragic and the comic formed an indissoluble entity. There are many examples. Among the Wintun during the winter festival, the most sacred of their initiation rites, a clown backs up in front of the initiate and does exactly the reverse of what the initiate must do; the struggle for personal-social identity is expressed in the ritual, but there is simultaneously a denial of identity. The point is that human beings construct the identity and also can destroy the identity; we are capable of both, and we are obligated to understand this and somehow transcend it. This perception also melded with the dual image of the deity itself in Radin's work. This particular fusion is a classic—if repressed—theme in the Judeo-Christian tradition; it appears in the Book of Job, except that Job does not finally defend his own occasional insight. In the end, God *knows*, and God is unequivocal; the universe is an ethical structure, and we must hew to the line. In the primitive perspective, nothing could be more alien than the conclusion of the Book of Job.

As far as the figure of the shaman is concerned, Radin worried about that. He understood very clearly that the rise of church and state were related, so that the shaman turns into a priest at a certain point of socioeconomic development, and the exploitative potential of that combination has been one of the marks of high civilization. He wrote about that in a yet unpublished manuscript on the rise of civilization. In primitive society the shaman is not yet a determinate establishment figure but is, among other things, an aspect of Everyman. Radin told the story of the Winnebago who, while watching a shamanistic performance, turned to the ethnographer and said, "Well, it's good that some of us are that way some of the time, but it would be disastrous if all of us were that way all of the time." His notion—not terribly original, I suppose—was that the shaman represents the unenacted portion of our consciousness and that the shaman represents in his person the humanity of any given culture balanced on the knife-edge between meaning and chaos, between mere biology and symbolic existence.

This view is related to his notion of the trickster. The trickster incarnates mere biological energy, which is capable of generating symbolic performances, but the symbolic construction is always in danger of collapsing back into the inchoate energy. The shaman is the more positive, more evolved figure of symbolic creation, which is part of the substratum of the mentality of all human beings; that is, it represents the cultural potential. But precisely because of that, when, with the appearance of class divisions, the state, and so forth, that consciousness is broken off from its moorings in the people at large (when it is no longer an aspect of the shaman in each one, so to speak, which is the cultural creating capacity), then the resultant monopoly and displacement of symbolic usage can be transformed and can be used against people. The priest emerges in a determinate, alienating, exploitative structure, which includes such affairs as the paying of tribute. The society at large—not as a reification, but as the concrete interaction of human beings—is no longer sacred. Radin was well aware of that transition.

MEGGITT: For Roheim, the shaman is the precarious ego and the trickster is the unpredictable id.

DIAMOND: For Radin, the shaman would be the symboling self, or rather, selves.

PAUL RABINOW: You painted Radin's picture as a traditional intellectual, a secularized Jew at the end of his tradition who attempted to bring together the contradictions in it through thinking about them, much as your description of the trickster also takes places on a mythological level. And you implied that we can't return to that as a model of the intellectual. In what way did you mean that?

DIAMOND: I don't think we *can* return to that as a model. I think that Radin, like most of us, was the result of a dialectic between his own temperament and the historical and socioeconomic circumstances in which he was reared. Radin was full of important, almost paradigmatic, contradictions. Despite his emphasis on the concrete, he was an extremely abstract thinker; he was, occasionally, even abstract in his insistence upon being absolutely concrete at every point. He was also an extremely bookish man, probably more than was necessary; he was something of a *yeshiva bocher*. He turned learning into a ritual. He believed that the intellectual professions were the highest occupations that a man or woman could engage in, despite his suspicion of the basic structure and reification of intellectual life in our civilization. He was not pragmatically engaged with the real problems of his own society (or even of his own daily life), though he wrote about them and was fully aware of them. There are a number of reasons for that. First of all, he was fearful. This is not unknown in the academy. But there is another dimension in Radin: although he came from a family that achieved economic security and became distinguished, he was an Eastern European Jew, basically, and he always had an immigrant mentality. That is, he was afraid of the ultimate authorities in our society. He was afraid of the police, for example. He was bewildered by our technology, as I have tried to point out. He was afraid to miss a train; he didn't know how to make his own arrangements. One should not confuse those characteristics with intellectual work per se. But they indicate Paul's fear of being and doing anything other than intellectually. All his energies—and he had great energy—were poured into a single mold. One can understand this culturally, but I don't think it would serve us as a model for the use of the mind in the immediate and relentless present. I loved Paul Radin. But I was aware, sometimes painfully, of the results of the narrow socialization and cultural deprivation to which he was subject, but which he managed to surmount in many astonishingly creative ways. If he hadn't had the kind of intellectual opportunities that were offered him, and if he hadn't used those opportunities to "cure" himself, he could easily have become an extraordinarily deformed human being. In short, he was in many ways a victim.

BIOGRAPHICAL NOTE

*Photo by Robert Adelman; reprinted with
permission of the University Press of Florida   1990*

STANLEY DIAMOND was born in New York City in 1922, into an intellectual and
progressive Jewish family, which included a grandfather who was a founder of
the Yiddish theater. He grew up in the ethnic potpourri of Greenwich Village
and attended the De Witt Clinton High School, along with classmates James
Baldwin and Paddy Chayefsky. By the time he graduated, he had become a political activist and a radical. Diamond went to the University of North Carolina
for two years and then to New York University, majoring in English and philosophy. A course with E. Adamson Hoebel introduced him to anthropology, but
its descriptions of types of arrowheads and of the "war to the death" between
Neanderthal and Cro-Magnon men aroused his curiosity rather than his enthusiasm.

When his B.A. was awarded in 1942, Diamond was in North Africa as an
American Field Service volunteer attached to the British Eighth Army. While
in this service, he came into contact with African tribesmen who had been sold
into the South African army by their chiefs. His experience with the British
army was an education in the hierarchy of colonialism and helped turn him toward the decision to become an anthropologist.

After the war, Diamond was accepted into the anthropology department at
Columbia, delaying his admission for a year while he worked in a variety of jobs.
At Columbia, he took courses with Julian Steward and Gene Weltfish, among
others, and studied with the MUS seminar (see general introduction), where he
first presented the library-based research on the Dahomey protostate that be-

came his dissertation. This groundbreaking work focused on how state formation is pitted against, and resisted by, kinship organization in prestate societies. After receiving his Ph.D. in 1951, Diamond spent two years in Israel doing fieldwork in a kibbutz and in an Arab village. Subsequently, he worked among the Anaguta, a marginalized people of Nigeria (1958–1960), and he wrote critically about the Nigerian state; he returned to that country during the Nigerian Civil War (1967–1970) and became an eloquent advocate of Biafran independence. He also carried out field research among the Allegheny Seneca Indians (1962) and supported Seneca efforts to halt construction of a dam near the reservation. Diamond conducted extensive research in the United States on the cultural background of mental illness and education: He studied the families of schizophrenics while in residence at the National Institute of Mental Health (1960–1963) and directed a Culture of Schools project based at Syracuse University (1965–1967).

Diamond taught at the University of California at Los Angeles (1953–1954), Brandeis University (1956–1960), the Maxwell Graduate School of Syracuse University (1963–1966), and Columbia University (1966–1967). In 1966 he joined the New School for Social Research, where he organized and chaired the graduate anthropology program. He served as a distinguished visiting professor at Bard College and the Free University of Berlin. In 1975 Diamond founded the journal *Dialectical Anthropology*, which he edited until his death. The subtitle he gave it expresses his own purpose as an anthropologist: "an independent international journal in the critical tradition committed to the transformation of our society and the humane union of theory and practice."

The major themes of Diamond's work are the character of primitive societies as prestate paradigms and the processes of state and nation formation. An intellectual heir of Marx, Rousseau, Montaigne, and Vico, his predominant concern was with the anthropological critique of Western civilization. According to a reviewer of his book of essays, *In Search of the Primitive* (1974), by "sensitively focusing on the human consequences of being born into a primitive society, Diamond simultaneously explores the human implications of civilizational existence." The book has also been described as "a prolegomena to a Marxist anthropology," a project Diamond pursued with an edited volume *Toward a Marxist Anthropology* (1979), in which he drew an important distinction between critical and ideological Marxism.

Diamond was as much a poet as an anthropologist; in fact, he claimed he went into anthropology because it was the next best thing to poetry. He published two critically acclaimed books of poetry and was in the forefront of the ethnopoetics movement, which aimed to join the concerns of anthropology and poetry. One of his last efforts was to organize a series of readings as a forum for anthropologist-poets. Stanley Diamond died in 1991.

Bronislaw Malinowski on his way to the United States in 1938. Courtesy of Helena Wayne Malinowska

4

BRONISLAW MALINOWSKI

Raymond Firth

◈

At the time that Paul Radin was studying under Franz Boas, Bronislaw Malinowski was reading about primitive cultures in Cracow, Poland. In 1910 Malinowski moved to England and began postgraduate work in ethnology at the London School of Economics (LSE). Academic anthropology had begun in England in the 1880s with E. B. Tylor's appointment at Oxford, and it had then been introduced at Cambridge by A. C. Haddon, a professor of zoology who organized the Torres Strait expedition of 1898. Haddon had also initiated a course in ethnology at the LSE in 1904. The year that Malinowski arrived, the course was turned over to C. G. Seligman, a physician who had volunteered for the Torres Strait expedition, had been drawn into ethnology, and then had carried out fieldwork in New Guinea, among the Veddas of Ceylon, and in the Sudan.

Malinowski was born in Cracow in 1884. His father was an eminent linguist who also did some work on Polish ethnography and folklore. Malinowski attended the university in Cracow, where he took a doctorate in physics and mathematics in 1908, but ill health forced him to give up his research in the physical sciences. This allowed him to follow up a favorite side interest, reading James Frazer's The Golden Bough and other works on primitive religion. He also read accounts of the Australian aboriginal family, which led him to do a "sociological study"; his publication on this study includes his first use of the concept of "function."/

At the LSE, Malinowski worked under Edward Westermarck and the sociologist L. T. Hobhouse as well as Seligman, his principal teacher. In 1914 Malinowski carried out his first expedition, to the Mailu off the coast of New

Guinea, making a brief visit to the Trobriand Islands as well. It was en route to New Guinea that he first met A. R. Brown (later Radcliffe-Brown). His report on the Mailu earned him a doctorate from the LSE in 1916.

Undertaking a second Melanesian field trip in 1915, Malinowski returned to the Trobriand Islands; he went there again in 1917, spending a total of about two years in fieldwork in the Trobriands. The Trobriand Islanders became the subject of an extensive series of monographs on economics, family life, magic and religion, and law, as well as the vehicle for Malinowski's analysis of culture as a universal phenomenon.

Malinowski taught courses at the LSE in 1913 and again in the early 1920s. When he was offered a permanent appointment there in 1923, he proposed that it be called a Readership in Social Anthropology, to indicate the sociological emphasis of the department as distinct from the cultural anthropology being developed at University College, a sister institution within the University of London. (Social Anthropology, he also pointed out, had been the title used by Tylor at Oxford and later by Frazer at Liverpool.) During his years at the LSE, which continued until 1938, Malinowski became a highly influential teacher, including among those who studied with him E. E. Evans-Pritchard, Raymond Firth, Meyer Fortes, Phyllis Kaberry, Edmund Leach, Lucy Mair, Ashley Montagu, S. F. Nadel, Talcott Parsons, Hortense Powdermaker, Audrey Richards, Isaac Schapera, Godfrey Wilson, and others.

Malinowski made three trips to the United States between 1926 and 1936. He returned in 1938 on what was intended as a year's sabbatical, but on being advised not to go back to wartime England, he accepted a visiting professorship at Yale. He remained at Yale until his death—three months before his permanent appointment there would have become effective. During the Yale years, he made two short field trips to Mexico, where he began a project on marketing among the Zapotec Indians of Oaxaca in collaboration with Julio de la Fuente. Malinowski died in 1942, the same year as Boas's death.

Reacting against both the speculative reconstructions of the evolutionists and diffusionists, on the one hand, and what he saw as the Boasian treatment of culture traits extracted from their contexts, on the other, Malinowski originated a functionalist approach to the study of culture. In his view, culture was an integrated system of institutions derived from human needs, and he saw the goal of anthropology as constructing a "science of culture." His program for fieldwork—emphasizing long residence in the field, use of the native language, and participant-observation—became basic features of anthropological method. Both his theory and his method were critical to the development of what came to be identified as the distinctive "anthropological approach"—the intensive, holistic study of functioning societies.

tensions between the social + scientific

There is still a paradox in the public image of Malinowski—a kind of disjunction between the very personal, critical estimates that have been given of him and the pervasive scientific influence that he seems to have left behind. A kind of wonderment seizes commentators as they review discrepant facets of Malinowski's life in the anthropological community and his contribution to its intellectual development. Two recent examples, one French, one British, can illustrate this. Michel Panoff, who has devoted a whole book to Malinowski (1972), begins with the observation that it has always been well understood among professional ethnographers that Malinowski was a very mediocre theoretician, then goes on to say that he was unequaled as a field-worker and credits him with some formidable anticipations of later French anthropological thought. Adam Kuper, poised between conflicting opinions of Malinowski's personality, complained that it is difficult to find a single objective portrait of him, and after granting him a grasp of the complexity of social reality "which amounted, almost, to a theory," does not hesitate to accuse him of theoretical naïveté, crude utilitarianism, and blindness to the notion of a social system (1973: 31, 36, 49).

In Malinowski's lifetime there were contrasting views about him, but the paradox was less of a puzzle. Things that he did or said could fascinate or shock, what he wrote could evoke enthusiasm or rejection, but his acts and utterances could more easily be seen and heard in context and interpreted as the outcome of a single, complex, highly intelligent, highly articulate, vigorous, sensitive mind. Now, when it is more than thirty years after he has died, no professional anthropologist under the middle fifties in age is likely to have known him, and curiosity about the character of this unusual man who is rightly termed one of the founders of social anthropology is understandable. Since I worked closely with him for some years in the most productive period of his life and retained ties of friendship (albeit at varying distance) with him until his death, it may be illuminating to some people for me to try and match what I remember of his personality with what has been written and thought of his theories, both by others and by me.[1] There will be no revelations, and I do not claim the portrait as objective. But I have tried to make it dispassionate, with a perspective that may be helpful to others in forming their own opinions.

It is a simplification, but not a great one, to see a triple paradox in the public image of Malinowski for people who did not know him. He suffered continually from bad health, and a tragic illness of his wife absorbed much of his attention, yet he managed to write so much. He has been generally applauded for the magnificent quality of his fieldwork and decried for his theories, yet he managed to inspire so many people. And while his fieldwork was long regarded as his prime achievement—depending upon his rapport with the Trobrianders, his sympathy and understanding—by his own account in his diaries he turns out to have been bad-tempered, contemptuous in some of his attitudes toward the people—the idol, as Clifford Geertz put it, certainly had feet of clay.

The first and last of these paradoxes can to some extent be put together. He had an undoubted history of ill health. Much of his early education took place at home because he was regarded as what in contemporary English terms would be called "delicate." In his twenties, after completing his doctorate in philosophy in Cracow, he was directed on medical advice to change his academic field. And between his Trobriand expeditions and his settling in England he had or was threatened by tuberculosis. Yet he had great intellectual energy and a constant, almost obsessional interest in maintaining his physical vitality. One of his friends has said that only someone as strong as a horse could have swallowed all the medicines he did without killing himself—but that may be an unwarranted gloss. Certainly he believed in exercise, in sunshine and clear air—which did not stop him from working in rooms with closed windows, and, in his early seminars at the LSE, with a roaring fire in the grate. But he also "lived on his nerves," in the colloquial phrase, with a physical and psychological sensitivity that burst out at times: against people; in shouting; in profanity; in a kind of cruelty springing from a mixture of exhaustion and egocentrism—and which broke down periodically into migraine that incapacitated him for twenty-four hours or so.

Given this cyclical pattern—a driving force of intellectual interest, with some amalgam of personal vanity and ambition that he never denied; also some components of physical weakness, always threatening, sometimes breaking out; given too the ordinary frustrations and trials of fieldwork compounded by his emotional turmoil over the separate attachments to two women revealed in his diaries—and his occasional outbursts against Trobrianders become explicable even where they are regrettable.[2] His output of scientific books and articles was accomplished by high focus, enlisting the aid of family, servants, research assistants, and friends and subjecting himself to a discipline of work that left much time for intellectual conversation but not too much for other pursuits. Walking he liked, but he played no games, did not garden, had no skills with his fingers and no hobbies that I can remember.

My own relationship with Malinowski covered nearly twenty years, from my first meeting with him when I was a graduate student in 1924 until his death in 1942. Before I ever knew he was in London, I had been fascinated by *Argonauts of the Western Pacific* (1922), which I came across by chance in a bookshop in New Zealand. Interested in the possibility of providing an economic dimension to anthropological data, I found in this book a superb example, based on intimate field experience, of what I had only vaguely dreamed of doing. So in London I was happy not only to have him as a teacher but also to become his research assistant. In 1925 and 1926, under a Laura Spelman Rockefeller Memorial grant, I worked with Malinowski on *Crime and Custom* (1926b), *Myth* (1926c), and *The Father* (1927b)—to use their shorthand titles—as well as the first part of *The Sexual Life of Savages* (1929) and various articles. His work habits were idiosyncratic. He came rarely to the Reading Room of the British Museum, where many academics then did much of their research; when he did

I had books ready, marked for him to see. I also abstracted much material for him, read to him sections of work for discussion, and acted as his amanuensis and critic. In London he did much work in bed; in Oberbozen, where he had a villa at which he spent most of the summer, he usually worked on the balcony, often nude in the sun, with a green eyeshade, scrubbing himself with a solution of iodized salt in the intervals of discussion about Trobriand myth or family life.

Whether in London or in Oberbozen he led an active social life, moving easily in multilingual conversation in a continental world of scholarly intellectuals, but without that pomposity which so often marked the senior academic of his day. But social life with Malinowski merged very easily into intellectual life. His seminars were famous: penetrating, with a quietly relentless Socratic approach broken by a sudden shaft of wit; impatient of any slick formal textbook definition; insistent on careful statement of a problem; yet generous in acknowledgment of any original contribution, however hesitant. But as much, or more, work with his students was done outside the seminar. Audrey Richards (1943) has noted how "they learned to discuss their theses on bus-tops or dodging the market-barrows down Holborn side-streets." His demands could be exigent. His research assistants could be worked late into the night, writing down many thousands of words—in longhand—more, they knew, than an article could possibly stand, with all protests met by such statement as, "First get it all down, then cut." But there were compensations—not only glasses of wine and meals, but also a stimulating flow of conversation, a genuine interest in the assistants' own ideas, and a sense of freedom in sharing a common intellectual atmosphere. Believing firmly in the importance of reciprocity, Malinowski also mobilized the domestic and professional world around him, particularly by exchange of gifts for services. Even his Oberbozen home was brought into the socioacademic orbit. Many of his graduate students stayed at the *Pfarrhaus*, the home of the priest at Maria Himmelfahrt near by, and joined in the teas at the villa and the walks through pine woods and alpine meadows in the evening, with talk ranging from the latest thesis chapter to more general problems of social theory or more personal problems of agreement and difference.

And at the back of all this, until 1935, was his wife, Elsie Rosaline Masson (the E.R.M. of the diaries). An intelligent, cultured, independent-minded Australian woman, she was very clear-sighted and she had a sense of humor. She realized fully what kind of being she had married and had accepted this from the start—she married against her parents' wishes and not from their home. She herself had already published a book on North Australia, and she had a fine sense of style and a good critical mind. But she devoted herself to her husband and children; they had three daughters. In the early years she spent much time reading and discussing his work, and he relied very greatly upon her judgment. She appears in his diaries as a person who could heal wounds and absolve from sins—and such she remained for him until the end of her life.

Malinowski's character is not easy to describe briefly. In intellectual matters he was widely if unevenly read, and he commanded a range of continental scholarship unusual in British anthropologists of his period—before European scholars wrote much in English or translations of their works became common. He was a vivid, often very frank conversationalist with very definite views on many social questions, including the effects of national shortcomings. Insistently theoretical in his professional approach, he was yet constantly applying concrete example and pragmatic test. Anthropology was for him a meaningful intellectual discipline that related to everyday life, not just an academic study of "the primitive." As in this discipline, so also in his personal relations—he was not satisfied with superficial appearances but wished to scrutinize motivation and effect. He enjoyed some measure of good living but was not impressed by wealth. He was careful, even mean, with money and counseled his students accordingly, but he was generous with his time and attention to their problems. He was conscious of the social value of flattery and sometimes used it blatantly, but he was scornful of hypocrisy and quick to identify it in himself and others. Loyalty was a prime virtue in his eyes—and loyalty commonly meant agreement in action, not necessarily in opinion. With a strong ego drive and more than a touch of hypochondria, he also had an intense interest in the human personality of others and so tended to make a strong impact on people at the first meeting.

Malinowski's personality then was complex, but it was not protean, not inconstant in change. Rather can he be described as romantic in the sense of subordination of form to theme, both in social action and in anthropological analysis. He was a romantic not in the sense of sentimentalism—he was a realist, a near-cynic on occasions—but in the sense of having his values in the sphere of human personality rather than in human constructs. He never surrounded himself with choice pictures or other art objects; he liked good food and wine but was no connoisseur. Even books, so important to his intellectual development, were cherished less than people's opinions, and he never built up any very substantial library. He looked for his values in people, not things—friendship, loyalty, truth were prime concepts to him and overtly appeared in his more personal relationships. Intellectually, he did not reject the principle of order, but order was of less significance to him than the dynamic forces that he saw at work. He was not a classic, not a structuralist in his interests. He was impatient of formalistic statement and did not always bother to be formally consistent. As part of these dynamic forces he recognized, and used, exaggeration, violence of expression, intellectual shock tactics, as instruments of exploration and understanding. Introspective, self-exploring, he also had a romantic attitude to faith. A lapsed Catholic who sometimes used his former religion for sociological display, he was actually a skeptic who would have liked to believe. He had a "nostalgia for belief." He felt strongly that in his own circumstances he was subjected to an overshadowing by fate; in such attitudes his intellect and his emotions went hand in hand. In the aesthetic field he was not artistic in the ordinary sense. He had a strong liking for music, especially the German nineteenth-century composers, including Wagner. But I do not remember that he took much interest in painting—though his second wife was a painter—and in sculpture and architecture he was distin-guished by keen sensibility rather than by specialized taste. As for literature, his other pursuits left him little time for lengthy reading, and it is my impression that he was knowledgeable rather than learned in this sphere. (But his recipe for learning a European language, which he himself used for Spanish and urged upon his students for Italian or German, was to invest in an armful of novels and read through them with minimal resort to grammar or dictionary!)

In the field of political and ethical values Malinowski was an internationalist and a humanist. As a product of a cosmopolitan education he spoke Polish, German, French, and English from an early stage, and at various points had added Italian and Spanish. All these he handled fluently, in addition to his New Guinea experi-ence with Motu and his command of Trobriand. Rhoda Metraux, in her excellent article on Malinowski, states that he spoke Russian (1968: 542). I don't think this is strictly true. When I was traveling with him on a train in North Italy about 1925, he was once away for about an hour, talking with a Russian, he explained. I said I had thought he did not know Russian. He replied that he did not, but had "made out" by combining the smattering of what he had "picked up" with his knowledge of Polish and other Slavic forms. His spoken *Hochdeutsch* was perfect—a *Gräfin* of our acquaintance whom I asked said that if anything it was too perfect! In later years he preferred to write in English, and I think from what he said he would not have wished to write a literary piece in Polish. But his English pronun-ciation was never quite perfect; in some particulars, as in "fud" for "food," he con-tinued to betray a continental upbringing. And despite his amazing linguistic facility he continued to count in his natal tongue even at a late date in England. (When I caught him once mumbling to himself what to me were some very odd sounds, he said rather sheepishly that in private he always counted in Polish.)

[margin annotation] emphasis on learning local language.

Given his cosmopolitan outlook, I did not see him as a Polish nationalist in any active sense. Of course in the '20s and '30s he was very conscious of the wrongs in Polish history, and he retained many Polish contacts. But though he had Pol-ish students—J. Obrebski and A. Waligorski, for instance—and perhaps had spe-cial ties with them, he did not give the impression of being first and foremost a Pole, and I don't think he was ever interested in returning to Poland to take a permanent academic position. In a generally admirable series of articles, Kon-stantin Symmons-Symonolewicz has taken me to task for discussing the problem of Malinowski's relation to Poland and things Polish "in a somewhat superficial manner" (1958: 16n). He cites Malinowski's frequent national self-identification as a Pole before the war as evidence of his Polish patriotism and nationalism. Now Symmons-Symonolewicz does add that it is more a question of the mean-ing of terms such as patriotism and national consciousness than of real discrep-ancy in interpretation of Malinowski's sentiments. But in turn, I think he has failed to realize how in conversation, as in writing, Malinowski used his Polish-ness as he did his Catholicism—as a counter in the play of argument, a kind of foil to the position he was adopting. There is no need to doubt the genuineness of his feeling for Poland; the question is the degree to which this outstripped other feelings, and my impression is that politically he thought in international rather than narrow national terms. But it seems that Malinowski's sense of Polish identification developed—or revived—quite markedly when he was in the United States during World War II. (I have in corroboration here the opinion of Feliks Gross, a long-time friend and colleague of Malinowski.) So the appearance in 1973 of Malinowski's portrait in a gold medallion on a 2-zloty stamp of Poland was a justifiable tribute to a Pole of international reputation.[3]

What Malinowski was, unequivocally, was an enemy of fascism and Nazism. Right from the beginning of the Mussolini epoch in Italy, he made no particular secret of his feelings of profound dislike of the regime, and his detestation of Hitlerism was even greater. But his reactions were of an intellectual rather than a political type. He attacked totalitarianism in public lectures and in the book he was preparing shortly before his death, *Freedom and Civilization* (1947), but as far as I know he joined no political party.

His friends, like his scholarship, were international. Apart from some of his British academic colleagues in anthropology and sociology and distinguished intellectual figures in Britain and the United States, his real friends included an English statistician and his wife, who was a very talented artistic woman; a Viennese Jewish industrialist (to whom *Sex and Repression* is dedicated) and his wife, with both of whom he had close ties ever since his Australian days; a French pearl buyer whom he had known in the Trobriands and who appears in the diary; a scholarly ex-missionary administrator, who directed the International African Institute; an English landowner of a great county family, who was also something of an anthropologist and an authority on Émile Durkheim and Friedrich Nietzsche. To these people he opened himself in friendship, which he treated as one of the sacred values.

Ultimate honesty—not superficial honesty—was another such value. He could not stand conventional codes; he used them but despised them. So some of his judgments of people were apt to run athwart of accepted norms. At a time when the French in general were often said to be the most polite people in Europe, Malinowski, seeing, as he thought, beneath the surface, described them as the rudest, except perhaps the Germans in some moods. The peasants of Italy—not the nobility—he credited with the best manners of all. The English he tolerated, and indeed admired "English" ("British" had not then come so extensively into vogue) democratic institutions. But he sneered at the concept of the English gentleman—"that stinky species" as he once wrote in a letter to me, as a warning. As I have said, he was a flatterer, especially to men and women in positions of power, but he was also quite willing to describe them offensively—mostly with words beginning with *b*—behind their backs. His flattery he treated as a kind of cheerful foible, a social instrument that he did not intend to be taken seriously, except by those stupid enough to believe in it. Also, he was not afraid to mingle flattery with solid criticism. I well remember after

we had once called on Marcel Mauss and Malinowski had been almost offensively critical, as we left the apartment I queried his manner. He laughed and
said, "The thing to do with these people"—he meant the *L'Année sociologique*
group—"is every now and again to give them a good sound kick." But under-
neath all this he attached great value to sincerity, to frankness, to a willingness
to put all the intellectual and emotional cards on the table, to admit to one's
own ambitions and vanities—and to a capacity to point out those of the other
person too. Friendship with Malinowski could be a wearing relationship. It
might demand a confrontation every now and again, with no or almost no holds
barred. But it had its compensations, not least of which was precisely to have
the benefits of this cuttingly analytical, realistic scrutiny of act and motive. Of
course, every now and then he got it wrong, or the friend committed some
blunder, and this could be difficult. (I have indicated elsewhere [Firth 1975: 6]
one such development in my own case.)

Much has been made of Malinowski's profanity, which was free and, in English at least, at times almost adolescent. People have been shocked by what he
said about the Trobrianders—but as one of his friends has said, that is nothing
to what he said about, or to, some of his British colleagues. I have no wish to
defend the vulgarity and prejudice revealed in some parts of his diary, including the expression translated as "niggers," which apparently might equally have
been rendered as "blacks." But two points are worth remembering in this context. The first is that the diaries were written in Polish, for his own private
record, as a kind of catharsis in which no ideas or feelings should be kept back;
there is no suggestion that they were ever intended as anything more than a
frank expression of his personal state of mind. Who among us has the courage
to set down his private thoughts, including his grosser thoughts, as openly? The
second point is that in his own idiosyncratic way Malinowski was a firm believer
in the universality of human rights. His consciousness of ethnicity is not to be
simply equated with a racist denial of such rights.

Malinowski was a humanist, in two senses. He had no belief in spiritual powers other than those of man himself, no faith in revealed religion. Though a
Catholic when young, he seemed to have lost all trace of this by the time I knew
him, in his forties—except for the occasional lighthearted reference for comparative purposes. Even when admiring with him the architectural and sculp-
tural grandeur of Catholic churches in North Italy, I had no hint that he had
any nostalgic interest in their rituals or that their beliefs formed any very active
part of his intellectual heritage. Perhaps one of the legacies of his Catholicism
was a certain preoccupation with the concept of death—though his intellectual
interest in the problem of the fear of death was perhaps more a reflex of his
personal temperament than of his religious heritage.

He was a humanist in a broader sense too. He believed intensely in the value
of man irrespective of individual status or condition. Superficially perhaps he
was a bit of a snob—it amused him to hobnob with a titled person. But it was a

game he soon tired of, and it was the quality of the person that he sought. He had plenty of titled peopled—some knights, a princess, a countess, and various continental nobles—in his wider circle of friends, but they stayed there on their merits. Retainers—family cooks, charwomen, college porters—he treated rather regally; he tipped them well and got them to do services for him (this was in prewar conditions) in an incredibly short space of time after he first met them. But then he also made a point of speaking to them, inquired about them personally, got small gifts for them—so after more than thirty years the face of one of them still lights up when I mention Professor Malinowski to him. He was not a philanthropist in the conventional sense. In the period I knew him best he contributed to few if any "good causes" that I can remember. But he spoke out continually in favor of what he saw as basic human values.

   I can exemplify this in a brief reference to his views on sex. He was a pioneer in the advocacy of what may be called modern enlightened sex values. Malinowski himself had strong personal heterosexual interests, which he made no great effort to conceal. But he was actively concerned with more general issues of the theoretical place of sex in social life and of the practical significance of anthropology in programs of sex education and social reform. He was a friend of Havelock Ellis—that noble, patriarchal, white-bearded figure (as I knew him in his late years) whose *Psychology of Sex* in six volumes was a more literate Kinsey of the 1920s, when writing scientifically about sex was a more perilous occupation than it is today. He was also a strong supporter of the British Social Hygiene Council, led by its formidable Secretary-General Mrs. C. Neville-Rolfe and counting among its members Julian Huxley, Cyril Burt, and J. Arthur Thomson. He contributed to the conferences of the Council and induced his younger anthropological colleagues to do likewise. Parallel to, and indeed a little earlier than, the work of Margaret Mead in the United States, he helped social and cultural anthropology to free itself from the legacy of orgiastic rituals and classical phallic symbolism, of being overly concerned with savagery and nudity. He wrote of "savages" but they were not naked—they were in fact quite prudish about genital exposure. When people said of Malinowski, "Ah yes, I've read his *book*," one never needed to ask which book. Yet the famous *Sexual Life of Savages* (1929) contains almost as much about the status of women, the obligations of marriage, the dogmas of physical resemblance, and relations between different kinds of kin as it does about sexual behavior. Malinowski put forward the Trobriand customs of premarital sex as aids to marital choice of a fairly rational kind.

    In an address, "Anthropology and Social Hygiene" (1926a), leveled at modern Western society, he argued against "preaching barren continence" before marriage, and he thought that with the restrictions on divorce then prevailing, many a man and woman would prefer to enter a free union rather than bind themselves in a marriage tie. He was in favor of early marriages and saw no objection to contraceptives on biological, social, or moral grounds. He held that divorce should be easier and that the moral tone that penalized the woman rather than the man in all sexual irregularity was unjust and ignoble. In much of this he was well in advance of the public opinion of his day—though his opinions are not outmoded. But central to all his thinking and writing was the view that the full attainment of sexual satisfaction cannot be realized except in a permanent union of deep love and mutual sacrifice. He held that man is neither inevitably promiscuous nor naturally monogamous, that the experimental component in sexual desire leads to new sexual interests and experiences, but that there is also a deep seeking for attachment and fidelity. Assuming, as we all tend to do, the mantle of his science, he declared firmly that "it is evident then that anthropology is a vigourous supporter of all schemes and plans which lead to the strengthening of monogamous marriage and of the individual family" (1926a: 84). But he added with a characteristic image, "On the other hand, no student of man can be an absolute follower of Mrs. Grundy—she has never studied anthropology."

This central notion of the basic importance of the individual family, which appears clearly in all his treatment of kinship and which first saw full expression in his book on the Australian aborigines, probably had several roots. It owed something to Edward Westermarck, whose dictum that marriage was rooted in the family rather than the family in marriage Malinowski often quoted. It was also in part a kind of common-sense reaction against the theoretical constructs of primitive promiscuity and group marriage, which earlier anthropologists had invented to explain certain kinship terminologies and associated behavior and which Malinowski thought were gross misunderstandings of the situation by people who had never studied what actually happened. But I think this notion was also related to his own deeper feelings of the need for stability in human relationships—linked in another aspect to his conception of friendship. There was also perhaps some reflection of his Catholic upbringing in his notion of a high ideal—of beautiful love, a stable marriage, and a solidary family—which the weakness of the flesh, "reality," is always threatening to impair.

With his zest for stripping off the superficialities from statements about behavior, it is understandable that Malinowski found much that was stimulating about Freudian theory. I gather that he never met Sigmund Freud, but Princess Marie Bonaparte, who was analyzed by Freud and did much to help Freud leave Vienna for London when the Nazi occupation of Austria took place, was his friend. So also was J. C. Flugel, author of *The Psycho-Analytic Study of the Family* (1921). Malinowski wrote that the open treatment of sex and of "various shameful meannesses and vanities in man"—the very thing for which psychoanalysis was most hated and reviled—was of the greatest value to science. But he became increasingly impatient of the exorbitant claims of psychoanalysis to explain the origins of human institutions, and he did not accept the full sexual basis advanced by Freudians in their interpretation of symbolism. Together, well after his first reading of psychoanalytical material in the Trobriands, we studied Freud's analysis of dream and delusion in Wilhelm Jensen's novel *Gradiva*, and other Freudian works including the *Drei Abhandlungen zur Sexualtheorie*. On the one hand, Malinowski rejected the idea of a primal horde adopted by Freud from J. J. Atkinson and used as a basis for much of the argument of *Totem and Taboo*. On the other hand, he refused to see sexual connotations in many mundane acts of living—he could not believe, he said, that eating a mutton chop was the equivalent of a sexual act. In this as in many other ways he was a pragmatist, not a symbolist.

Malinowski's pragmatism has been examined by Leach (1957), fairly on the whole, though in my view Leach got carried away a bit by his defense of Charles Peirce against William James. Malinowski's formulations were at times a bit naive. But the point is that he was never a rigid doctrinaire but was willing to be guided by what he saw as the empirical facts of a situation. This comes out in his attitude to psychoanalysis, including his Trobriand modification of the Oedipus complex. Since in the Trobriands the authority over children recognized by Europeans as inherent in the father was exercised by the mother's brother, Malinowski inferred that the hostility expressed in myth for the authority figure could be expected to take on another form—and this he found. It was the rigor of the Freudians, led by Ernest Jones, that helped to alienate him from their theoretical approach as they attacked his interpretation. But his was a sociological interpretation, based on a consideration of the structure of social and economic relationships. Malinowski described the Oedipus complex as "essentially patriarchal in character," and the "avuncular complex"—hatred of mother's brother and incest wish for sister—as essentially matrilineal. He reversed the psychoanalytical interpretation: "The nuclear family complex is a functional formation dependent upon the structure and upon the culture of a society."[4] (Note that this is an intensivist rather than an extensionist form of argument!) Malinowski, like later functionalists, has been accused of not looking below the surface of social phenomena, of failing to recognize the abstract systematic qualities of interconnected events. But in Trobriand myths he saw not merely a charter for rights and privileges but also the expression of some deep relations in the structure of the society. He saw the repressed hatred of the mother's brother breaking through in the Tudava myth, which he described as containing a "typical matrilineal drama which forms its core, and which is brought to its logical conclusion." He even, in language with which we are now much more familiar, said in interpreting the presentation of an ogre's head in a pudding to be eaten by the startled guilty uncle, that the story "contains then in reality one villain and one conflict distributed over two stages and duplicated into two persons" (1927a: 105). The reinterpretation by Jones of Malinowski's views—that a basic hatred of the father had led to a Trobriand denial of him and to transference of the father's role to the mother's brother—seemed to Malinowski a very strained position and not supported by the symbolic speculative material of the "primal horde" myth type.

Malinowski's relatively straightforward view that the Trobrianders did not know of physiological paternity or at least consistently denied it as an intellectual matter has been borne out by the field experience of Reo Fortune. The interpretation of what such denial means has been modified by commentators such as Radcliffe-Brown, Montagu, Leach, and David Schneider, but it was Malinowski who first developed the sociological significance of the Trobriand data, from an earlier Australian model.

Malinowski's acute self-awareness was perhaps channeled to some extent by his acquaintance with psychoanalysis. But his almost clinical attitude of exploration of the self was marked not by the sometimes humorless detachment of the professional analyst, but by a lively expression of self-mockery. This has rarely been understood by his commentators, though his friends knew it well. A few brief extracts from letters to one of his students will illustrate this aspect of his character. In April 1939 he acknowledged a letter as "a lovely birthday present on my sad 55th anniversary of the most calamitous event which befell in my life—except perhaps the one which preceded it by 9 months; or else my decision to become an anthropologist." In a letter of May 1940 he disclaimed having taken any offense at what might have seemed a critical note by his correspondent:

> Now, as you know, "Malinowski is as touchy as he is conceited," to quote the majority of my colleagues, pupils and friends. So the phrase cannot be in any way offensive. At the time I probably reacted to it as an indication that you plan and propose to develop Malinowski's theory and to replace it by something bigger and better.[5]

I have mentioned Malinowski's humanism in regard to religion, to sex, and to international affairs. In the field of applied anthropology too he shared the attitudes of liberal humanists of his day in believing in the broad developmental and philanthropic aspects of colonial government. He recognized many of the inequalities and injustices in the colonial situation, but he regarded moves to self-government as likely to be distant (as indeed they seemed in prewar days). He accepted that the ultimate political decision lay in the hands of the governing power, and he was more concerned that the local people should have good government than that they should have self-government. (I remember arguing with him strongly on one occasion that in "indirect rule" the "indirectness" was less important than the fact that "rule" was still maintained.) He was on good terms with Lord Lugard, one of the architects of indirect rule; and he fought Sir Philip Mitchell, a noted colonial governor, on the issue of the practicality of applied anthropology rather than on the objectives of government. "Practical" anthropology to Malinowski was primarily getting an understanding of the facts of a social situation—polygyny, female "circumcision," "brideprice," land tenure, labor migration—by careful functional analysis. It meant also not ignoring the effects and implications of agricultural improvement and medical and educational advance, as well as noting the results of settler greed, bureaucratic ignorance, and missionary intolerance. He was not afraid to draw attention to "race prejudice, political and economic imperialism, the demand for segregation, the safeguarding of a European standard of living" (1945: 23) as forces that denied to Africans an equality of treatment with their colonial rulers.

He also held that the anthropologist had a moral obligation to be "a fair and true interpreter of the Native." He was very conscious of the rights of indigenous peoples, both material in respect to landholding and immaterial in respect to the dignity of personality. It was no accident that he was associated with Norman Leys, who wrote bitterly against white policies of land annexation in Kenya, or that both Jomo Kenyatta and Z. K. Matthews, strong African nationalists, owed much to him in their anthropological studies and academic life.[6] But for him the duty of the anthropologist to "speak as the Natives' advocate" stopped at laying bare the sources of maladjustment; he did not envisage any more active political commitment. Hence it has been easy for modern critics, in a very altered situation, to impute to him a tolerance, if not actual support, for colonialism, and a shaping of his anthropological theory accordingly. What the modern revulsion from political imperialism often overlooks is the challenge fairly consistently offered by social anthropologists to any form of intellectual imperialism, that is, to attempt to dominate by organizational and sometimes even by physical means the freedom of opinion and the development of ideas by people under a variety of forms of government. In expressing such challenge Malinowski was unequivocal. He wrote, "The absence of political freedom destroys all other liberties." But at the same time he noted the dangers of misuse of words like democracy and freedom, of inflation in ideals, and of contempt for ideas as slogans become commonplace. "The spiritual foundations of public opinion have to be watched with the same eternal vigilance with which we look after the physical foundations of our national defenses" (1947: 13, 336).

So far I have tried to sketch some of the salient features of Malinowski's character as an introduction to a more direct comment upon his theories. But in passing I should perhaps make reference to some rather more adverse opinions of the man and his intellectual contribution, as expressed by colleagues who knew him. The most outspoken of these was by Max Gluckman, in a review of Malinowski's posthumous *Scientific Theory of Culture.* While acknowledging Malinowski's notable services to anthropological fieldwork, Gluckman denigrated his theoretical contributions and linked their inadequacies with Malinowski's personal failings. According to Gluckman, Malinowski, as the only specialized social anthropologist of his "generation" in Britain after the 1914–1918 war, stood alone, a solitary king; his dissident pupils had hived off; he either quarreled with or absorbed the views of his juniors. "He is noted for his distortions of the views of preceding or foreign or filial rivals. Power corrupts. . . ." (Gluckman 1963: 243). The thesis is interesting on structural grounds, but to those who knew Malinowski well it is a travesty. The "solitary king" is a view of hindsight. It is true that Evans-Pritchard, with acute perception, had left Oxford to come to the LSE—an almost unheard-of move in those days. But Gregory Bateson, Reo Fortune, Monica Hunter, and Camilla Wedgwood did their major anthropology at Cambridge; Gluckman himself, with his Rhodes Scholarship, preferred to go to Oxford; and in London Daryll Forde

[handwritten marginalia: maybe this makes him different from those like Durkheim Bocs]

studied primarily with W. J. Perry. In the 1920s and 1930s Malinowski was certainly outstanding, but in the contemporary scene he was a leader in a field of choice, not a unique potentate. With entirely different personalities and other monarchs around, any authority position can lead to trouble, with filials becoming rivals, as the history of many anthropology departments has since demonstrated. Moreover, few of those around Malinowski were neutral personalities, and some themselves generated much heat as well as light.

It is no secret, for instance, that Evans-Pritchard and Malinowski were at daggers drawn for personal as well as for professional reasons and that Evans-Pritchard did his best to destroy Malinowski's reputation long after his death. (In 1934 Malinowski begged me to serve as one of the editors of the Festschrift for Seligman, so that, he said, his name would not have to stand next to that of Evans-Pritchard on the cover of the book! But Evans-Pritchard was not noted for his charity. He refused after some delay to contribute to the memorial volume for Malinowski.) The point of this is that when, for example, Evans-Pritchard said that Malinowski "seldom made abstractions" and showed "little originality or distinction of thought" in his explicitly theoretical writings, these statements have to be read in the light of such strong personal feelings of antagonism. Evans-Pritchard was an expert in the glancing blow. His dismissal of Malinowski's theory of religion and magic as a pragmatic one which "might have come straight out of the pages of William James, *as indeed it may have done*" (Evans-Pritchard 1965: 48; italics mine) carries more than a suggestion of plagiarism but ignores some basic differences between the approaches of the two men. James, for example, held that it was certain that the whole system of thought that leads to magic and allied beliefs may just as well be called primitive science as primitive religion; Malinowski, as is well known, insisted that the division between magic and primitive science was clear-cut, each with its own separate function. James was concerned with the pragmatic value of immediate personal experiences in religion and regarded these as realities in the fullest sense of the term; Malinowski argued that while the roots of religious experience lie in the individual, the realization of religious acts and beliefs requires collective efforts, the controlling force of society. Again, in criticizing Malinowski's "emotional" theory of magic, Evans-Pritchard suggests the possibility that much of Malinowski's observation of rites was of those performed for his benefit, for payment, in his tent (1965: 46). But not only does he cite no evidence for this opinion but he omits to mention, as a dispassionate critic should, that Malinowski specifically states that he was present, by permission of the officiating magician, at every garden rite in Omarakana agriculture, and also witnessed the reciting of spells "in the solemnity of actual performance" in the magician's own house" (Malinowski 1935, vol. 1: 86, 94). In other words, more generally, when what are ostensibly scientific judgments—either positive or negative—are passed in a circle of people who have known one another personally, they must be regarded as a function of the total situation and may have to be interpreted in the light of considerations not always immediately apparent.

In considering Malinowski's position in theoretical anthropology, many commentators have separated his fieldwork sharply from his theory. They have praised him for the quality of his fieldwork as if he were an indefatigable collector of facts, in rapport with the Trobrianders because he lived in a tent among them and spoke their language fluently, and had a keen eye for the minutiae of behavior. Such views have ignored Malinowski's cardinal principle—no fact without a theory—as clearly set out in the last section of the "Baloma" essay (1916). As more perceptive analysts have seen, Malinowski's real ethnographic gifts lay deeper. He was keenly aware of the complexity of the sociocultural reality. He had an acute perception of how the meaning of cultural items had to be reached (initially at least, we might add) through an understanding of their functional interrelations. He realized that significant problems lay not only in the study of conformity, but also in that of discrepancy—between what people said and what they did, between the norms of social order and the pursuit of individual interests. In some aspects of his field technique Malinowski may well have been stimulated by the example of Edward Westermarck, by whom he was much influenced in his few years at the LSE. He contributed to Westermarck's *Festskrift* in 1912 and in later years talked of Westermarck with a kind of respectful affection, rather different from his somewhat contemptuous affection for Sir James Frazer, to whom he also felt much indebted. Now Westermarck, a cultivated European, spoke the vernacular of the field in which he worked—unlike either Rivers or Seligman, with whose field experiences Malinowski was well acquainted, or Radcliffe-Brown (then A. R. Brown), who gave Malinowski some useful field advice before he went to the Trobriands. Between 1898 and 1914, when Malinowski left London for Australia and New Guinea, Westermarck had paid at least a dozen visits to Morocco and accumulated a vast mass of field material in Arabic, as well as engaging in close relations with some sectors of Moroccan society. So Malinowski had the example of a man whom he respected, a theoretical sociologist as well as a vernacular-using field-worker. In a sense, then, he may be said to have been following one thread of the European Orientalist tradition in his immersion in the field—a point I do not remember to have been noted before.

But what Malinowski certainly did not get from Westermarck were two elements in his work. One was his more lively, more sophisticated sense of a theoretical problem in a systematic social order. (When Malinowski is accused of "lacking the notion of a system," his work should be compared with that of Westermarck, in which the lack of a concept of a systematic framework of society is much more apparent.) Here the influence of Durkheim and *L'Année sociologique* was probably very important. Another element was of a much more personal kind—his sense of awareness of the anthropologist as a factor in the total field situation. Geertz, by no means uncritical of Malinowski, has stated that this was among Malinowski's prime contributions to anthropology. Panoff (1972) has seen it as a "demand for authenticity," in clearly analyzing the relation between the perceptions of the ethnographer and the actions and reactions of the people he studies. In more than a superficial sense, Malinowski may be regarded as a precursor of some of the developments of "cognitive anthropology." However this may be, there is no doubt that for those within his ambience, fieldwork was never the same after the publication of *Argonauts*. In particular, the use of the vernacular was necessary not just as an instrument for collecting better data, but also as a means of relating more effectively to the people and so gaining a fuller understanding of their society and culture.

While participant-observation in field anthropology owes a great debt to Malinowski, I have the impression from my talks with him, as well as from his *Diary* and other works, that his participation was almost always secondary to his observation. In his relations with the Mailu and even with the Trobrianders, his cerebral functioning had almost complete ascendancy over his "gut" reactions of involvement. His preoccupation with the intensely personal quality and significance of his experience was not, however, a mere self-absorption. He saw this experience as having a more general quality, as typifying categories of the human condition. With this, I think, is linked his attitude to anthropological theory. He has sometimes been called "a mediocre theoretician" because some of his specific theories no longer fit the modern idiom or have been shown to have clear imperfections. But his major contribution lies not in his specific theories but in his insistence on the need for theory, the relation of the particular to the general, at every stage of anthropological enquiry. So even the most mundane piece of ethnography, for example an article on stone implements, is shot through with suggestions about art, social status, symbolism, and political and economic power. This is why some commentators, such as Panoff, have been impressed by what he calls the "architecture" of the presentation of material in the *Argonauts*, and why Bateson and others have acknowledged the stimulus of ideas implicit or immanent in Malinowski's work.

Where Malinowski does display weakness, especially by contrast with much modern analysis, is in his failure to supply many "middle-range" generalizations from his studies. Meyer Fortes has pointed out with justice that one of the paradoxes in Malinowski's work is that his theoretical writings are mostly couched in terms of the highest generality, and the specific variability of cultural phenomena tends to disappear. To some extent, I think, this was a response to a very widespread intellectual interest of the time, going far beyond anthropology. There was a strong focus on problems of the concept of a human nature, of what was meant by instinct, of the relation of human culture to innate drives, of the relevance of nonhuman animal behavior to human behavior. There was much talk of the theories of W. McDougall and A. F. Shand; Malinowski opened his *Sex and Repression* with a quotation from John Dewey's *Human Nature and Conduct*; Julian Huxley lectured to the University of London Anthropological

Society on the mating display of great crested grebes; and he and Malinowski had discussions on the role of sexual selection as part of natural selection. It was a period of much speculation and little systematic evidence. With his background of general sociological theory and his recent vivid Trobriand field experience, Malinowski was easily drawn into this seductive but somewhat elusive field of reflection.

Comment on Malinowski's more concrete fields of enquiry is easier. His studies in social and cultural change have attracted much attention, most of it critical, from Africanists who preferred other frameworks for analysis of the material. His formalist approach by means of charts indeed seems better adapted to preliminary sorting of data than to final conceptualization of results, and his reliance on the notion of "institution" as a unit of culture contact is clumsy. But some of the criticism was rather wide of the mark. Take his attitude toward the study of history. It is true that he himself used little historical documentation in his studies of social change. But a broader charge has often been repeated: that he ignored history, that he was confused about what history is, that he had an obscurantist bias against history. It is worth remembering, then, that on Malinowski's first introduction to New Guinea, he proposed as a possible study the "process of transformation and adaptation of the Koita *iduhu*" involved in the Koita migration from inland to the coast during the last fifty years; and that in the Trobriands he collected material on historical changes in canoe types, in clan chieftainship, in trading patterns and transfer of magic, and in inter-island migration. What he said about the value and limitations of history, as cited in *Dynamics of Culture Change*, can always provide material for argument. But there is no reason to doubt that such expressions as: "I would be the last to underrate the value of historical knowledge"; "To oppose history and science is futile. To neglect either of them makes any humanistic pursuit incomplete"; and "[S]o-called functionalism is not, and cannot be, opposed to the historical approach but is indeed its necessary complement" represented his considered opinion (1945: 33, 34).

In some other spheres there were clearer gaps in Malinowski's approach. He was a pioneer in the study of economic anthropology, but as I have indicated elsewhere, his contribution must be regarded as inadequate in some important respects (Firth 1957: 209–27). I do not think he ever really thought about resource allocation and its implications in formal economic terms, or—since "formal" has now become a loaded word in this anthropological context—in a systematic manner. He was too concerned with rebutting the caricatures of primitive economic experience given by Karl Bucher and by the Economic Man stereotype of the classical economists. He did not realize that for a long while this stereotype had never been intended as anything more than a fiction, a model construct for the development of propositions by logical inference. Yet if he himself was not very sophisticated along economic lines, at least he set others off on the path; his contribution on the Trobriand economy in the *Economic Journal* of 1921 was a really new development, remarkable for its freshness and originality. His sociological contribution to concepts of labor organization was limited, but that to the theory of transactions was seminal. In the theory of transactions his presentation was rich in conceptual distinctions—for example, between levels or spheres of exchange—which I myself, Paul Bohannan, and others later developed.

The concept of reciprocity, of which Malinowski was one of the prime formulators, has borne most fruit. Explicit in the *Argonauts* (1922), it is developed in *Crime and Custom* (1926b), by which time Mauss had published his "Essai sur le don" (1923–1924). I was Malinowski's research assistant during the writing of *Crime and Custom* (see the preface) and with others regarded Mauss's essay as giving a new dress of comparative classical and ethnographic documentation to Malinowski's basic formulation on the Trobrianders. Malinowski had discussed the issues with Mauss and had accepted Mauss's point about *mapula* being not "free gifts" from husband to wife but diffuse compensation for sexual services. But he did not regard Mauss as an "independent inventor," so to say, of the reciprocity principle—whereas he did so regard Richard Thurnwald. In statements about reciprocity as a weapon for enforcement of rights and as part and parcel of a whole system of mutualities, it was to Thurnwald alone that he referred. In translation (Malinowski quoted only the German): "We name the symmetry of transactions the principle of recompense (*or* repayment). This lies deeply rooted in human experience (*or* feeling *or* perception) . . . and the greatest meaning attaches to it in social life."[8] After his tribute to Thurnwald, with whose work he was much in sympathy, Malinowski in a prophetic mood stressed the importance of the "inner symmetry of all social transactions, of the reciprocity of services," and foretold that symmetry of structure would be found in every "savage" society, as the indispensable basis of reciprocal obligations.

In political anthropology Malinowski's contribution was quite limited. But there have been some distortions of his handling of Trobriand materials by later commentators. An interesting review of Malinowski's findings has been published by J. P. Singh Uberoi (1962), looking at *kula* relationships as a model of the political organization of small-scale stateless societies. This work does pull out some aspects of the situation to which Malinowski gave too little attention and provides a useful overview of *kula* politics. But produced under Gluckman's aegis, Uberoi's book tries to treat Trobriand chieftainship as a kind of headmanship of African style and much underplays the significance of the crouching and other signs of ritual respect paid to Trobriand *guyau* leaders. There was room for reassessment of the status of the officeholder whom Malinowski sometimes dubbed the "Paramount Chief," the headman of highest rank in the Trobriands, and H. A. Powell has dealt very adequately with this problem (1960, 1969). But Gluckman's extravagant style of writing led him to the regrettable statement that Malinowski's characterization of the Tabalu chief To'uluwa as a Paramount Chief was "well on the way to becoming social anthropology's Piltdown Man: not that Malinowski was a forger, but he certainly attributed to this man a position which he did not have."[9] Yet if Gluckman had bothered to read Malinowski's own accounts carefully, he would have found that Malinowski had taken over the term—too loosely perhaps—from Seligman and other earlier writers; that he often used it in lowercase initials, not capitals; and that he clearly indicated that it was intended to apply to supremacy of mystical status, not political jurisdiction. He specifically states that the "tributary grasp" of the headman of Omarakana and chief of Kiriwina (i.e., To'uluwa), though considerably restricted by white control, used to reach over all the northern half of the island—that is, was restricted to this area—and that only two miles away lived another chief who, though in several respects his vassal, was also his main foe and rival. That Malinowski had no intention of ascribing to the Omarakana chief a political suzerainty over all the Trobriands is clear from his statement that another district on the western coast of the northern part of the island "possesses no paramount chief." Politically, he clearly meant the term to indicate no more than district headship. That he was sensible of the complexity of the situation is indicated too by his statement that it was impossible "to enter here into all these shades and singularities of political organisation" (1922: 65–69; 1932; 1935, vol. 1: 328). In the light of all this, one may borrow a form of expression from Gluckman himself as it appears in his account of the judicial process among the Barotse and talk of his characterization of Malinowski's "Paramount Chief" as "The Case of the Inappropriate Analogy."

What is more interesting is the contrast between the position of Malinowski and that of Gluckman in the theory of conflict. In reviewing Malinowski's analysis of culture change, with special reference to South Africa, Gluckman (1963: 207–34) said that Malinowski did not recognize the significance of conflict, that he refused to see conflict as a mode of integrating groups and to recognize that hostility between groups is a form of social balance. This is the Radcliffe-Brownian thesis of social opposition in another form, and I think Malinowski would have regarded it as too bland. I think Malinowski did fail to comprehend fully the theory of feud, but I also think Gluckman imported this theory into the interpretation of situations of such heterogeneity that it failed to apply. I myself still cannot understand how Gluckman, with all his knowledge of the South African situation and his strong reaction against racial discrimination, could write of "the cohesive effect of *conflict* in a modern African situation" (Gluckman 1955: 140; italics mine). Reciprocal economic interest and shared or parallel aims in education, religion, even friendship have been such that participation in the overall social system has engendered some cohesion, but to juxtapose conflict and cohesion as if one could be translated into the other in South Africa seems to me to be near to absurdity. Malinowski, on sounder ground, regarded conflict as divisive, except where it was ritualized (as in sex antagonism in Trobriand gardening). Gluckman praised Malinowski for his studies of conflict in the Trobriand analyses—as he did more generally for the fruitful hypotheses, suggestions, and implications in his work as a whole (Gluckman 1963: 241). But Malinowski's analyses, vivid and enlightening as they were, did tend to depict conflict rather too much in individual focus. The classic dramatic quarrel between To'uluwa's son Namwana Guya'u and his sister's son and heir Mitakata was rendered by Malinowski as occurring largely on personal grounds: Namwana Guya'u the son had received gifts which Mitakata the heir thought should legally have been his; Mitakata had slept with one of the wives of Namwana Guya'u, who had got him jailed for it (1926b: 101–5). Powell has supplied a more sociological focus. He has pointed out that Namwana Guya'u was the leader of a political group traditionally rivals of the Tabalu, of which To'uluwa and Mitakata were leaders (1960: 129–31). Mitakata had scored by marrying a "sister" of Namwana Guya'u, thereby putting himself in a position to demand marriage tribute from the latter; Namwana Guya'u had countered by getting Mitakata jailed for adultery; and the latter's kin had retaliated in turn by expelling Namwana Guya'u from his father's and their village. There was a personal side to the quarrel, but the political dimension was more important.

In kinship too it seems clear that despite Floyd Lounsbury's linguistic support, the general point that Fortes and Leach have made about Malinowski's failure to think widely enough in role and category terms is fair. Powell (1969) has reviewed this whole field of argument, bringing in additional Trobriand evidence of great interest and putting forward his own interpretation of the material. Broadly, while somewhat critical of the earlier commentators, who he thinks have departed from Malinowski rather less than they imagined, Powell essentially concurs with the view that Malinowski tended to confuse individual requirement and category response in kinship, to see phylogeny as too much a repetition of a somewhat speculative if plausible ontogeny. At an earlier period I too found myself in disagreement with Malinowski on this issue, in regard to the acquisition of kinship speech by children. Malinowski, as is well known, argued for an extension theory, for an adoption of a term for mother's sister from that for mother, and so on. In my Tikopia study I pointed out to the contrary, that there was no good reason to assume exclusively maternal conditioning of an infant; that a process of definition, of narrowing down of the mother from a wider female universe was as likely as one of extension (Firth 1936: 272–76). But Malinowski's focus on what he later called the "initial situation of kinship," from his early work on Australian aborigines, did a great service to anthropological studies. He brought a sense of reality into the discussion of kin relations, a concept of a dimension of service and manipulation of service, of flexibility in verbal and nonverbal behavior, essential to a sophisticated understanding of kinship.

Malinowski's treatment of language, and of symbols, brings out the close relation between his personality and his theories. Able to converse effectively in half a dozen languages, he was very conscious of the power of words as instruments, as stimuli to action as well as communicators of information. Questions of translation were often before him. To him, use of language—even when writing with the help of an amanuensis—was an active involvement in a social situation, not just a mental exercise. Hence, his theory of meaning focused upon contextual-ization. Malinowski's article on meaning in primitive languages (1923), arguing that words have no meaning in themselves but are symbols, was important—even novel at the time—to anthropologists interested in language. His emphasis on speech as a mode of action, in which the meaning of words would be defined by what he called "context of situation" (broadly equivalent to C. K. Ogden and I. A. Richards's sign-situation), was stimulating to those engaged in research or interpretation of field material. Malinowski's contextual theory of meaning has been analyzed by D. T. Langendoen (1968) in conjunction with that of J. R. Firth. Langendoen's Chomskyan aloofness is at the opposite pole from Mali-nowski's engagé attitude, but his estimate seems basically acceptable to me; a contextual theory of meaning if taken literally is inadequate.

Malinowski's intensely pragmatic attitude to language led him to concentrate upon the use of words in an action frame of reference. Even in the most abstract and theoretical aspects of human thought and verbal usage, it seemed to him that the real understanding of words was ultimately always derived from active experience of those aspects of reality to which the words belong. But his notion of "reality" left many questions open, as did his contention that ultimately all the meaning of all words is derived from bodily experience (1935, vol. 2: 20–22, 58).

His treatment of the notion of symbolism was curiously uneven. In his article on "Meaning" in 1923 he even said that words must be treated only as symbols, while in the language volume of *Coral Gardens* in 1935 he hardly used the term or the idea of symbol at all. He was much concerned with the mystical and bind-ing power of words, as against their mere communication uses, and he gives a vivid illustration of how canoes were guided in complete darkness through in-tricate channels by instructions shouted from the shore. He was much im-pressed by the "mysterious" power of speech in such situations, its pragmatic effectiveness as a medium for coordinating action, but not by its symbolic qual-ity. In his Frazer lecture on myth (1926c) he explicitly denied that myths were symbolic. There was little room for symbolism in primitive man's ideas; myth was a hard-working cultural force; we can certainly discard all symbolic inter-pretations of myths of origin; myths are not symbolic of hidden realities (1926c: 14, 79). Only in his article "The Group and the Individual in Functional Analy-sis" (1939) did he revert to treatment of words as symbols and give what he called the "cultural definition of symbolism." It was very general: "Symbolism is a component of human culture, with language as its prototype. . . . Symbolism must make its appearance with the earliest appearance of human culture. It is in essence that modification of the human organism which allows it to transform the physiological drive into a cultural value" (1939: 955).

What does all this add up to? I am not sure. Malinowski's handling of the "symbol" concept was very elliptical and idiosyncratic. But I think that it em-bodied a shift of focus rather than of opinion, that he never deserted his early idea of the significance of words as symbols, with their meaning to be got pri-

marily from their context. I think, as Langendoen admits, that Malinowski included in his idea of context the transmitted, traditional elements of language.
He stated, "Society and its component groups are the carriers of verbal—that
is, symbolic—tradition" (1939: 964). (But Langendoen's objection to this, in
the work of J. R. Firth, is that it is unusable as a concept—nothing can be said
about it in any relevant way.) I think Malinowski's dropping of the term "symbol" in the middle period of his writing was a reaction against intellectualistic
interpretations of language. His denial of symbolic interpretations of myth was
a rejection of the *particular* symbolic interpretations current in his day. He
said he hardly attempted any complicated or symbolic interpretation of myth,
any artificial and symbolic rehandling. It was not, then, that myths were
asymbolic—after all, they were composed of words—but that what he wanted
was a focus on the immediate, overt, instantaneous relationships of what was
said, before looking for symbolic values. He put this in another frame by first
denying that myths have etiological/explanatory value and then—in a passage
that is often overlooked—saying "once we have realized that myth serves principally to establish a sociological charter . . . it becomes clear that elements
both of explanation and of interest in nature must be found in sacred legends"
(1926c: 121).[10] (In the introduction to a new edition of *Coral Gardens*, Jack
Berry has pointed out that Malinowski was dealing with speech rather than
with language, which seems to me to be another way of indicating the primary
emphasis that Malinowski placed on the here and now, and on individual components of a situation.)

The same sense of pragmatic urgency, which led Malinowski to transpose
the historical dimension of events into the present, to view myth as primarily
social charter, and to concentrate on speech even when he wrote about language, emerged in his treatment of Durkheim. Malinowski has been criticized
for having distorted or failed to understand the views of Durkheim; I would
hold that he simply selected for criticism Durkheim's more reified abstract
concepts. He criticized the "collective effervescence" theory of religion and
said Durkheim did not distinguish the collective profane from the collective
religious. He said (in a final footnote to "Baloma") that he was purposely not
using the term "collective idea" introduced by Durkheim and his
collaborators—although in the writings of Henri Hubert and Mauss it had
proved extremely fertile—because nowhere was there a clear candid statement
of just what was meant by a collective idea, nothing approaching a definition
(1916: 423). The postulate of collective consciousness he felt to be barren and
absolutely useless for an ethnographical observer. He criticized, too, the emphasis Durkheim laid on the phenomena of material symbolization—the
churinga, the national flag, the cross—as generating religious attitudes. But
Malinowski also wrote of Durkheim as having developed one of the fullest and
most inspiring systems of sociology—albeit marred by certain metaphysical
speculations and a lack of reference to the biological basis of human behavior

(1944: 19). He praised Durkheim and his followers for their exploration of the notion of obligation and of the relation of moral conduct to society. In putting forward his own views about the mystic binding power of words, Malinowski took occasion to reaffirm his debt to Durkheim, saying that his own sociological explanation was obviously a reinterpretation of Durkheim's theory that mysticism is but an expression in belief of man's dependence on society. We can hardly sympathize with Malinowski's view that in one way his whole theory of culture consisted in reducing Durkheimian theory to terms of behavioristic psychology. But his statement that he was trying to reinterpret Durkheimianism in empirical terms is more acceptable and much more positive than he is often credited with being (see 1935, vol. 2: 235–36).

In the spiral of critical appraisal, the views of Malinowski on Durkheim have in turn been countered by those of Claude Lévi-Strauss on Malinowski. Malinowski criticized Durkheim's metaphysical outlook on social phenomena; Lévi-Strauss has criticized Malinowski's "naturalistic, utilitarian, affective" interpretations of totemism. Malinowski's critique of Durkheim's theory of religion is matched by Lévi-Strauss's critique of Malinowski's theory of magic. (Here, we can enter an occasional caveat. Referring to Malinowski's notion of risk as an element in predisposing to magical performance, Lévi-Strauss says there is no objective criterion for deciding which undertakings are held by human societies to be more or less risky, independently of the fact that some of them are accompanied by rituals [1962: 82, 96–97]. This seems a little far-fetched; what about statistics of automobile accidents and the use made of them by insurance companies?) But Lévi-Strauss has paid tribute to Malinowski's "incomparable" fieldwork, has credited him with the basic materials from which Mauss's "Essai sur le don" emerged, and has praised him, together with Mauss, for truly innovative procedures toward the establishment of proof in the ethnological sciences (1950: xxxii; 1973: 16).

On the face of it, the approaches of Malinowski and of Lévi-Strauss to the anthropological scene have been diametrically different, as functionalism has been outmoded by structuralism in a plangent way. Each man has applied a distinguished mind to elucidation of problems of the human condition. But whereas Malinowski explored the subtleties of conduct, in the field, Lévi-Strauss has explored the subtleties of thought, in the study. The conclusions of Malinowski, bold and assertive in their simplicity, had a very narrow ethnographic base; those of Lévi-Strauss, equally challenging, are much more developed and elaborate, and refer to a very wide range of comparative scholarship. Yet I think there is something in common between Lévi-Strauss's grand attempt to chart the unexplored territory of basic human thought and Malinowski's attempt to lay down a framework for the understanding of the essentials of human culture. Both have been heroic endeavors, the one perhaps more successful than the other. But in the course of their efforts, both have provided new ways of looking at social phenomena that will continue to be of lasting scientific value. Basically, while Malinowski concentrated on modes of action and Lévi-Strauss on modes of thought, there are certain similarities in their approaches. Both have been much preoccupied with the nature–culture dichotomy, Malinowski in the bio-social, Lévi-Strauss in the conceptual sphere. Both have been criticized for disparaging history, and both while denying the charge—Lévi-Strauss with a dazzling display of argument—have clearly found totality of social phenomena of more significance than continuity. Both have seen in myth a clue to the nature of society; to Malinowski myth was a differentiating charter, to Lévi-Strauss a differentiating code. Malinowski's idea of symbolism as a process that transforms physiological drive into cultural value seems to me to have something akin to Lévi-Strauss's idea of the "symbolizing function" of the human mind. They start from different sides of the basic problem of human culture, but one wonders whether if Malinowski were alive now the kinship of opposites might not be recognized in subtle debate.

Malinowski died in May 1942. In his obituary notice of Frazer, who died almost exactly a year earlier, he wrote: "The death of Frazer symbolises the end of an epoch." I think it might have been more truly said of his own. Functional identification and analysis of data had been the basis on which British social anthropology had been built up; in the immediate postwar period structural considerations took over. In her perceptive biography Metraux (1968) states that Malinowski's place in anthropology is as yet exceedingly difficult to assess. While there is still much room for argument, I think his role is becoming clearer. Leaving aside the slick comments about his seldom making abstractions or being a superb field-worker and a poor theorist, and also recognizing the modifications that have been made to most of his theoretical propositions, what he did for anthropology seems to me to basically comprise three areas. He directed attention to and powerfully formulated fundamental problems of human social and cultural life, in a manner difficult to avoid—he enforced confrontation with them empirically and as a personal experience of the anthropologist. He showed with great ingenuity and sophistication how data could be collected to bear systematically and critically upon such problems. He put forward a range of propositions of theoretical order—on magic, on myth, on matrilineal kinship, on transactional theory—which if overly pragmatic and individual-centered for most modern tastes, have still provided jumping-off hypotheses for a great deal of contemporary theory. What he himself said of Frazer can apply to Malinowski: he had an artist's power to create with great integrative capacity a world of his own (an empirical, not a visionary one), and he had the true scientist's intuitive discrimination between relevant and adventitious, fundamental and secondary issues.

BIOGRAPHICAL NOTE

Photo by Hugh Firth   c. 1970

RAYMOND FIRTH was born in Auckland, New Zealand, in 1901. As a schoolboy he discovered early accounts of Polynesians, and he encountered Maori people in areas of rural New Zealand where his father and maternal grandfather farmed. These early experiences led him to nourish ideas of one day studying a traditional island community, a notion that was reinforced when, at the age of twenty, he took a hiking trip through New Zealand's North Island and again met some Maori.

Firth attended the University of Auckland, taking his first degree in economics and history and continuing on to an M.A. in economics. Choosing for his thesis the topic (unusual for the time) of a marginal economic institution, kaori-gum extraction, he joined his study of documentary evidence with brief fieldwork among the gum-digger workers, an ethnically diverse group that included indigenous Maori.

Firth had come across social anthropology by reading Lowie's *Primitive Culture* and then some articles by Malinowski on his Trobriand research, and he decided that this was exactly what he hoped to do: to combine Pacific anthropological materials with economic theory. In 1924 he went to England and began postgraduate studies at the LSE, planning to take his degree in economics and to read anthropology "as a hobby." But that was the year that Malinowski took up his post there, and meeting Malinowski was momentous for Firth. He was among the initial group in the famous Malinowski seminar, along with Evans-Pritchard and Schapera. Malinowski, remembering the time, said he began his teaching career with Firth "as chief arbiter of argument and catalyser of discussion. . . . We vindicated the theories of Westermarck and of E. Grosse; we redemolished Morgan and Bachofen; we learned from Rivers and Andrew Lang, without accepting their doctrines" (1936: viii). Firth received his Ph.D. in 1927, with a thesis based largely on Maori texts, published as *Primitive Economics of the New Zealand Maori* (1929).

On a visit to Sydney in 1927, Firth met the newly arrived professor of anthropology at the University of Sydney, Radcliffe-Brown. There was an unexpected opening in the department and Firth was hired to fill it, an opportunity that also gave him funds for his next research. Wanting to do fieldwork in a Polynesian society not yet touched by economic development and where a pagan religion was still practiced, he chose to go to Tikopia. This was the beginning of what he called his long love affair with Tikopia. His work there resulted in a large body of monographs and articles, including one of the great ethnographic classics, *We the Tikopia* (1936).

During Firth's years at Sydney, he came to be influenced by Radcliffe-Brown's structural views—much to Malinowski's disappointment. In 1933 Malinowski called him back to the LSE to take up a lectureship, and in 1944 he was appointed to Malinowski's chair. After his retirement in 1968, Firth served as a visiting professor at the Universities of Hawaii, British Columbia, Chicago, and California (Davis and Berkeley); Cornell University; the City University of New York; the Australian National University; and the University of Auckland.

In addition to his extensive studies of Polynesia, Firth did fieldwork in Malaya, beginning in 1939. The book based on this work, *Malay Fishermen: Their Peasant Economy* (1946), represents one of the first analytic uses of the concept of peasant. Firth was also a pioneer in urban anthropology, organizing two studies of kinship in London during the 1950s and early 1960s.

Firth carried his initial interest in economics into his anthropology, looking at economics as aspects of human social relationships; his essay in *Themes in Economic Anthropology* (1967) is his summation of issues and problems in that field. However, he extended this interest to a more general theoretical approach, and his *Elements of Social Organization* (1951) and *Essays on Social Organization and Values* (1964) mark significant advances in social anthropology. The major theme of this work is the concern with social process, which he called "social organization" in contradistinction to "social structure." This approach focuses on problems of social continuity and change, and gives central place to individual choice. It anticipated much of the development in social anthropology of decision-making theory and of attempts to relate structure and process. Raymond Firth died in 2002, still writing and lecturing at the age of 101.

Ruth Benedict (c. 1925). Courtesy of Rhoda Metraux. Photographer unknown

5

RUTH BENEDICT

Sidney W. Mintz

Ruth Fulton Benedict was almost a contemporary, in age, of Paul Radin and Bronislaw Malinowski, but at the time they were doing their early ethnological studies she was living within the roles available to a well-bred woman of her day. After graduating from Vassar in 1909 she spent a chaperoned year in Europe, did volunteer social work, taught in a girls' school in California, wrote poetry, began some work in biography, and, after her marriage in 1914, attempted to be a dutiful wife. She became an anthropologist only when she was in her mid-thirties, taking her Ph.D. in 1923. From that time on she worked closely with Franz Boas, training most of the generation of Columbia anthropologists of the period between the world wars.

Benedict's first anthropological study—her dissertation—was on the distribution of the guardian-spirit theme among North American tribes. She followed this with some comparative work on American Indian folklore, which still stressed diffusion but also showed a concern with the way traits and themes were integrated in different cultures. She had her initial fieldwork experience among the Serrano Indians of California, under Alfred Kroeber's supervision; she then worked among the Zuni. It was in 1927, during a field trip to the Pima, that she was struck by the marked differences between Pueblo and Plains cultures and began to think of each culture as a "personality writ large." Her view of cultures as integral configurations—conceiving of a process whereby each culture selects and elaborates upon certain portions of the vast range of human potentialities—was fully developed in the book Patterns of Culture (1934). Immensely popular and influential outside of anthropology as well as within it, it formed a link between anthropology and the humanities, on the one hand, and psychology, on the other. This work, along with her papers dealing with the cultural patterning of psychological mechanisms and of behavior defined as "abnormal," became foundations of the field of personality-and-culture.

The advent of World War II drew Benedict into applying her approach to modern cultures. Improvising techniques for the study of cultures that were not directly accessible, she produced under government auspices a series of depictions of "national character" relevant to the war effort—most importantly, on Japan. After the war, this interest developed into a large-scale interdisciplinary project on seven national cultures—the Columbia University Research in Contemporary Cultures—which was continued by Margaret Mead after Benedict's death in 1948.

Ruth Benedict, whom Margaret Mead described as "one of the first women to attain major stature as a social scientist" (Mead 1974: 1), came to anthropology relatively late in life, in comparison with her contemporaries. She discovered anthropology only after a long search and after having sought fulfillment in many other pursuits, only one of which—writing poetry—seems to have provided her with deep satisfaction. Having discovered anthropology, she was to become one of its most distinguished and distinctive practitioners. It is because certain of her unusual and highly original contributions now appear to have been forgotten or ignored that I will offer here what is only a narrow view of her scholarship.[1]

She was born in 1887, the elder of the two daughters of Dr. and Mrs. Frederick S. Fulton. Her father died while she was still a baby and only a few weeks before the birth of her sister. The girls' mother did not remarry and grieved her loss unremittingly. The emotional qualities of her widowhood lay very heavily on the children, as did, it appears, the economic constraints it imposed. Reading Benedict's own words, quoted at length in Mead's two books about her (Mead 1959, 1974), one gets the impression of a saddened, often dreary childhood, wherein the moments of happiness came most freely when the little girl could play by herself and enjoy her own fantasies. She was partially deaf, due to a childhood illness, and Mead gives the impression that most people (including her mother) preferred her more cheerful younger sister, Margery.

Ruth Fulton went to Vassar College, where she studied English literature. After graduation she taught school, somewhat desultorily. In 1913, when she was twenty-six, she affianced herself to Stanley Benedict, who is described as a prom-

ising young biochemist. The ensuing years, when she lived in a Westchester sub-
urb and worked at being a good housewife, must have been barren and bleak.
Mead's citations from Benedict's letters and journal document her attempts to
keep up her spirits and to accept her role as a dutiful wife. But she was not happy.
At some point she learned that she could not have children, at least not without
what Mead calls "a very problematic operation," for which her husband would
not give his consent (Mead 1974: 18). Though she finished her long-planned essay on Mary Wollstonecraft—a portion of an important work on women she had
conceived earlier—it was rejected for publication. Only in her poetry did she
manage some early success. There, she concealed her own identity with pen
names until well into her anthropological career, and though poetry remained
important throughout her life as a form of expression and as a basis for strong
bonds of friendship, it never became enough to fulfill her wholly.

In 1919 Benedict happened upon anthropology; she took courses at the New
School for Social Research with Alexander Goldenweiser and Elsie Clews Parsons and was deeply affected by what she began to learn from these two radically different teachers. At that time she had been married for five years, and
while neither she nor her husband appears to have been ready to confess failure, their marriage by this time was merely standing still. As Benedict's interest
in anthropology grew, her husband's interest in her life seems to have declined
the more. Much stimulated by what she was learning, Benedict became Boas's
student; he accepted her on Parsons's urging. With Boas's blessing, she completed her doctorate at Columbia in three semesters.

From the publication of her dissertation in 1923 until Boas's retirement in
1936, Benedict remained at his side almost uninterruptedly. After his retirement, she continued to play a key role—though it was often obscured—both at
Columbia and in the profession at large. Her work won her an international
reputation, especially after the publication of *Patterns of Culture* (1934). But
she was not elected president of the American Anthropological Association
(AAA) until 1947, and it was only in July 1948 that Columbia saw fit to bestow
upon her a full professorship, in a shamefully tardy attempt to make up for its
previous treatment of a great scholar. At that time, Benedict had been teaching
at Columbia for twenty-six years, the final twelve of them as an associate professor. She died two months later.

During her lifetime, Benedict's work was the subject of many reviews and
evaluations. After her death, Mead wrote two important biographies of her—
startlingly different in emphasis and interpretation, it seems to me—and others
have also taken Benedict as their subject (see, for instance, Modell 1975, 1978,
1983). In the accounts that have been written of her, much has been made of
the enigmatic qualities of her character and of the contradictory forces that appear to have governed her—such as the conflict of marriage and motherhood
versus a career, and of poetry versus anthropology. I should like to suggest that
these contradictory forces are to a large extent played out, enacted as it were,

in Benedict's scientific work: not that she "solved" any of her personal conflicts by becoming an anthropologist, so much as that the kind of anthropology she did actualized those conflicts. My feeling is that in Ruth Benedict, as in few others, a consistency of character, of calling, and of theoretical conception can be identified. That is, her anthropology was, in some basic way, her own self embodied.[2]

I will mention three themes of her work to illustrate what I mean. First, the concern with coherence. This reverberates in Benedict's work; she was, from her first papers onward, very sensitive to what looked like coherence or consistency within a cultural system. It would be fair to hazard a guess that Benedict liked it when it all fell into place, that she got aesthetic satisfaction out of closure in her descriptions of culture. Second is the concern with a dominant strain as the expression of that coherence. This reveals itself particularly in *Patterns of Culture*. In Boas's slightly evasive introduction to the book, he indicates his feeling, much as Benedict does herself, that some societies reveal a coherence and a dominant strain, and others do not. I think her work shows that Benedict found it aesthetically more satisfying, intellectually more gratifying, to deal with cultures that could be summed up in rather limited, dense terms. The adjectival renderings that typify her descriptions of the three major cultures in *Patterns of Culture* express this notion of a dominant trend. Finally, and most surprising in view of her training, was Benedict's repeated reversion to the notion of choice—that societies, or cultures, choose some particular direction out of the great arc of human variability, that there is choice for them much as there is choice for individuals.

I suggest, then, that these three themes—the search for cultural harmony of parts in a single system; the preference for those systems that seemed to her to manifest some single dominant theme; and above all the idea that peoples choose their cultures, get only one, and then sometimes lose it irrevocably (remember her phrase about the cup that is fashioned and the cup being broken) embody the conflicted personality of their inventor and the particular life circumstances in which she found herself. One had the feeling with Benedict that beauty and calm, and tolerance and humor, and life itself, had been very dearly bought. How was that communicated? I have not the slightest idea. But as with no one else I have known, I had the sense that Ruth Benedict was a person who all along had made choices and that the notion of making choices was immensely important to her as an integral personality.

I wish to touch on two aspects of Benedict's work before referring briefly to her personal influence on me. The first has to do with Benedict's contribution to an anthropology of the immediate, the relevant, and—lest it be forgotten—the political; the second relates to Benedict's contributions to an anthropology of modern life, particularly through her efforts to study national states and cultures.

"In the 1930's," writes Mead (1974: 49), "Ruth Benedict often chafed at the amount of energy Boas devoted to 'good works' and lamented the time lost to research and writing. But as the Nazi crisis deepened in Europe and World War II approached, she who had so vigorously rejected such good works was in the end drawn into them." Because of her espousal of cultural relativism, Benedict has sometimes been thought to have been politically uncommitted or neutral. This is a misreading, I believe, of her ideas; nor did her cultural relativism mean she was politically naive.

In his paper "American Anthropologists and American Society," Eric Wolf has elegantly described American anthropology of the period during which Benedict's work had its early impact: the faith in human malleability, seen as nearly infinite; the educational process as an Aladdin's lamp of progress; democratic pluralism as the American way; and an unconcern with power and its nature (Wolf 1969b). I think Wolf's argument is illuminating, persuasive, and generally accurate. But I don't think Benedict was at all unaware of, or unconcerned with, the nature of power. Indeed, I think both Benedict and Boas were well aware of the problem power posed, and I am not even sure that they were really guilty of an overgenerous optimism about power, even if they sometimes may have seemed actuated by such optimism. Anthropology at Columbia clearly suffered because Boas was outspoken and willing to take controversial stands—much more would have come his way had he kept his mouth shut—and his colleagues and students suffered with him. Long before Benedict became an anthropologist, Boas had managed to make himself highly unpopular in the United States, particularly in connection with his views on World War I. As a German and a Jew, he was already suspect; the stands he took on war, peace, spies, and nationalism only made him more so. His stress upon the equal potentialities of different races, upon culture as the distinctive attainment of the human species as a whole, upon the difficult social and psychological position of nonwhite people in the United States, and upon other politically sensitive issues earned him the enduring enmity or hostility of many of his professional contemporaries. To a varying degree, his students suffered because of his courageous outspokenness. Some imaginatively enlarged the distance that separated them from his views; others merely ignored the positions he took. Benedict seems to have paid little attention to Boas's public political stance until long after she received her degree. But she emphatically did not seek to disassociate herself from him.

During the years of World War II, Benedict became actively involved in the winning of the war itself; the intellectual achievements of her later years are intimately connected to the war experience. Beyond the meaning to her of personal involvement in a crucial test of American survival, however, in this work Benedict grasped fully—perhaps for the first time—the profound political implications of anthropology. Many of us are, I believe, familiar with the principal limitations of the cultural relativism and pluralism that Benedict espoused and believed in; perhaps we should be equally aware of the very positive aspects of these perspectives.

To begin, Benedict devoted a substantial portion of her intellectual energies from 1940 onward to fighting racial prejudice (e.g., Benedict 1940, 1941, 1942; Benedict and Weltfish 1943). Those of us old enough to remember what the treatment of racial minorities in this country was like at that time (even if we cannot be consoled by the present) ought to be able to see why the positions taken by people such as Boas and Benedict were absolutely essential to change. Yet it will not be enough simply to yea-say their work. Some of Benedict's views (Mead 1959: 358–68) are worth citing at length these days—which is to say, the days of Ardrey, Jensen, Schockley, and Herrnstein, not to mention DeFunis, Bakke, and Weber:

> Those who hope for better minority relations need to consider equally, when they think out their strategy, the assets as well as the liabilities. The greatest asset we have in the United States is the public policy of the state. This is not to say that our Federal government, our states, our police forces, and our courts have been blameless; of course they have not. But as compared with the grassroots discriminations and segregations current in the United States, public policy has been a brake, and not an incentive. This would not necessarily be remarkable in a country run, for example, by a benevolent dictator, but in a democracy where the people have a voice in selecting their legislators and their judges, it is something to ponder. The correspondence between popular prejudices and state action has been far from being one-to-one. In states where opinion polls and strong labor unions and powerful industries have been against hiring men without regard to color or creed or national origin, it has still been possible to get Fair Employment Acts passed. In cities where there is a quota for Jewish students in privately endowed colleges, there is no quota for Jews in the tax-supported city colleges. When New York State Negroes protest today that private medical colleges are willing to train such a bare minimum of Negro doctors that the supply is totally inadequate, they unquestioningly propose a state medical college to remedy the situation. In areas where there are restrictive covenants and "Jim Crow" city blocks, city and Federal housing authorities have been able to insist upon and administer housing projects which have both Negro and white tenants. Even in this present postwar year [1947] when the record of civil liberties has been deteriorating, Chicago ruled against a "lily-white" policy in its new veterans' homes, and when a mob attacked the houses let to Negroes, the largest police force Chicago had ever called out was stationed to protect them. In Gary, Indiana, when white school children and their parents struck against allowing Negroes in the schools, the mayor broke the strike by use of the tenancy laws and upheld the city's policy on nonsegregation. On October 30, President Truman accepted as "a charter of human freedom in our times" a strong report on civil liberties for minorities written by the Civil Rights Com-

mittee which he had "created with a feeling of urgency," and which recommended laws to end segregation, poll tax and lynchings, the enactment of permanent Fair Employment Acts and of statutes to prohibit Federal or state financial assistance to public or private agencies "permitting discrimination and segregation based on race, color, creed, or national origin."

This state policy is of the utmost importance in the United States. Of course it cannot be fully implemented in a democracy where there is so much free-floating racial and ethnic prejudice. But the fact that public authorities take such stands, often in the face of public sentiment, is a remarkable fact. For the great crises of racial and ethnic persecution have occurred in all countries precisely when the government gave the green light. From the pogroms of Czarist Russia to the mass murder of Jews in Hitler Germany, the constant precondition was a favorable state policy. The government in power was following a policy of eliminating the minority or was at least allowing matters to take their own course without intervention. The importance of whether the state is on the side of racism or is against it is just as true in matters of discriminatory behavior as it is in pogroms and violence. In a democracy or a dictatorship the state can use law and the police to defend the rights of minorities or to abuse them. When by Federal or city ordinance or by industrial negotiation umpired by the state, a new and less prejudiced situation has become a *fait accompli*, even those who protested most actively against it while it was under consideration tend to accept the arrangement and to become accustomed to it. Certainly in the United States it seems clear that more can be accomplished by these means toward ameliorating the job and housing discriminations than by any amount of work by good-will organizations.

This is not to say that informal, private, and nonlegislative efforts to improve social relations and eliminate prejudice are therefore unimportant. In a democracy laws and court decisions must have the backing of interested citizens, or they become dead letters. The ultimate goals of all who work for better race and ethnic relations can never be achieved merely by enforcing laws, which can forbid only the most blatant and overt acts of discrimination. No fiat has ever made any man over so that he can respect the human dignity of a Negro or a Jew if he has lived all his life in a community which acted on premises of white supremacy and anti-Semitism.

Any strategy for lessening our national shame of race and ethnic discrimination before the eyes of the rest of the world must therefore value interracial meetings of the women's auxiliaries of a Massachusetts town, and the We-Are-All-Americans pageants of a Middle Western city. But unless people who participate in such activities see to it that their efforts feed into a demand for Federal and state and city action they are guilty of bad tactics. For it is clear that the state can be used in America as an asset in their endeavours, and if they overlook this they are neglecting a major resource.

Such workers have often been too idealistic to join hands with politicians who want minority votes, but it is by such means that measures are put through in a democracy such as ours. If the powers that be are not moved to act for the good of the total community, perhaps they can be prevailed upon to court a substantial group of voters. And these voters may be able to press for enforcement also, thereby gaining first hand experience in the business of acting as American citizens. (Benedict n.d. [c.1947]; from Mead 1959. Reprinted by permission.)

I find it nothing less than remarkable that Benedict should have called attention more than thirty years ago to the fact that the most important force for the elimination of institutionalized racism in America was the U.S. government. Perhaps this is obvious, but if it is, we all must be disposed either to forget it or to bury it beneath our catalogue of complaints about that same government. Heaven protect us from the goodwill organizations—and I emphatically include here the elite private universities of our fair land, with their eloquent defenders of privilege—whose vaunted struggle against racism appears ultimately to hinge on the pressure, however feeble, to which they are subjected by governmental bodies. What seems, after all, to rise above the pronunciamentos, the indignant denials, and the litanies about quality are the triumphs of the U.S. Army, the U.S. Post Office, and the State Department—of all things!—in providing minority citizens with a fair opportunity to perform and to excel.

In 1943 Benedict and Gene Weltfish published the pamphlet *The Races of Mankind*, a delightful item of popular education, to the fate of which an anecdote is attached. This pamphlet set forth a familiar position: it declared that races—insofar as one could speak of such categories in dealing with humankind—were equal in their potentialities. Mead writes that the pamphlet was denounced in Congress as subversive, "mainly because of a tactical error committed in the writing, in stating baldly that some Northern Negroes had scored higher in intelligence tests than had some Southern whites" (Mead 1959: 353).[3] In this instance, as in others, Benedict's view turns out to have been very militant for its time, and depressingly apposite today. Who among us has been more outspoken on the issue of racism than she; who has done as much to use his or her professional stature to impel our country toward social justice?

While I believe these materials exemplify Benedict's scientific and political posture in the postwar years, I am struck when I recall now, in the retrospect of three decades, some of the commonly held opinions of the time: that her views were retrograde, unscientific, even irrelevant. Such negative opinions had to do in part, I believe, with the "psychological" determinism she was thought to espouse and with the lack of congruence between her theoretical positions and the evolutionary and materialist perspectives then in the process of rehabilitation at Columbia University. I am certainly as sure now as I was then that her critics, including some of my friends and classmates, were missing the point; though just as certainly I often found myself in disagreement with her views. No one sought to gainsay Benedict's position on race, but I suspect many persons thought that the belaboring of such views was superfluous. If so, then surely Benedict was right, and we who thought otherwise were wrong—not only was she right in what she thought, but also in her conviction that it had better be said, loudly, clearly, and repeatedly. She is, plainly, still right.

This brings me to another aspect of Benedict's scholarship to which I wish to refer: the studies of national cultures and national character for which she was famous. Her work in this regard is of special interest to me because I was both her student and Julian Steward's. Both of these scholars were interested in the anthropological analysis of large-scale, complex modern societies; their approaches were radically different. Steward's approach was very much in the ascendant in the midforties, Benedict's was not. With her death in 1948, research of the kind for which she had fought, and of which she herself was surely the most distinguished practitioner, went into a sort of eclipse. In spite of some work by Mead and others consistent with Benedict's approach, national-character studies along the lines Benedict advocated have only grown rarer over the years.

The scientific promise of such research still needs to be evaluated. But my purpose here is rather to point to an aspect of the intellectual history of the time. Both Steward and Benedict were trained in the particularistic study of small-scale, non-Western societies, within some broad Boasian outlook. Though they took markedly different directions in their research, their interests overlapped, sometimes surprisingly. For instance, Steward's doctoral dissertation was on the ceremonial buffoon in native North America, while Benedict's paper on property rights in bilateral societies (1936) was published in the same year that Steward's paper on primitive bands appeared in the Kroeber Festschrift (Steward 1936). Their interests intersected, in other words—perhaps even more, at times, than either of them recognized or acknowledged.

Both of these scholars moved from the study of small-scale societies toward the problems posed by big ones, at or about the same time—in the postwar years. Steward's view was ecological and stratificational, emphasizing the environment, the means and relations of production, the organization of institutions, and the role of class, among other features. Benedict's view was configurational, thematic, and value-oriented; differences in values and attitudes were expected to occur both within and between sectors of the same society, but underlying, generally shared understandings were also thought to typify the society at large.

This is not the place to attempt to evaluate or compare these two radically different approaches. But it does seem appropriate—particularly since they have often been seen as mutually exclusive theoretically—to stress that some scholars have benefited from both views and that time has left the similarity of intentions of Benedict and Steward honestly revealed. Both wished to transfer interpretive procedures from small, relatively homogeneous societies

to large, class-divided societies. Both believed such societies might be ana-
lyzable in terms of fundamental value orientations. Both were interested in
the practical or policy implications of their findings. To note these similarities
does not diminish in any way—nor should it—the very important differences,
both methodological and theoretical, between the Steward and Benedict approaches.

But neither should the differences obscure similarities of intent or of their
aspirations for the future of the profession. The critics of Benedict and the
critics of Steward were usually of different sorts, but often they espoused a
kind of anthropology equidistant from the work of both of these scholars. On
the one hand, Steward was ostensibly not (or no longer) interested in the real
subject matter of anthropology (which is to say, "primitives"), and his interests
showed a discomfiting concern with what was happening in the real world. On
the other hand, Benedict similarly had supposedly lost her interest in so-called
primitive peoples, and had become attracted by real-life problems. Worse, she
thought peoples had underlying values or orientations that might not be explainable either by class or by ecology—thus managing to be heretical in even
more ways than Steward. Though Steward's students continued to work along
the lines he had developed—and, of course, he survived Benedict by more
than two decades—other anthropologies became the wave of the future in the
1960s and 1970s. Neither Benedictian configurationism nor Stewardian ecology would lead the way in those decades, when it was becoming clear to some
that the New Ethnography would soon solve all important anthropological
problems. Boas and Benedict were not the only optimists, it seems. Today, it
may still be worthwhile to touch anew on Benedict's approach to the study of
national cultures.

In that work, Benedict revivified concepts she had developed in the study
of technically simpler societies and gave them new meanings: the idea of coherence within one culture, the presence of some dominant strain or theme as
the expression of that coherence, and the relationship between cultural
"givens" and the culturally constrained evolution of personality. Readers of
The Chrysanthemum and the Sword (1946a) are unanimous in the opinion
that this is Benedict's crowning achievement in the study of national cultures.
There have been innumerable criticisms; but in the light of the methods Benedict had to employ to write the book, few scholars would gainsay the penetrating originality of her analysis. In the years following the publication of that
book, Benedict continued to work on national cultures and provided many
graduate students and colleagues with the opportunity to join her in the research.

A short presentation to the New York Academy of Sciences (Benedict
1946b: 274–79), made the same year as the publication of Chrysanthemum,
provides as clear a statement as any of her research aims at the time. In it,

she discusses the problems posed by a plentitude of information ("Vast quantities of material are a handicap only when the crucial problems to be investigated are not formulated"), the lack of homogeneity in modern nations ("The conditions do not mean that investigation must be abandoned. The solution is to multiply the number of investigations"), and class differentiation

("The trained anthropologist . . . has to present both parties as actors in a patterned situation. He can see it as a kind of see-saw, and by studying the height of the fulcrum and the length of the board [in the study of classes, laws about property and land, general conditions of social security, and the like], he can show either that the group on the high end of the see-saw is necessarily very far up and the group on the low end very far down, or that they are more nearly balanced").

Most important, it seems to me now, was Benedict's insistence on the study of culture as a way to explain. This may seem obvious to a new generation of scholars, but it is historically interesting to observe how many decades it has taken some of us to discover that understanding class does not obviate the study of culture and that culture is not reducible to class, when all is said and done.

Her view of the values of a culture as underlying its surface manifestations, resonating in different institutions and providing thematic unity to overt diversity, has been criticized and defended with equivalent zeal. It seems to me that nothing is likely to convince the skeptics; in my own case, I have always been uncertain how Benedict's hypotheses might be tested. But her attempts to distill the value essence of a social group by identifying some core of beliefs, then to show us how those beliefs serve as the mortar of the cultural edifice, impress me all the same with their daring and penetration. I have been unable to find any citation for a remark she once made in passing about the relations between conquering and conquered peoples in the history of European imperialism. She said that she thought the English had always done well with martial and bellicose subjects, like the Masai, the Sikhs, the Maori, or the Gurkhas, while the Dutch had always done well with submissive subjects—while neither had ruled wisely those of opposing temperaments. I recall being struck by the observation (without being certain either that it was true or that it could be tested). What impressed me was that it seemed like a way of summing up a very great deal swiftly and neatly—and that it touched on a very important issue, one I had never heard or read a scholar comment on before. Benedict's unusual gift for providing highly original cameo accounts of this sort, as well as her extraordinary sense of humor—the sense of humor of a great lady—were revealed to me first in her classes and again in the teacher–student conferences I was privileged to have with her. But perhaps I will be excused for mentioning how I came to be a student of Benedict's.

My first encounter with her in the fall of 1946 was part of my own search for a profession or occupation that would feel worth doing. One has the impression that similar searches have become popular again—or, at least, that they were for awhile following the end of the Vietnam War. Like so many of my classmates, recently discharged from the armed forces, I was seeking with some bewilderment a career having "something to do with" the study of society. I cannot now remember who first suggested to me that I attend a lecture by Benedict, but I remember the lecture well. She was describing the organization of several societies by means of analogies, and I recall her employing "hourglass" and "siphon" designs to dramatize indigenous structures of power for the collection and distribution of valuables. She talked about the *kula* and about *potlatch*—new words for me. (It was a year or two later before the precise images came back to mind, this being when I first heard a lecture by Karl Polanyi.) Benedict stood before us, tall, spare, seeming rather distant, her voice startlingly low and slightly hoarse, plainly dressed, her silver hair short and severe, what I judged to be her shyness heightened by the contrast between the penetration of her ideas and the somewhat absent gaze with which she regarded us. I was astonished by her and by her lecture. It simply had never occurred to me before that a total culture might be looked upon as if it were a work of art, something to be coolly contemplated, something utterly unique and distinctive, yet available to be studied, analyzed, understood. That any teacher at that time in my life could have impelled me to think of Keats—when I had not so much as looked at a poem in five years—was wonder enough for me. I decided to become an anthropologist because I heard Ruth Benedict give a lecture. And that is about as close to the truth of it as I can come.

Benedict first asked to see me after I had written a short paper for her, comparing the Passover seder as it had been observed by my grandfather, my parents, and my siblings. I remember clearly sitting nervously before her while she explained that she had enjoyed the paper. I made an inane remark about having wanted to make the paper less literary and more scientific. She smiled and said only: "Oh, I have no objection to good writing!" I was, of course, grateful and very flattered. In the course of the subsequent year and a half, I attended courses given by Benedict, received her advice, and was employed by her in her project, Research in Contemporary Cultures. One of the sturdiest memories I have of those times is of her complete evenhandedness with her male and female students, even though we returning male veterans were quite thoughtlessly shouldering out of the way our female contemporaries. While there was—as I remember it—an antifemale bias among many of my male classmates that extended itself to Benedict, it was not reciprocated. Throughout, I recall Benedict as serene, generous, and courteous—more so, certainly, than she needed to be.

I have been asked several times whether I can specify how Benedict's anthropology affected my own work, and I have been at a loss to answer, mainly because I never tried seriously to think about it. I think I know the answer now, at least in one particular regard.

In 1948, when Benedict died, I was in Puerto Rico as a member of a graduate-student group that, under Steward's direction and John Murra's supervision, was at work on the project Steward had initiated there. I had studied with Benedict in the period 1946–1948, but my interest in Steward's perspective and the chance to do fieldwork abroad had led me away from Benedict's research. By the time that I had returned from the field and written my dissertation, I had begun to do a kind of anthropology that was heavily historical, with particular emphasis on the economic history of the plantation system and the evolution of forms of labor. That emphasis emerged when I studied the Puerto Rican south coast community I had chosen in early 1948; in subsequent years, I became a Caribbean specialist.

In the summer of 1953, I returned to Puerto Rico to start a new fieldwork project, this time entirely on my own. My aim then was to record a single life history, but that of a person from the community I thought I already knew fairly well. I did not realize at the time—though I certainly do now—how much my interest and my theoretical aims had been influenced, partly by my undergraduate training in psychology, but considerably more by the training I had received from Benedict. In her sensitive analytic movement from cultural standard to individual response and back again, Benedict made us aware of the dominant place of culture in the profile of the individual; but she never portrayed culture—nor, I believe, conceived of it—as some impersonal monster, some bloodless computer, "encoding" us, or pouring us into rigid molds.[4] Because I knew Taso, my chief informant, well, long before our work on the life history began; because I spoke his language comfortably (if not fluently); because I knew his family, friends, and neighbors, their work, the place they lived and a fair amount about its past—for these and other reasons, I hoped that the life history we prepared together would be of a piece with the study of the community that had preceded it. That, at least, was my aim. My search for congruence, though, was not a search for harmony. Benedict's work makes clear that while individuals are certainly "products" of their cultures, they cannot take on their characteristically distinctive identity, while growing up, without strain and suffering. The relationship between culture and individual, then, is neither straightforward nor simple, and Benedict's nuanced view of how cultures work, in and through persons, had surely affected me profoundly. But while I worked with Taso, I had only the dimmest notion of the ways my teacher, the person whose words had made me try to become an anthropologist, had given shape to my ideas and inspired me to test them, years after her passing.

One of Benedict's last published works was her presidential address to the AAA, "Anthropology and the Humanities" (1948). She argues here that anthropology, more than any other of the so-called "social sciences," stands at the boundary between science and the humanities; she deems this not only proper but necessary, calls her own view "heretical," and concludes: ". . . once anthropologists include the mind of man in their subject matter, the methods of science and the methods of the humanities complement each other. Any commitment to methods which exclude either approach is self-defeating." In this late paper, Benedict waxes particularly eloquent on the illumination provided by fieldwork. She points out that "the humanities . . . were an intense cross-cultural experience . . . their aims were often couched in the same phrases as those of modern anthropological investigation of an alien culture." She argues that "the mind of man . . . man's emotions, his rationalizations, his symbolic structures" are commonly included in American anthropology's definitions of culture—and that this inclusion makes of the humanities anthropology's greatest resource. Her plea is emphatically not an attack on science, though it is perhaps worth mentioning that her science was much damned by some colleagues in the final years of her career as being "no more than" art.

Rereading her presidential address recently, I thought back to the life history I had attempted to record and to fit within what I understood of the history of a community, a region, and a class. "For more than a decade," Benedict had written,

anthropologists have agreed upon the value of the life history. Some have said that it was the essential tool in the study of a culture. Many life histories have been collected—many more have been published. Very little, however, has been done even with those which are published, and field workers who collected them have most often merely extracted in their topical monographs bits about marriage or ceremonies or livelihood which they obtained in life histories. The nature of the life history material made this largely inevitable, for I think anyone who has read great numbers of these autobiographies, published and unpublished, will agree that from eighty to ninety-five per cent of most of them are straight ethnographic reporting of culture. It is a time-consuming and repetitious way of obtaining straight ethnography, and if that is all they are to be used for, any field worker knows how to obtain such data more economically. The unique value of life histories lies in that fraction of the material which shows what repercussions the experiences of a man's life—either shared or idiosyncratic—have upon him as a human being molded in that environment. Such information, as it were, tests out a culture by showing its workings in the life of a carrier of that culture; we can watch in an individual case, in Bradley's words, "*what is*, seeing that so it happened and must have happened." (1948: 592)

Benedict makes her point again—what she calls "the common ground which is shared by the humanities and by anthropology as soon as it includes the mind and behavior of men in its definition of culture" (1948: 593). "But if we are to make our collected life histories count in anthropological theory and understanding," she writes:

> we have only one recourse: we must be willing and able to study them according to the best tradition of the humanities. None of the social sciences, not even psychology, has adequate models for such studies. The humanities have. If we are to use life histories for more than items of topical ethnology, we shall have to be willing to do the kind of job on them which has traditionally been done by the great humanists. (1948: 592)

But this important plea for anthropology's crossroads does not forget what anthropology itself has to offer. In a prophetic reference, Benedict tells us:

> Only with a knowledge of what the current ideas were about ghosts and their communications with their descendants can one judge what Shakespeare was saying in *Hamlet*; one can understand Hamlet's relations with his mother only with an acquaintance with what incest was in Elizabethan times, and what it meant to contract "an o'erhasty marriage" where "funeral baked meats did coldly furnish the marriage tables." (1948: 593)

It seems to me that Benedict's insights here about the relation between culture and individual were lessons I had begun to learn from her at an earlier time, quite without realizing it. What Clifford Geertz has referred to as "Zola's maxim that character is culture seen through a temperament" (1962: 13) is a maxim that was well understood by Benedict and one she sought repeatedly to teach.

In the three decades since her death, Ruth Benedict and her work have been overshadowed to some extent by the enormous proliferation of anthropologies and anthropologists. I believe that what she offered us, however, is still fresh and penetrating, for those of us willing to contemplate it. That she gloried in diversity seems less and less quaint, in a world the sameness of which grows ever grayer. That she underlined our common humanity seems less and less academic, in a world still so unsure of what makes us human or whether we are unique. That she wanted an anthropology of modern life made her a pioneer of our profession. That she wanted social justice for all Americans, without regard to gender or race, makes her as modern as our times.

DISCUSSION

SYDEL SILVERMAN: Do you have any thoughts on Ruth Benedict's problems as a woman at Columbia?

MINTZ: There is no question but that she was systematically discriminated against by Columbia University. Among the pictures that hang on the balcony at Fayerweather Hall, hers is the only one of a female. For many years anthropology was not assimilated to the Faculty of Political Sciences because it would have meant that the faculty would have a woman taking lunch with them and participating in the conduct of their affairs. This is stated by Robert Lynd in his memoriam to her. Beyond that, there is the history of her relationship to Boas and to Ralph Linton. I never heard Ruth comment on Linton, but his hostility toward her was intense. After I went to Yale in 1951, he was a colleague of mine until his death on Christmas Eve 1953, and when he referred to Benedict, it was always with a good deal of animus. He would occasionally boast publicly that he had killed her, and he produced for me, in a small leather pouch, the Tanala material he said he had used to kill Ruth Benedict.

ALEXANDER LESSER: There was another factor at Columbia that caused discrimination against Benedict, namely, that the whole department was discriminated against. For many years Boas was given no opportunity to put anyone into any position; that included Ruth Benedict. If she had been a man she wouldn't have been appointed much earlier. Goldenweiser wasn't. Of course, when the chips were down, the fact that she was a woman was against her too.

MINTZ: I would agree. As you have demonstrated, Boas paid very dearly for the challenges he posed publicly in American life. Benedict was in some ways the unwitting victim of Boas's stands, but I think she suffered in additional ways because she was a woman.

GENE WELTFISH: Before Linton came to Columbia, anthropology was part of the Faculty of Philosophy, Anthropology, and Psychology. It was Linton who engineered it into the social sciences.

Another point about Benedict at Columbia. When Columbia wanted to fire me, Ruth Benedict stopped a meeting of the board of trustees of Columbia to protest. I think it was the only time that the board of trustees at Columbia has had a meeting stopped.

LAURA THOMPSON: We should remember that *The Chrysanthemum and the Sword* was one of the first attempts by an anthropologist to describe the culture of a whole nation. Benedict used all the empirically based information that she could find, and then she filled in the gaps by insightful use of internal evidence from the culture itself in order to describe the configuration or pattern of Japanese culture. In *The Chrysanthemum and the Sword* she shows us how she achieves the pattern at a distance, and she projects it backwards. Then she shows us how to project the pattern forward; that, of course, is prediction—limited prediction within certain boundaries. She's talking about how she thinks a group, a nation in this case, will behave, under certain likely circumstances in the future. At the time she was working for the Office of Strategic Services.[5] I think she was given this assignment in 1944. This work was very important during World War II. The winning of the war in the Pacific depended, we felt, upon this kind of information being accurate, and we can now see that it was. In addition to the military need, there was also the need to know what to do when we won, because by that time we thought we would win and knew we would then have the problem of the occupation. We don't think of Ruth Benedict as an applied anthropologist, but that's the way I'm thinking about her now. The whole last chapter of the book, called "The Japanese Since VJ-Day," deals with predictions. Since that was written thirty years ago, we have thirty years of reported behavior on the part of the Japanese and the Americans, and we can test her predictions against the historical facts. In that way we can judge what kind of a scientist she was and the insights she had. It would be difficult to find any statement she made about what should be done regarding the Japanese that has not been shown to be correct.

MINTZ: I remember being told that a question was put to her that went something as follows: There were about 350,000 Japanese soldiers on the Chinese mainland; on the basis of her analysis of Japanese culture, when the Emperor surrendered would those soldiers put down their arms or continue to fight? Answer yes or no. She concluded on the basis of her study that they would surrender, which indeed they did. Now, whether one is able to demonstrate convincingly that her analysis of Japanese culture was the basis for what indeed ensued is a genuine problem of the social sciences. But one of the things that certainly excited my interest when I was her student was her daring and her willingness to work intuitively. There is a tendency in the more scientific of the sciences to assume that intuition plays no role in scientific hypotheses; I find that view uncongenial. It seems to me that without some capacity to intuit, it is hard to develop operational schemes that allow us then to see whether or not we can either retrodict properly or predict. I think the persisting problem with the work of Ruth Benedict and others who followed in that kind of research has always been the question of confirmation—to what extent can you establish that there is a relationship between the generalizations set forth causally and the events that do in fact occur post hoc?

THOMAS BELMONTE: I have always been impressed not just by her search for consistency and coherence, but also by her awareness of its absence and by her awareness of the dialectic of culture—for instance, the title of *The Chrysanthemum and the Sword*. She never turned away from contradictions, from paradox. In some ways she even presages structuralism. The reason her books are still read and are still exciting to beginning anthropology students is because of the incredible breadth of her vision and the acuity of her insight.

MINTZ: I would agree substantially, and I did not mean to suggest that her search for coherence, her interest in dominant strains, and her emphasis on choice meant that she didn't see a dialectic in this. In fact, I was trying to suggest that the tension that marked Benedict's character persisted throughout her entire life; and that same tension—which is a tension of dialectic, a tension of contradiction—seems to me to mark her attempts to describe how societies are organized and how competing elements function in giving societies their dynamic.

ROGER SANJEK: In the criticism of *The Chrysanthemum and the Sword* on the part of Japanese scholars, one of their main points was her lack of concern with Japanese history. They felt that she had mixed together information from different periods of what was in fact a very changing hundred years before World War II. What were her feelings about history, and how did she communicate this in her teaching? This is puzzling, especially considering Boas's interest in history and your own.

MINTZ: So far as I can recall, in the classes I took with her Benedict made absolutely no reference to history. She was, in some very pure way, a functionalist in her explanations, and it was particularly interesting that she took the position she did given the nature of her early work; she had been schooled very carefully in the use of historical inference and in reconstruction. I think she was very much interested in the way things fit and not at all interested in their historicity. She would occasionally make offhand comments about how there are some cultures that aren't very coherent but perhaps at some other time in their history they were. References of this sort always were rather obscure and not helpful. Surely one reason I find difficulty in tracing my own thinking to Benedict directly is that I find her ahistoricity so uncongenial; another reason is her lack of interest in class.

WELTFISH: Benedict took no courses with Boas. She took her work at the New School under Goldenweiser. Boas simply transferred the credits from the New School to Columbia and then she wrote her thesis. Her real thrust was toward religion, mythology, and symbolism, which came from Goldenweiser, who was so interested at that time in totemism and was not really emphasizing history. So she was never exposed to that very strong historical streak in the Columbia department.

PAUL RABINOW: How would you place her importance in American anthropology?

MINTZ: Let me begin to answer that not with Benedict but with someone else. Allow me to refer to what I regard as Robert Redfield's importance in American anthropology. I learned a great deal from reading Redfield. One reason he was so instructive to me—and I don't mean this to be at all depreciatory—was because I thought he was so dead wrong, and he was so eloquent in his wrongness that I always found his books immensely stimulating and continue to find them so. I don't think Benedict was dead wrong, but she was wrong some of the time. One of the important things she did for American anthropology was to pose in a daring new way—much as Redfield did— formulations of an unusual and original kind against which lesser figures could lapidate their own ideas. I was interested to read, for instance, a comment by Melville Herskovits on Redfield's description of the city in relation to the folk–urban idea. Herskovits remarked quite indignantly: Professor Redfield doesn't take into account the fact that cities in West Africa are not heterogeneous, nor disorganized, but that they are mosaics of neighborhoods, composite, that kinship relationships are maintained, and so on. To which Redfield with characteristic graciousness responded, I am so happy to be able to help Professor Herskovits to point that out. When we look at people in the history of science over time, we have to give them credit for what they have done, and one of the things people do is help us get smarter, or at least they help us think better; that may be because we think they are right or it may be because we think they are wrong. One of the things that has haunted me the whole of my professional life is that when I read Benedict I don't know how to operationalize what she says, but over and over again I feel convinced that she is right. I don't know how to deal with that feeling, but it's one of the reasons I don't dwell on the distinction between the humanities and the sciences.

BIOGRAPHICAL NOTE

Photo by Max Hirshfeld   1996

SIDNEY W. MINTZ was born in 1922 in Dover, New Jersey. His father was a cook; his mother had been a garment-trades organizer for the IWW (Industrial Workers of the World) before her marriage. He was the youngest of their four children, the only boy. After finishing high school at the age of fifteen, he went to live with a sister in New York City and attended Brooklyn College, majoring in psychology. In the one anthropology course he took (with Alexander Lesser), he earned a C. A week after his graduation in 1943, he joined the Army Air Corps.

After the war, Mintz took a job as a group worker, hoping to win admission to a school of social work. He also registered for a sociology course at Columbia, which he hated. As he recounts in his essay, a lecture by Ruth Benedict led him toward anthropology. Though he was a student of both Steward and Benedict, he thinks his basic professional outlook was shaped by the MUS (see introduction) and by his research experience on Steward's project in Puerto Rico. There Mintz studied a U.S. corporate sugar plantation, which was the basis for his dissertation; he received his doctorate in 1951. There followed some important theoretical statements on plantation systems, including the earliest anthropological discussion of the "rural proletariat." His subsequent work in Puerto Rico also resulted in the book *Worker in the Cane* (1960), the life history referred to in his chapter.

After Puerto Rico, Mintz turned to other Caribbean locales, Jamaica and Haiti. His work there included landmark studies of peasant markets and a reformulation of the nature of Caribbean slave life. Bringing both historical and political-economic perspectives into his analysis, he coined such concepts as "proto-peasantry" and "reconstituted peasantry." His unique vantage point of field experience in Hispanic, French, and English islands has enabled him to write extensively on the comparative ethnology and the political, economic, and cultural history of the Caribbean (1974). In later decades, he also did fieldwork in Iran and Hong Kong.

Mintz's first teaching was in temporary appointments at City College, Queens College, and Columbia. He began teaching at Yale in 1951, became a professor in 1963, and stayed until 1975. In 1972 he won the De Vane Medal for teaching, awarded yearly by Yale's Junior Phi Beta Kappa; because of his devotion to undergraduate teaching, he regards this as the most important prize of his career. Mintz moved to the Johns Hopkins University in 1975 to help create a new department of anthropology; its pioneering development of Atlantic studies and its stress upon history brought it national attention. Mintz remained at Hopkins until his retirement in 1997. He has also taught in Munich, in Paris at the École Pratique des Hautes Études and the Collège de France, at the Massachusetts Institute of Technology, at Princeton University, and since retiring, at the University of California at Berkeley and Florida International University, as well as in Australia, New Zealand, and Hong Kong. He was the T. H. Huxley Medalist of the Royal Anthropological Institute (1994), Distinguished Lecturer of the American Anthropological Association (1996), winner of the Fernando Ortiz International Prize (2002), and the W. E. B. Du Bois Lecturer at Harvard (2003).

Mintz's central concern has been the relationship between anthropological concepts of culture and materialist philosophy. He has had a major role in the study of Western agricultural systems and in advancing historical analysis in the anthropology of complex societies. His landmark book on the history and anthropology of sugar consumption, *Sweetness and Power: The Place of Sugar in Modern History* (1985), marked the beginning of his serious scholarly interest in food. He pursued this interest in historically informed studies of eating habits, cuisines, and food complexes such as soybeans and seafood. His *Tasting Food, Tasting Freedom* (1996), a series of essays on eating, power, and morality, takes up topics ranging from how Caribbean slaves created their own cuisines in the Americas to how Coca-Cola gained international renown.

Sidney Mintz continues his active retirement from his home base in Baltimore, Maryland.

Julian Steward during fieldwork among the Carrier Indians, 1940. Photo from the University of Illinois Archives (15/2/21-19), with permission of Gary Steward

6

JULIAN H. STEWARD

Robert F. Murphy

In 1921 the department that Alfred Kroeber had founded at Berkeley added
to its faculty Robert Lowie, one of Franz Boas's first students, who had spent
thirteen years with the American Museum of Natural History doing ethnological research on North American Indians. That same year, Berkeley began systematic graduate training in anthropology. Among the students in the
department during the 1920s was Julian Steward.

Steward was born in 1902 in Washington, D.C., where his father was an
attorney in the U.S. Patent Office. The family were Christian Scientists.
When he was sixteen, Julian was sent to the Deep Springs Preparatory
School, on the Nevada–California border, near the Owens Paiute reservation. It was there that he first formed his attachment to American Indians
and that he developed an interest in both archaeology and ethnology.

Steward began his undergraduate studies at Berkeley, where he took the
introductory course in anthropology that was given jointly by Kroeber,
Lowie, and Edward Gifford. After a year at Berkeley he transferred to Cornell, for financial reasons. There was no anthropology at the time at Cornell,
although its president, Livingston Farrand, was an anthropologist trained by
Boas. After graduating, Steward returned to Berkeley in 1925 to study anthropology. He received his Ph.D. in 1931 with a dissertation entitled "The
Ceremonial Buffoon of the American Indian." The dissertation (which
Steward would later claim, incorrectly, to be the first Ph.D. thesis in personality-and-culture) combined distributional study, encouraged by Kroeber, with behaviorist psychological interests stimulated by Lowie.

Steward began teaching in 1928 at the University of Michigan, where he initiated instruction in anthropology. In 1930 he was replaced by Leslie White, and Steward moved to the University of Utah, where he instituted programs in both ethnology and archaeology. He returned to Berkeley in 1933, teaching there for a year.

Steward started his research career in archaeology, working during the late 1920s in the Columbia River Valley. During the Utah years he became the first state archeologist of Utah; he worked on early Shoshoni and desert remains, then shifted his attention to the Pueblo expansion into southern Utah. He carried out his important ethnological research among the Shoshoni from 1933 to 1935. Thereafter, apart from one summer (1940) among the Carrier Indians in British Columbia, he did no more field research but became a research director and promoter. In 1935 he joined the Bureau of American Ethnology of the Smithsonian Institution, where he stayed until 1946. During this period he organized the work on the seven-volume Handbook of South American Indians (1946–1959). He also became director of the Smithsonian's Institute of Social Anthropology; in that role he inspired and funded research on Middle American and South American peasantry.

In 1946 Steward went to Columbia University. Along with his teaching and supervision of a large number of doctoral dissertations, he undertook a comprehensive study of the island of Puerto Rico. Steward stayed at Columbia until 1952, when he moved to the University of Illinois. He remained there until his retirement, initiating during these years an ambitious collaborative research on the modernization of traditional societies. Julian Steward died in 1972.

Coming into American anthropology at a time when it was dominated by historical particularism, cultural relativism, and functionalism, Steward played a leading role in the revival of interests in generalization and in the development of modern materialist approaches. Regarded as a scientist by some because of his attempts to formulate cultural laws and as a historian by others because of his limiting comparison to selected cases, Steward himself defined his endeavor as a lifelong search for causality. He brought ecological interests into modern anthropology through his own studies of Indians in which he sought causal processes in the interactions between culture and environment, his according priority among the elements of culture to "core" features over "secondary" ones, and his explicit concept of cultural ecology. His efforts to define culture types, his concept of levels of sociocultural integration, and his outline of cross-cultural regularities in the development of civilizations became part of the new evolutionism. Finally, his programs for research in complex societies marked a break from folk–urban polarities, from global depictions of national character, and from the study of communities as microcosms, focusing instead on the relationship of "subcultures" to regional and national contexts.

It is a Durkheimian, and Freudian, maxim that the ancestors do live among us, they are imbedded in our thoughts, they motivate us, they limit us, they restrain us, they shape our view of reality, they endow us with the language in which we speak of the world and ourselves. This has long been intuited among many peoples through the institutions of ancestor worship, which speak of the organic and continuing social and psychological links between the generations, links that symbolize the corporate nature of society. The ties between our anthropological teachers and founders and ourselves may not be as primary as those of kinship, but they are commonly modeled on these attachments and share some of their qualities. They are multistranded, or functionally diffuse, they are hierarchical and entail varying degrees of authority, they are incorporative, and they are ambivalent. We may not follow the paths set by the ancestors, but our very deviations have been conditioned by them.[1]

The reality of the ancestral spirits is manifest in Columbia University's Department of Anthropology, for the department has spent this entire century centered in the fourth floor of Schermerhorn Hall. Each office is known for its past occupants. Alfred Kroeber's office is across the hall from mine, and the couch on which he took his mandatory afternoon naps is still exactly where it used to be.[2] At the end of the hall, Franz Boas's office is currently occupied by Marvin Harris. Harris, it should be noted, has attacked almost every position ever taken by Boas, but he does so with a sense of immediacy and intensity that one would usually extend only to the living. It might be said that Boas is dead, but this would be irrelevant, for Harris remains inescapably his heir. It could even be added that Harris's sallies against "historical particularism" are part of the ritual that keeps Boas alive, at least in spirit.

The office next to my own has had a wooden bench outside its door ever since the Boasian period. On it, generations of Columbia-trained anthropologists have waited their turn, as in a doctor's office, to see their professors. The bench is still there and students still sit in waiting, just as they used to, but the office's tenants have changed. Julian Steward, a former occupant of the office, died six years before this writing, and he left Columbia twenty years before that, but as a true ancestor his intellectual presence continues. It is noteworthy that the present tenant of the office studied under a Steward student, and the one before him took courses with Steward in the early 1950s. Several of the current members of the Columbia faculty wrote their doctoral theses under Steward's direction, returning to Columbia to teach, and they help continue a perspective, if not a specific theory. Beyond this influence, the department's graduate students seek out Steward's writings year after year, for they still find him lively and topical. It is indeed hard to realize that over a quarter century has passed since he taught at Columbia.

Steward's influence at Columbia is reminiscent of that of A. R. Radcliffe-Brown at the University of Chicago. Both were compelling teachers who attracted devoted followings, and both had an impact upon the local anthropological culture proportion to their relatively short tenures—Radcliffe-Brown spent ̣ at Chicago, from 1931 to 1937, and Steward was at Columbia only six ̣o, from 1946 to 1952. The persistence of the tradition in each case was due ̣art to a tendency of both departments at the time to hire their own graduates, a practice that has ended with the diversification of anthropology and the institution of affirmative-action programs. But the impetus of the ancestral ideas at both universities has been carried on more vigorously by the students than by their mentors, for Steward and Radcliffe-Brown have had something of lasting importance to say to their respective audiences.

Steward's influence at Columbia was great, but so also was Columbia's upon Steward. He fitted into a preexistent theoretical tradition, which he served to shape and crystallize; it was as if he and Columbia's graduate students had sought and found each other. I will review the salient features of Stewardian anthropology in detail in later pages, and I give here only a few highlights to help clarify Steward's preeminence at Columbia. Its primary characteristic was a naturalism through which cultures and societies were viewed, much as a physicist would view matter and energy. Implicit in this positivism was a faith that culture is caused, and causal, and that we can find these chains of determinism, and thus explain culture, through proper methodology. Coupled with this assumption, Steward's anthropology had an earthy and common-sense orientation that regarded the exigencies of work and livelihood as among the most important of these determinants. He was not a systematic philosophical materialist by any means, but more than any anthropologist of his day, he saw the key to much of human culture in food-getting activities. Steward's theories also stressed the active and sensate over the symbolic and conceptual in social life, a logical enough outcome of his preoccupation with work and groupings. The approach was realistic, unetherealized, self-consciously tough-minded, and dynamic. It found its subject matter in the more mundane aspects of culture, and it sought explanation in sinew and sweat.

Steward's anthropology would seem, at least superficially, to be a sharp departure from the Columbia tradition set by Boas. There never was a Boasian "school," however, and Columbia's Ph.D.s were remarkable for their diversity of interest and theory. What they did get from "Papa Franz" was a cultural realism that was shared by his students Alfred Kroeber and Robert Lowie, and by their student Julian Steward. Added to this was Boas's politics, expressed in pacifism during World War I and radicalism in his later years. This orientation was also characteristic of most of his students during the 1920s and 1930s, a community of opinion that had nothing to do with Boas's anthropology but which could only have been encouraged by his politics. One of Boas's students fondly recalls a conversation with him in which the dilemma of being young and starting out in life during the depression '30s was raised. The old man disagreed, saying these were the best times in which to launch a career. Conditions were indeed miserable, he added, "but if I were young, I would do something

about it." To the extent that the anthropological theories of the Columbia students reflected their political orientations, Boas must be considered a primary
influence. Ironically, it would appear then that Boas was the spiritual founder
of Columbia's so-called materialism.

Boas's influence was strongly reinforced by time and place. The Depression
era germinated radicalism of thought and action within anthropology, as within
all intellectual pursuits. That some departments of anthropology remained un-
affected by the mood of the times was symptomatic of moral and physical isolation from their social milieus, a smug aloofness that used to be paraded as
"objectivity." Columbia, however, was located in New York City, then as now a
center of intellectual innovation and ferment as well as a staging area for all the
malaises of urban society. If the politics of the Columbia students stressed human exigency and struggle, it was because these were a part of their way of life.
And it is not surprising that their anthropology was based upon the same premises and worldview. Such was the ambience at the Columbia to which Julian
Steward came in 1946.

The specific theoretical heritage of Boas, and that of Ralph Linton and Ruth
Benedict, may not have been congenial to the ideas brought by Steward to Columbia, but the basic epistemology was the same and the student culture, as opposed to faculty thought, was even more receptive in 1946 than during the
depression '30s. The Columbia students of the late 1940s were a new breed. As
in the past, there was a large contingent of New Yorkers, but the postwar generation differed in significant ways. Most of the students had come of age during the Depression and, haunted by the failures of their parents, were prone to
economic anxieties and driven to succeed. They had also gone through a war; a
majority had been in combat zones and most had been enlisted men. It may be
conjectured that the division between officer and enlisted person contributed
to the political climate of the student body and to their affinity for the world's
losers, and their overseas experience must surely have whetted their appetites
for other cultures. The student body of the period also included a higher proportion from the lower class and lower middle class as compared to past
decades, for their studies were largely supported by the educational benefits of
the G. I. Bill. Finally, the universities of the entire country were inundated by
male students who had postponed higher education for up to four or five years,
and, as a consequence, the Columbia anthropology department had a lower
percentage of female students than during any time in its history. The composite picture that emerges from these traits is of a student group that would have
no trouble understanding the compelling motivations of an empty stomach or
seeing authority as emerging from the muzzle of a gun.

This short sketch does not, of course, do justice to the variety of interests and
personalities of Columbia's students, but the characteristics were sufficiently pervasive to set the tone of the department. The materialism of the postwar students
ranged from Marxisms of variable orthodoxy through Leslie White's "culturology"

.only, an eclectic concern for economic and environmental factors. , least, it was a view of the world that was both agonistic and realistic. ,vas some division within the student body between the new students and .w who had entered somewhat earlier. The latter were holdovers from Linton and Benedict, were in varying degrees influenced by Freud, and were more interested in symbolic systems than in concrete social action. Having lost Linton by resignation in 1946 and Benedict by death in 1948, they found themselves with a faculty that was uninterested in their work and fellow students who were antagonistic to it. One of the credos of the evolutionists and materialists of the 1940s and 1950s was that there is a necessary contradiction between cultural explanations and psychological ones; this is not at all true, of course, but the notion persists to this day.

Steward did not have to establish a "school" at Columbia—he found one waiting for him. The student temper combined with Steward's theories and persuasiveness as a teacher to produce an almost instant following. The Columbia faculty at the time were few in number, consisting of Steward, Benedict, William Duncan Strong, Harry Shapiro, George Herzog, Gene Weltfish, Marian Smith, and Charles Wagley. The size of the student group was, however, larger than at the present writing, due to the pressure of the returning veterans and a very loose admissions policy at that time. The result was a badly overworked faculty, a situation that was somewhat ameliorated by the fact that the few undergraduate offerings were taught by the junior members, Weltfish and Wagley. The sheer weight of numbers and the attraction of his ideas placed a heavy teaching burden on Steward, a problem that was complicated by bouts of poor health throughout his Columbia tenure. But even in the semesters in which he was unable to teach, he held seminars and discussions at his house in Alpine, New Jersey.

Steward's classes were large, his audiences attentive. He was neither flamboyant nor charismatic in the classroom, but his lectures were masterpieces of integration of fact and theory. Though noted as a theoretician, he held to the principle that theories must be based on facts and that facts, in turn, were unintelligible without theory. I particularly remember his one-year course "Greater Southwest Culture Sphere," which was an organizational gem. He covered the standard ethnography and archaeology of the Southwest United States in exhaustive detail, but he did it within a framework that he first outlined in his paper "Ecological Aspects of Southwestern Society" (1937). He interwove and contrasted the concepts of culture area and culture type, analyzed the varieties of society in terms of his method of cultural ecology, and attempted to see the entire picture as episodes in evolutionary process, from pre-Basketmaker horizons to the modern period. The empiricism was painless for being placed in context; this also made it retainable in our minds. Only a few members of the class had a deep interest in the area as such, but the course was a better introduction to Steward's thinking than some of his more theoretically slanted seminars.

There was a certain magnetism in Steward's lectures that was created in large part by his remarkable gift for synthesis. He also radiated a sincerity and conviction that welled from a certainty that he was on the right track. This was conveyed without undue dogmatism or authoritarianism, and the students sensed that he wanted them to join him in the quest. The theory was not complete, the answers were not all collected, but, we thought, if we develop the theoretical structure further and flesh it out with the right kind of data, then we would surely break through to a true science of man. Like another great teacher, Leslie White, his closest intellectual associations were with students and he treated them as partners, albeit junior ones. Steward conveyed a sense of excitement and purpose to us, and he took us seriously; the latter was probably his most important gift to his students.

Columbia University, in common with other institutions, was profoundly affected by the political moods of the postwar period. Want and struggle were part of the life experience of many of the Columbia anthropology students, and they were understandably attracted to a theory that took adequate account of this aspect of society. This basic view of social life also contributed to a political climate that, in terms of the prevalent ideology of the country, was radical. Although eschewing organizational ties that would involve endless meetings and passing out mimeographed circulars at subway stations, many students of the time were influenced to varying degrees by Marxian thought. They found in Steward's ideas a sympathetic resonance, an alternative to a rigid philosophy that would nonetheless preserve an emphasis on the material conditions of life. Moreover, it was a theory developed in the language of anthropology and using anthropological data. The ponderous terminology and obsessive concern with class struggle of orthodox Marxism were replaced by a more open-ended theory dealing with human labor in its natural setting. To his students, Steward was pioneering a new road to the understanding of history, a road that did not lock them into a fixed system.

The growing tensions of the Cold War in the late 1940s and the appearance of McCarthyism in the early 1950s cast a pall over academic inquiry that drove Marxian thought underground and rendered somewhat suspect even the non-Marxian materialisms of Steward and White. It is difficult for today's students to understand the mood of the period or to empathize with its victims, for there has been a profound liberalization of moral and intellectual norms since the early 1960s. The subject is certainly beyond the scope of this essay, and I can only note that thought was constrained by fear for livelihood; the 1950s were chill, narrow, rigid, and fearful years, and this had an inevitable effect upon the discipline of anthropology.

To his credit, Steward did not modify his theories under this pressure. It could be argued that it kept him from taking a more avowedly materialistic position, but this would ignore the fact that he had maintained a pluralistic stance throughout his career, as documented by several of his earlier publications (see, e.g., Steward

1941). Actually, Steward was quite frank about the political implications of his theories and used the Chinese Revolution as an example of an independent evolutionary change, contrasting this to the conspiracy theories of the right, which he saw as a kind of diffusionism. Harmless though this may seem today, it was bold talk in 1951. Contemporary students often note that Steward never referred to Karl Marx's writings, despite some of the common ground between them. This may have been in part a matter of discretion—few other anthropologists of the day mentioned Marx, for that matter—but I believe it arose more from a lack of deep interest in Marxism. He had done his student reading of Marx and was well aware of the theory, but he never gave any indication that he had given it close study. To the best of my knowledge, most of his scholarly reading was restricted to anthropology, and his entire intellectual frame of reference was couched within the discipline. There are, of course, profound differences between Steward's theories and the Marxism of the time, which will come out more clearly in the pages below. It can be stated summarily here, however, that Steward gave greater attention to technology and environment than did Marx, and his view of historical process was wholly nondialectical. The chief area of overlap was a common concern for labor process. In the final analysis, Steward was a liberal, and his anthropology was consistent with his politics.

Steward's Columbia students are now a few years older than was their professor some thirty-odd years ago, a thought that will dismay them. They include Pedro Carrasco, Stanley Diamond, Louis Faron, Morton Fried, Sidney Mintz, Robert Manners, Elena Padilla, Vera Rubin, Elman Service, Elliott Skinner, Eric Wolf, and many more.

Several others were indirectly influenced by Steward. Marshall Sahlins entered the department at about the time Steward was leaving, but his studies with Fried and Service were in the ecological-evolutionary tradition. Marvin Harris was not a Steward follower during his graduate student days, but he later acknowledged him as a principal source of his ideas on "cultural materialism" (Harris 1968, 1979). All of these people have pursued their own courses, their own interests, and their own ideas. What unites them, however, is a basic assumption, a premise and axiom, that social thought emanates from social action and that the imperatives of work, power, and sex are prior to the symbolic forms that encapsulate them. It is this very elemental and general kind of materialism that prevails to this day at Columbia, and not one or another particular theory. Despite the departmental sobriquet as "the cowshit-weighing capital of the Western world" bestowed by one wit, who will remain nameless as well as tasteless, its faculty and students display a variety of talents and inclinations that range over the gamut of current anthropological theory. But beneath this diversity there exists a community of understanding and a common language that was inspired by Franz Boas and crystallized by Julian Steward.

In sketching Steward's influence at Columbia, I do not mean to underplay his important role in the history of the Bureau of American Ethnology and the

Smithsonian Institution, nor am I ignoring his impact upon another generation of students at the University of Illinois.[3] I am merely writing about what I know best and hope that others will write of their own experience of the man. Actually, much of the following account of Steward's theories will be based on his work during the Washington years from 1935 to 1946 and his tenure as a research professor at Illinois from 1952 until his death in 1972. Thus, I am not at all suggesting a view of his work seen exclusively from a New Yorker's perspective. (Like the lady who, when asked what route she had taken on her drive from New York to California, replied, "The Lincoln Tunnel.") Columbia, however, was a special high point in Steward's career, for he came into intensive interaction with a large group of involved and supportive students, most of whom have become major figures in the profession. Moreoever, fortyish to fiftyish is a good age for anthropologists, though advanced senility for physicists and molecular biologists. By the midforties, the anthropologist has acquired the necessary background in empirical research and is ready to start putting it all together, and by the midfifties his talents are best used in issuing retrospectives and benedictions, such as I am giving here. Steward came to Columbia at the age of forty-four and left when he was fifty. He had come at the right age to the right people in the right place at the right time.

The appeal of Steward's anthropology to his Columbia students derived in good part from his approach to culture. He was not greatly concerned with the concept as such and generally accepted the classic definition of Tylor or its modifications by his teachers Kroeber and Lowie. Rather, it was his basic fieldwork method and the kinds of data he collected that distinguished his research from that of most of his contemporaries. By the 1930s, when Steward did his principal ethnographic research, there were no autonomous native social systems left in the United States. Indian culture was carried about in the memories of the aged and was unevenly and fragmentarily transmitted to the young. However well or poorly remembered, traditional cultures found little expression in concrete social behavior. Many practices, such as those connected with etiquette, child rearing, body usage, household ritual, and the like, continued with only moderate alteration, but other areas of social behavior had lapsed, leaving only disembodied traditions. The economic life of most Indian societies had been disrupted and totally transformed, reducing groups to absolute dependence on the whites. The native political orders had been smashed with the defeat of the Indian nations, and the political patterns remaining were usually either creations of government officials or responses to reservation life. Religious practices had been suppressed by the Bureau of Indian Affairs; the people proselytized by Christian missionaries. What was left of native American life was little more than memories.

Due to the historical situation of the American Indian, most attempts to document aboriginal cultures were based on informant interviews and not on direct observation. An old man could tell the ethnographer how buffalo were hunted, but there was no way that such an event could ever again be observed. The result was that the researchers collected skewed data. The informants idealized and rationalized past custom, and they also standardized it. What was often elicited was not how a certain practice was done, but how it should have been done. The varieties of situation and expression were reduced to neat normative systems, a process of reduction that was aided and abetted by the investigator's own search for regularity and order. As most ethnographers have learned, it is extremely difficult to achieve even the most rudimentary quantification from an interview and virtually impossible when the informant's culture lacks developed systems of enumeration. This same problem extends to the collection of case material, or slices of real life, from interviews. The informant may know that there was once a preference for cross-cousin marriage, but he will usually be hard-pressed to supply instances of such unions from the past. In short, the entire realm of concrete social behavior was of necessity underreported in Americanist research. But this was exactly the kind of data needed for Steward's theories—and it was the kind he gathered in the field.

The primary characteristics of Steward's classic monograph *Basin-Plateau Aboriginal Sociopolitical Groups* (1938) are its meticulously detailed descriptions of local groups, their subsistence-seeking activities, and seasonal changes in their composition and organization. I retraced some of Steward's footsteps when doing research among the Shoshoni in 1954 and found myself unable to collect the same kind of material. The twenty years that had elapsed had taken their toll of older informants, but I believe that other factors were also responsible for Steward's striking compendium of behavioral data, as opposed to normative information.

The Shoshoni had not all been settled on reservations, and there were small Indian settlements scattered throughout the towns and ranches of Nevada. This not only continued the dispersed settlement pattern of native times, but kept the people in contact with the land. Not all of the old subsistence activities had disappeared. People still went out each fall to gather pine nuts, some of which were sold to be marketed as "Indian nuts." The native wildlife had been reduced by the whites, but deer, rabbit, and antelope were still taken and constituted an important source of meat during the depression '30s. People still knew where to find roots, they still used the old springs for water, and even their work for the whites took them into the land. They had not been as completely uprooted as most American Indians. Moreover, their aboriginal groups had been small, their memberships more easily remembered than would be true of societies based on large bands or villages. All these factors made the behavioral data accessible, but it took hard work to get it.

Steward crisscrossed the Great Basin, visiting every part of it, no matter how remote, and interviewed every single Shoshoni with knowledge of times past. Paradoxically, this geographical exhaustiveness, so essential to the development of cultural ecology, was made necessary partly because Steward was also doing a culture-element survey of the region as part of Kroeber's distribution studies. Whatever the motive, in doing so he pioneered a brand of social anthropology that was based on behavioral observation and that saw the normative order to be derivative from this matrix of social action.

Steward's concern with behavior, and with the environmental and situational restraints on that behavior, is often overlooked by commentators, though it lies at the heart of his theory. Steward's peers considered the concept of "culture" to be the governing principle of anthropological research and its main contribution to the social sciences. This is fair enough, but most went on to stress the normative, symbolic nature of culture and its unidirectional determination of conduct. There was little scope in the concept for dynamic interplay between norms and behavior, for the path between them was a one-way street. As for the mechanisms by which culture was derived, it was no less a materialist than Leslie White who wrote that "culture causes culture." And if culture is a symbolic and not a behavioral affair, which White also maintained, then symbols are the causes of other symbols. Finally, given the fact that symbols are ideational, we are led into a total idealism. But it was an idealism that was well adapted to the normative memory-data being collected on the American Indian reservations. Paradoxically, the students closest to a dialectic between norm and action, at the time, were those identified with the personality-and-culture school, a group that was commonly charged with idealism. But a basic sociological materialism—as opposed to simple economic determinism—places activity as prior to idea and finds norms to be crystallizations of behavior; Steward's approach did exactly this.

Any focus upon social activity per se must account for the fact that behavior is carried out within the framework of constraints both internal and external to the social system, for failure to place it in context would result in complete nominalism. And it was Steward's isolation and analysis of these constraints—notably the external ones—that produced the theory of cultural ecology. One of the concomitants of anthropological positivism is a view of society and culture that posits inherent tendencies toward stability—if not toward outright homeostasis. The result has been that the roots of most social and cultural evolution and change have been traced to exogenous factors—to diffused technology, population growth, contact with other societies, and relations with the natural environment. Steward's theory was concerned with all of these, for he found a principal source of constraint upon, or determination of, behavior to be the patterns of work called for in the pursuit of subsistence.

The behavioral outcome of any social situation is partially governed by norms and partially by sheer necessity, by accommodation to certain inescapable facts within situational reality. In recent years, anthropologists have come to recognize that actors are by no means blindly impelled by the dictates of culture but, rather, often look to culture for meaning and rationalization of prior acts. Among primitives practicing cross-cousin marriage, it has been discovered that most everybody has far more cross-cousins than parallel ones, a phenomenon that would be remarkable if it were genetically true. What happens, of course, is that a nice girl meets a suitable boy and the genealogies are brought into line with the romance. In our own society it has been found that, despite clichés to the contrary, morality can be legislated, as in antidiscrimination laws. All of this is to say that people often do what they have to do and then manipulate the symbolic system to give justification and meaning to their actions. In the cultural-ecological method, the necessity of certain ways of behaving is imposed by the absolute imperatives of subsistence and survival and the limited ways in which these imperatives can be satisfied.

Steward's effort to escape the whimsical arbitrariness of cultural relativity and unilateral normative determinism led him to search for the less flexible factors within any social situation. Symbols and groupings are capable of endless permutations, but other elements are given; culture must adjust to them rather than vice versa. One of these given elements is technology. Most of the tools and techniques of any culture are derived from other societies, and the material inventory of a group is highly dependent upon its position along routes of cultural diffusion. The presence or absence of items of technology is not, of course, wholly a matter of historical accident, for every culture screens and selects diffused traits, and some inventions are autochthonous. But however much necessity may be the mother of invention, the reverse proposition is more commonly the case: Needs are defined by available technology—and resources. The resources offered by the natural environment are the second important given category in Steward's theories. Resources and technology cannot, however, be considered separately, for it is through tools and knowledge that natural features become culturally useful and humanly accessible. Thus, if there are no metallic ores in a region, one would hardly expect metallurgy to arise there. On the other hand, unless a group has a knowledge of metallurgy, the ore-bearing strata are just so much useless rock. This is all very rudimentary, of course, but it is well to remember that technology and environment are not completely independent variables and that the two together define the life chances of societies.

The heart of Steward's anthropology is the analysis of the ways that the two givens, technology and resources, are brought together through human labor. Just as the possibilities of any society are promoted or inhibited by the natural environment, and just as technology is contingent upon history, so also are there limited ways in which specific tools can be used on specific resources. That is, certain operations may entail quite delimited and narrowly defined forms of labor, involving characteristic patterns of collectivization and individuation of work, cycling of activities, specialization of tasks, and so on. This does not imply that one and only one form of labor is effective in any operation, but rather that there are limits of variability in patterns of work contingent upon the tools and resources exploited.

A few examples may be in order. There are many kinds of fish and many de-
vices for catching them, but how people go about fishing depends much upon
the instruments and the type of fish being sought. In the Amazon basin, the
main aboriginal fishing techniques were with the bow and arrow and with fish
poisons. Bow-and-arrow fishing is usually done from a canoe and requires at
least two people, one to shoot the fish and the other to paddle. The paddling
can be done by a woman or young boy, whereas the bow and arrow are always
handled by men; this type of fishing can thus entail cooperation within the conjugal family. Fish poisoning, to the contrary, often draws entire villages into cooperation. The poisonous sap of certain vines and roots is released into smaller
streams or lagoons by men who beat sheaves of the vines with clubs. The toxic
substance drifts downstream with the current and paralyzes the gills of the fish
which, dead or stunned, are easily taken from the water by other men and by
women and children. The operation involves the coordinated labor of many
people. There must be enough men pounding the vines to achieve a certain
concentration of the poison in the water, and large numbers of people must be
stationed downstream to prevent the stunned fish from escaping. In contrast,
hook-and-line fishing, introduced by the whites, can be carried out by solitary
individuals. Most species of fish can be caught by any of these means. The gi-
ant pirarucu fish, however, is best taken with hook and line, though this technique cannot be used for piranha, which are able to bite through the leaders.

The constraints upon labor imposed by certain technologies when applied to
specific resources are evident in hunting as well as in fishing. Herd animals,
such as peccary, bison, and antelope, are usually hunted by collective means, for
a lone hunter may kill only one animal before frightening away the herd,
whereas a group of men may dispatch enough to provide meat for an entire
community. The Plains Indians hunted bison from horseback, the riders flank-
ing the running herd and killing the outliers with bow and arrow or lance.
Groups of unmounted Shoshoni hunted the fleet antelope by driving herds
down valley floors to pens, and hunting parties in the South American forests
bring peccary bands to bay with dogs. Deer, mountain sheep, and other nonherd animals, to the contrary, are most commonly taken by individual hunters
through stalking and ambush. The weapons used are also critical in determining the organization of work. In almost every instance in which firearms have
been introduced, there has been a tendency toward more individualized hunting. The greater range and striking power of guns make it less necessary to
bring a concentration of firepower to bear upon the animals. White bison
hunters, for example, used powerful rifles to pick off the lead animals in a herd
from a long distance; the systematic killing of the lead bisons kept the herds
from stampeding.

These are not invariant patterns, for collective hunting parties often encountered and killed nonherd game, and individuals could and did prey upon herds.
Rather, a strain was set up toward a certain mode and organization of work that

conformed to the practical needs of the task. Steward sometimes referred to this simple process as "adaptation" to the environment, a choice of words unfortunate for its rather biological and Darwinian overtones. We need not, however, posit blind mechanisms of natural selection of the most efficient forms of work, for the matter is more simple. The subjects of anthropological inquiry, be they primitives, peasants, or whatever, must be assumed to possess a good store of pragmatic common sense and a comprehension of their situation at least equal to that enjoyed by the ethnographer. They are perfectly capable of understanding and acting upon the usefulness of certain modes of work. This does not necessarily lead to the single most effective way of getting a job done, but it sets a sharp limit on the alternatives.

In my own experience among the Mundurucú Indians, I watched large collective garden-clearing ventures fritter away time in sociability and side diversions, clearly sacrificing efficiency for social solidarity. But the Mundurucú saw this just as clearly as I did, for they knew very well that in some villages the work of clearing was effectively carried out by two or so men. This was regarded, however, as further evidence of the abandonment of proper traditional ways by such people. What must be remembered in interpreting seemingly wasted time is that the Mundurucú had the time to waste—there was nothing else that they urgently needed to be doing, the job eventually got done, and they had a good time doing it. With the general erosion of social solidarity, however, the pattern of garden-clearing work became more individualized, as befitted the new social system and the technology of steel axe and machete. It also fitted into a new economic order in which work had become intensified due to the demands placed upon labor by trade with the whites. As the Indians' appetites for Western goods increased, "spare time" became scarce and pressure grew to carry out tasks in the most expeditious ways possible. One result has been the attrition of forms of collective activity that had their source in the social system rather than in technical necessity.

That most subsistence operations were seen to allow for a degree of flexibility kept Steward's ecological approach from being monistic and rigid, while empirically demonstrating the limits of this flexibility. Steward recognized that the range of such variation was itself dependent upon environmental and technical factors. A crude technology permits small latitude; conversely, the extent to which a society can control and alter the environment is a measure of freedom from some of its constraints. And environments that offer fewest resources and are most forbidding to human occupation will be those that allow for least flexibility. This was brilliantly demonstrated in Steward's study of the Great Basin Shoshoni, a people possessing only a rudimentary technology and living in a harsh landscape.

Steward's study is too well-known to warrant detailed recapitulation, but its main argument is that the very structure of Shoshoni society was a reflex of its habitat and exploitative patterns. Possessing none of the technology needed to realize the full potential of the environment, the Shoshoni scavenged from it, subsisting on its sparse game population and its thinly distributed wild vegetation. Steward painted a picture of a people reduced to the bare essentials of life, living in a society that was all infrastructure. The Basin Shoshoni had no stable political organization beyond parental authority and the prestige given by age. There were no chiefs, and leadership was a temporary and ad hoc matter, a situation that was consistent with the fact that there were no stable or formally defined sociopolitical units beyond the conjugal family. The Shoshoni had no tribes, no bands, no villages, no clans, no lineages. They were found scattered in small clusters of a few families each across an enormous terrain extending from southern California to Idaho and Utah; egalitarianism, individuation, and amorphousness characterized the social system.

Steward found the roots of this system in the processes of work, as shaped by tools and resources. The division of labor was along sex lines, the women gathering wild vegetables and grains and the men responsible for the protein in the diet. The female labor of root digging and seed gathering scattered the women out, for the plants were thinly distributed and the work completely individual. No help was needed, nor was there any division of tasks, in unearthing roots with a digging stick or beating seeds from grass with a basketry flail. Most hunting was similarly pursued by individual men. Deer, rodents, and other small game were taken by lone hunters by stalking and ambush. Large-scale, cooperative, and organized hunts for antelope and rabbits took place, but these were infrequent and occurred in shifting locales. Leadership was temporary and the roster of participants always different, and stable cooperating groups did not emerge from these occasional and movable feasts.

The cultural-ecological method took Steward from a consideration of known and useful resources and technology to the labor involved in exploitation of the environment to a final consideration of the causal influence of that labor on other social institutions. The latter involved a kind of functional analysis that, unlike some varieties, always took the organization of work—the cultural-ecological nexus—as its starting point. In the case of the Shoshoni, it would be almost tautological to say that work was a determinant of social structure, for the foraging units were the principal segments of society. Work is a social activity in the strictest sense, and work groups are preeminently social groups. There is interchange and equivalency by definition between the artificial categories of the "social" and the "economic," and it is an artifact of the anthropological imagination that reifies the two classes and attributes a sort of causal energy to them. Of course, they are related! In terms of concrete social behavior, they are the same. Nonetheless, Steward took the trinity of resources, technology, and labor to be a priori, for they were acted upon by elements exogenous to the social system, and they involved a kind of inflexibility and necessity. There were strict limits to the extent that this nexus could be shaped to fit other institutions; in the final analysis, most of the accommodation would be *to* the cultural-ecological situation and not *by* it.

The key element in Steward's anthropology, then, is not economic or environmental determinism, but a view of social life that sees social behavior as situationally shaped and constrained and that then goes on to derive cultural norms from regularities in that concrete behavior—this is a point I made before, but its importance merits repetition. It is this underlying principle that guided Steward's Shoshoni work and most of his subsequent writing. The approach was not unique to Steward, nor was it originated by him. Germs of it can even be found in the writings of his old teacher, Robert Lowie. For all of Lowie's fulminations against materialism, he was among the first anthropologists to understand the central importance of rules of residence in the formation of descent principles. In a critique of the evolutionists' idea that kinship and territory are mutually exclusive criteria of organization, Lowie declared flatly that kinship may simply be the language in which territorial, or spatial, relationships are phrased. People are kin because they are brought together and not the reverse. And the reasons for bringing them together, or keeping some of them apart, may lie in the necessities of livelihood. Lowie attacked Lewis Henry Morgan's notions that the American Indians were at a higher evolutionary stage than the Hawaiians and that matrilineality preceded bilaterality by citing the bilateral Shoshoni, whom he put at the bottom of the evolutionary ladder, and certainly below the complex societies of Polynesia, for essentially technological reasons. Lowie's thoughts were phrased in cautious and hesitant hints typical of his style, but Steward went far beyond them, erecting a theoretical edifice that was uniquely his.

Labels are ways of aborting thought and of endowing the complex with a counterfeit simplicity. Cultural ecology, from its sound, connotes a kind of environmentalism that was not at all a part of Steward's anthropology. He had little patience for some latter-day ecological approaches that embed their human subjects in ecosystems, rather than sociocultural ones, or that are concerned with biological populations rather than societies. He did not see the ultimate goal of cultural ecology to be a systematic statement of humanity's relation to nature. Rather, he saw cultural ecology as a method for studying and understanding the causal processes by which societies are formed. And the key element in these processes was the very social factor of work.

In a similar vein, Steward's name has been associated with cultural evolutionism, but he was never much concerned with developing general evolutionary schemes; evolutionism, too, was a method of study and not an end in itself. His approach, commonly known as "multilinear" evolutionism, was an extension of anthropology's comparative method into the temporal dimension. Steward was already combining his cultural-ecological method with comparison by the mid-1930s, when he wrote a well-known article on patrilineal hunting bands (1936). In it, he argued that a type of exogamic, territory-holding, patrilocal, and patrilineal band tended to be associated with the hunting of nongregarious, nonmigratory animals. The regular recurrence of this basic pattern in a number of societies, he argued, demonstrated that a common causality was at work. This was a fair conclusion at the time, although later research showed that most of his representative groups were not formally patrilineal and that some were bilocal or even tended toward matrilocality.

Whatever the results, Steward's methodology was clear. One can examine a series of societies having common social-structural features to see if their ecological situations are similar, and one can also scrutinize societies living in similar environments under similar technological regimes to ascertain whether they have common features of social structure. As in his article on patrilineal bands, Steward preferred the former strategy, for it was consistent with the fact that he considered societies to be the proper units of analysis and regular recurrence of social institutions to be the basis for their scientific study. Moreover, he was not an environmental determinist, a position he sought to stress in "Tappers and Trappers" (Murphy and Steward 1956). In this article, we showed that similar processes of social change had occurred among the Mundurucú Indians of Amazonian Brazil and Canadian Algonkians. Despite radical differences of environment, contact with the whites had resulted in native dependence on trade goods, which were bought by the Mundurucú with latex rubber and by the Algonkians with animal pelts. The exploitation of each resource involved individualized work in small, delimited territories and resulted in both cases in the fragmentation of the population into residence on these holdings and their reorientation from village or band life to the trading stores.

The "Tappers and Trappers" essay sought to show the causal influence in social change of new economic pursuits and new forms of labor. And since the piece was both comparative and historical, it was also an exercise in the methodology of multilinear evolution, although I do not believe we used the term at all. The article most commonly associated with Steward's kind of evolutionism is "Cultural Causality and Law" (Steward 1949), perhaps his single most influential paper. Starting from the writings of Karl Wittfogel, who found in the history of China an association between the practice of irrigation agriculture and the rise of the despotic state, Steward extended the inquiry into other areas in which there had been autochthonous development of the state— that is, of states that were not spin-offs or derivative phenomena from other states—including those of the Indus Valley, the basin of the Tigris and Euphrates Rivers, the Nile Valley, the Valley of Mexico, Yucatán, and coastal Peru. The recurrence of large-scale irrigation agriculture and the intimate association of this mode of production with centralized political power were striking in most of the areas. There has been some evidence that the state preceded irrigation in the Valley of Mexico and it was clearly not a factor in the Mayan development, but the case for the rest of the world was strong.

In its essence, the methodology of "Cultural Causality and Law" followed the same lines as Steward's previous work. A relationship between irrigation and the state was posited for China and found to be recurrent in other parts of the world—a demonstration, to Steward, of similarity of cause. To clinch the argument, he took each society in his study from its earliest beginnings through the development of agriculture and on to the rise of cities and states, showing in each phase a causal sequence that explained it and paralleled the sequence in the other societies. The actual method of analysis was much the same as that used in his Shoshoni work, however different the subjects; multilinear evolution had merely added new controls and criteria of proof. In his analysis, Steward started from certain characteristics of the natural environment, in these cases climatic aridity and highly fertile soils, which provided the need for irrigation and the potential for great productivity. The technological factor was agriculture, which originated in dry farming and then became coupled with the new techniques of irrigation as cultivation spread into the arid zones. Given these elements, certain forms of organization were needed to carry out production. First, large concentrations of collective labor were required to build canals, weirs, and flood-control works and to maintain these facilities. The control and direction of this labor force, and the expertise needed to undertake these complex engineering projects, called for a specialized leadership group having coercive powers over the population. Such an elite would also have the responsibility of allocating the water to the communities served by the irrigation systems. The process inevitably produced class stratification and the state. It was not the only way the state could evolve, but it was indeed the source of much of civilization.

As in his labeling of the comparative-historical method as "multilinear evolution," Steward always sought new concepts and nomenclature to delineate what he was doing. Thus, there were "levels of sociocultural integration," "sociocultural types," and "culture cores," all of which had the heuristic value of communicating a complex set of premises or strategies under a single rubric. At times, the terminology acquired an ultimate reality that it never truly had. Steward, Wolf, and I spent hours and days discussing whether the "culture core" contained other institutional features than those relating to the productive system—until we finally recalled that "core" had no meaning other than what we thought useful. Rubrics and labels can block thought as well as facilitate it, but Steward's methodological lexicon had the merit of glossing and stressing his ideas and making them more communicable. We should not, however, allow the verbiage to overlay and hide the fact that there was an amazing consistency of method and purpose in Steward's writings, from his first articles on the Shoshoni to the mature reflections of his retirement. This consistency centered on the mode of production as a mediating activity between environment and culture and on the socializing effects of labor.

It is through their ideas that the ancestors live on, and Steward's legacy has a vitality that derives from its continued relevance to anthropology and to our society in general. But the special quality of excitement and discovery that Steward's students of thirty years ago experienced has passed and can never be recaptured—by them. Anthropology's special deliciousness is based upon a continuing opening up of new vistas, a finding of the totally new or a refinding and a different perspective on something familiar. We are constrained always to press on, to seek progress through research and imagination, but it is necessary to remember that the bases of our concepts were laid in the past. Under every innovative and heady idea lies the shadow of past thought, and some of our greatest discoveries are restatements of what had been known before. Students will be rediscovering Steward, in spite of themselves, for generations to come.

DISCUSSION

GENE WELTFISH: You say that Steward was not a dialectician, but I wonder if you wouldn't admit some kind of dialectics, that I do see in Steward and that to a certain extent explains Marvin Harris's unwillingness to let Steward fully into the materialist cadre. If you are going to allow ideology a causative role in a model of causality in culture, then I think that constitutes a trap door—the kind of trap door that Harris would hate to see opened—that once opened allows for all kinds of theoretical jumping around in a dialectical way.

MURPHY: I suppose you could reinterpret or help him along a bit; for example, in "Cultural Causality and Law," the progression from the Formative Period to the period that he called Cyclical Conquests comes about with the growth and development of irrigation agriculture and with the soaring of population until the previous forms of society are inadequate. But I'm not sure that this is the kind of dialectics that either Hegel or Marx had in mind. For example, the idea of the growth of population being an outcome of increased subsistence causing certain changes can be handled in straight mechanical causal terms. This is the way Steward tried to handle it. There was no necessary development of contradictions within the social systems themselves in Steward's work, although maybe you could supply it for him.

Incidentally, Steward's convictions about the causal role of subsistence did not always carry over into his view of things in his own life. During the years that Eric Wolf and I were his research associates at the University of Illinois, we occupied a little suite in a corner of one floor of the College of Agriculture, space released only because the main part of the College of Agriculture had moved into more sumptuous quarters. Down the hall from us was the office of the Department of Meats, which was chaired by a gentleman named Sleeter Bull. Julian had a series of secretaries, none of whom could spell. Finally he got a young lady who could spell beautifully, type perfectly, an absolute gem. He treated her with the greatest of care, he pampered her. But the Department of Meats would cook up rashers of bacon every morning; and as Eric and I would sit in our office going out of our minds at the smells, Sleeter Bull would come tiptoeing down the hall and say to the secretary, "Why don't you come down and have a little bit of breakfast, dear?" and she would go. Every now and then he'd say, "You look sort of peaked, looks like you could use a steak tonight for dinner," and he would take a great big thick T-bone out of his locker and give it to her. She left Julian for him. Julian was very cut up about this and thought this was manifest disloyalty, poor repayment for all the consideration he had given her. Eric and I tried to tell him, "Look, this fits very well with all of your theories. First things first. There is a bit of the Shoshoni in every one of us." Julian said, "Well, that may very well be, but people should have some principles before thinking of their stomachs all the time."

ALEXANDER LESSER: I would like to go back to the question of what Steward meant by multilinear and unilinear evolution. It seems to me that biological evolution is inevitably multilinear; that's what it was in Darwin, and that's what it always has been. The interpretations of the term "evolution" as unilinear have nothing to do with factual work in biological evolution. Multilinear evolution would mean that evolution takes place differently in relation to different forms; for instance, the bird is an end of evolution, just as man, but the bird is not on the way to man, nor man on the way to the bird. Julian's use of "multilinear," as you have explained it, ends in an effort to find a single cause of cultural evolution. In his studies of the comparisons of high civilizations, or the conception of levels of sociocultural integration, what he seeks is actually a unilinear development, *one way* in which basic evolution is taking place. I can't see that "multilinear evolution" has anything to do with his effort, except insofar as he was trying to get away from oversimplified conceptions of unilinear evolution.

MURPHY: You might see a multilinear evolutionism becoming a unilinear thing, in the phases of the development of civilization. The question then becomes, what are the ways of getting primary states other than through the development of irrigation? I'm not sure that Steward had a hard time dealing with the fact that all the evidence indicated that the influence of irrigation was problematic in the Valley of Mexico, and certainly absent in the Maya case, and that there might be other ways that the state could be reached. I think that the only person in anthropology who used a Darwinian model, a biological evolutionary model, was Fred Eggan. This appears in Eggan's "method of controlled comparison" (1954) even though he doesn't look upon that approach as an evolutionism. In his original attempt to understand Siouan kinship, Eggan always tried to deal with what happened: He started off with a linguistic group, such as the Sioux, and he then tried to see what were the ramifications of Siouan kinship, what various lines it took, how it diverged from what was presumably a uniform proto-Siouan kinship. Some people have called that a genetic model.

LESSER: But the ways in which Steward worked on, say, the development of the state, are unilinear and not multilinear evolution. The concept of multilinear evolution which he developed has really nothing to do with his work on the development of types, because he always looked for a unilinear pattern of development: one way in which bands changed, kinship forms changed, states developed. Maybe his procedures and his derivations are correct, but they are unilinear, and his concept of multilinear evolution is irrelevant.

MURPHY: The nearest that you come to a really unilinear scheme in Steward is in the idea of levels of sociocultural integration, the idea that there are, within any system, certain levels: Within the state, for example, are certain regions, within the regions communities, within the communities kin groups, within the kin groups families. Many people tried to make that into a unilinear evolutionism. He developed the notion of levels of sociocultural integration in his book on area research (1950a), and he proposed it as a means of trying to handle the study of acculturation. The point he made was that the history of contact in South America indicates that those institutions and aspects of culture that went first were the ones related to the broadest levels of integration, while the narrowest, most parochial levels of integration were least affected in the acculturation process. The Spaniards came into Peru and smashed all the idols, completely destroyed the state cult and substituted Catholicism, but afterwards there were left local shrines. As the Spaniards consolidated their control, they eliminated the local shrines; there were still family practices left, and so forth. Three or four hundred years after conquest the people were still being socialized as Indians; they were still sitting and walking like Indians, because these are things that you learn earliest and in the most primary, localized level of integration. Now this was very much like a unilinear evolutionism. I think that the idea of a progression from family level of integration to band level of integration to chiefdoms to states—for example in the work of Elman Service—these evolutionary taxonomies, I think, derived straight from Steward's levels of sociocultural integration. I do believe this is a kind of unilinear evolutionism. But not Steward's other ideas.

ROBERT CARNEIRO: I think Professor Lesser is right in thinking of "Cultural Causality and Law" as essentially the expression of unilinear evolutionism. Even though Steward originally meant it to apply to areas that were arid or semiarid, since he was using the Wittfogel hypothesis, he nevertheless pointed out that he had six or seven stages by which he could accurately characterize cultural development in various areas. He pointed out that in the Maya lowlands and in Southeast Asia, which were not arid areas, these stages still applied. He thus discovered that he had a unilinear sequence. But something surprising happened, and I wonder if you can shed any light on it. The article had created a sensation in 1949, and a few years later there was a symposium at the AAA meeting in Tucson, at which a number of scholars familiar with each of the areas that Steward had dealt with examined his sequence and his theory of causation in detail. The result was as you suggested: In the Valley of Mexico there did not seem to be evidence of irrigation very early, and in Mesopotamia, too, large-scale irrigation came after the state was formed. The causal basis for Steward's developmental theory was severely undercut. Steward, reacting to this, backed away from the sequence of stages he had proposed to characterize development. One archaeologist on the panel was displeased at this and told Steward, "You should not throw out the baby with the irrigation water." "Cultural Causality and Law" was the high-water mark of Steward's evolutionism. From then on he began a retreat, which became very marked by 1953. He made such an enormous advance. Why did he back away from trying to consolidate it and from finding as much order and coherence as he could? The rest of his life was retreat, as far as cultural evolution was concerned.

MURPHY: I think this gets back to my point that fundamentally he wasn't really interested in evolutionism. He didn't consider himself an evolutionist. To the extent that he found it useful for discovering laws, yes, he was an evolutionist. To the extent that he looked upon history as not being a hodgepodge concatenation of events one after another but as involving some orderly unfolding, yes, he was an evolutionist. He was an evolutionist in many ways. Everybody is a unilinear evolutionist, if you use the basic premise that evolution is characterized by a progression from simplicity to complexity. But it depends on how you define evolutionism.

MICHAEL HARNER: Something that is very distinctive about Steward is his preoccupation with causality, which I think was at least as important, if not more so, as his search for law. I wonder about the origins of this preoccupation. Certainly the Berkeley academic scene may have played a role in this, if only in a negative way. For example, Gifford's famous required course, "World Ethnography." Edward provided the students with the annual rainfall, temperature ranges, and many other environmental facts related to perhaps twenty cultures in the world, and the students were left to absorb it all and were not given any explanation as to why these facts might be significant. This was typical of the Berkeley undergraduate program; there was a tremendous variety of area courses and virtually no theories to explain why all this cultural diversity developed. I wonder if you have any insights into this very salient aspect of Steward's character, his search for causality.

MURPHY: I really don't. I know Gifford's course contained every known fact; people learned more about world ethnography than they ever wanted to know. (After Gifford retired, the course was always given to the youngest faculty member joining the Berkeley department. Very optimistic, bright young people used to be driven into absolute despondency by the information that they were to teach "World Ethnography." Then somebody would take them aside and say, "It consists of the group you're studying and anything else you want to throw in.")

Certainly Steward never got this preoccupation from Kroeber, who was concerned only with culture, not with social institutions qua social and not with social activity qua activity. He didn't really get it from Lowie, who said he was interested in causality but then imposed such strict scientific canons for determining causality that they simply couldn't be met in most of anthropology. But at the same time this aspect of Steward's work began to show up early. It might partially have come out of Steward's work in the natural sciences at Cornell. In part it may have been a reaction to his Christian Science mother. In part it derived from the Shoshoni experience, in which he saw the direct, dramatic, and irrevocable impact of the limitations of environment on an entire way of life.

LESSER: I don't see that an interest in causality needs to be explained. It seems to me that to be a scientist you have to be interested in causal relations, otherwise you're not doing anything. The fact that Steward followed the interest up in a particular way was the particular theory that he had, but even functionalists doing synchronic studies are interested in finding causes and effects and influences and interrelationships, when they look for connections that involve interinfluence. I don't see any problem with an interest in causality. The fact that he—unlike other people—tried to pursue it through broad cultural comparisons is one of the things that he added, but he didn't have to expound multilineality, because that was irrelevant to what he was trying to do. When Lowie used the *Kulturkreise* as an illustration of multilineality he had a good point, because that was supposed to describe different developments. But when you are looking for similar or parallel development you are looking for some kind of unilineality, and you have to use causality; otherwise you've got nothing.

MURPHY: Obviously there are all sorts of causes; Steward was interested especially in a causal sequence that showed some organic and regular unfolding of tendencies. He was interested in those causes that could be adduced from, that were contained in, autochthonous internal developments in societies. It was that interest that led him to engage in long dialogues about diffusion versus independent invention (which was one of the favorite problems of anthropologists of that time, of course). Steward always came down on the side of internal development as the thing to look for in the first place, because diffusion always seemed to him too adventitious and accidental. He wasn't denying its importance, but he always took the attitude that any society that was going to adopt some very important trait was probably ready for it anyhow. It was this attempt to see causal developments as emanating internally, autochthonously, from within the society, as having some sort of inevitability, and as being connected in some organic way with the unfolding of the society, that made him, in a real sense, an evolutionist as well as a student of causality.

BIOGRAPHICAL NOTE

Photo by Paul Byers, courtesy of Columbia
University Department of Anthropology

ROBERT F. MURPHY was born in 1924 in Rockaway Beach, Queens, where he grew up. He attended Far Rockaway High School—a school that produced an unusually large number of anthropologists (among them Alexander Lesser and three members of Murphy's own graduating class of 1941), although anthropology was not taught (or even mentioned) there. Murphy's first exposure to other cultures, apart from growing up as an Irish Catholic in a Jewish neighborhood, came through naval service in the Pacific during World War II. After the war, he enrolled in Columbia College under the G.I. Bill, and a course in anthropology (chosen because he had heard it was easy) introduced him to the subject. His interest aroused by his teacher, Charles Wagley, he went on in 1949 to do graduate work at Columbia. Although at the time it seemed unlikely that one could make a living out of anthropology, he "found the university to be more agreeable than was either home or the navy."

At Columbia, Murphy worked with both Steward and Wagley (a student of Ruth Bunzel and Ralph Linton, and Marvin Harris's teacher as well). Given the Latin American interests of these professors, Murphy decided to do his initial fieldwork in South America among the Mundurucú Indians of Brazil (1952–1953), whom he describes as the most persuasive of all his teachers. The Mundurucú were the subject of Murphy's Ph.D. dissertation (completed in 1954) and two monographs, *Mundurucú Religion* (1958) and *Headhunter's Heritage* (1960). Beginning in 1953 he spent two years with Steward at the University of Illinois, one of several research associates Steward brought to work with him there. Murphy's association with Steward in these years led to fieldwork among the Shoshone and Bannock Indians of Idaho and Wyoming (see Murphy and Murphy 1960). He also coauthored with Steward the "Tappers and Trappers" article (Murphy and Steward 1956) comparing Mundurucú and Algonkian responses to white contact, and he later coedited a collection of Steward's essays (Steward 1977).

In 1955 Murphy was appointed as an assistant professor at the University of California at Berkeley. There he came to know Robert Lowie, whose biography he later wrote (Murphy 1972). Among his Berkeley colleagues, David Schneider was the most important for him. In this period, Murphy carried out another major field project, among the Tuareg of Niger and Nigeria (1959–1960). In 1963 he returned to Columbia as a professor and remained a pivotal member of the anthropology department for twenty-seven years. He served as department chairman from 1969 to 1972.

Murphy's field research covered an extremely wide range of interests and areas, including societies in Africa and both North and South America. His work addressed a series of basic problems in ethnology, exploring a number of anthropological contradictions: The Mundurucú were patrilineal and matrilocal, the Tuareg were Muslim and matrilineal, the Shoshoni survived on the brink of starvation. At a time when theories of primitive society focused on cross-cousin marriage, he wrote an important analysis of the structural implications of parallel-cousin marriage (Murphy and Kasdan 1959). Murphy's theoretical orientation was (by his own description) "deliberately and happily eclectic," combining an early and persistent cultural-ecological bent, a strong dash of Freud (who first attracted his attention while he was an undergraduate), a middle period of structural-functional influence, and a later absorption with Lévi-Strauss—interests that "were cumulative, not substitutive" and that resulted in "an intellectual stew, well seasoned with Marx." The combination was expressed in his theoretical synthesis, *The Dialectics of Social Life: Alarms and Excursions in Anthropological Theory* (1971).

Murphy said that he thought of himself first as a teacher and second as an anthropologist, and that he did both because he liked to. He continued to do both into the last years of his life, when he was afflicted with an inoperable tumor of the spinal cord. Even as his malady worsened into quadriplegia, he scarcely slackened in his teaching and research supervision, assisted by a devoted coterie of his students. He remained the anthropological observer of his own experience and wrote analytically about it in a poignant book, *The Body Silent: The Different World of the Disabled* (1987). At the time that he died in 1990, he was preparing what was to be the Distinguished Lecture at the following year's meeting of the American Anthropological Association. He was planning (he wrote to a friend) to do "a number on the postmodern-deconstructive-reflexive-dialogic anthropology of our age."

Leslie White in his office at the University of Michigan, 1967. Photo by Beth Dillingham

7

LESLIE A. WHITE

Robert L. Carneiro

A contemporary of Julian Steward's, Leslie White was as instrumental as he in moving American anthropology toward generalizing theories of culture and toward materialist explanations. Like Steward, White was educated by students of Franz Boas: Alexander Goldenweiser, with whom he took courses at the New School for Social Research, and then, at the University of Chicago, Edward Sapir and Fay-Cooper Cole (an ethnologist-archaeologist who had studied under George A. Dorsey at the Field Museum before taking his degree with Boas). Like Steward, White had an early flirtation with psychology and then fieldwork experience among Indians in the American Southwest. While the two men are linked for their both having departed from the Boasian tradition, for their interests in formulating laws of culture, and for their respective contributions to the revival of cultural evolution, their concerns and their approaches were very different—often at odds with each other—and there was little direct contact between them.

Although White got his Ph.D. a few years earlier than Steward, his breaking of new theoretical ground began somewhat later. Until the late 1930s his writings dealt with Pueblo Indian ethnology and were fully consistent with his Boasian training. During the 1940s, however, White published a series of seminal statements setting forth a comprehensive theory of the evolution of culture and redefining anthropology as a science of culture—"culturology." Iconoclastic and bitterly opposed at the time, White's ideas on evolution, energy, and the concept of culture eventually came to be widely accepted.

Like Steward, White was at the height of his development as a scholar and teacher when anthropology entered a period of explosive growth after World

War II. Thus, the two men had a profound influence in shaping contemporary anthropology—including the shaping of reactions to their views.

✿

Leslie White was, without question, one of the intellectual leaders of contemporary anthropology. But he was more than this. He was one of the major instruments by means of which anthropology became a full-fledged science. When
he entered it, anthropology was dominated by a negative and critical particularism. When he left it, it had become a positive, expanding, and generalizing discipline. And this transformation was due in no small part to White's own efforts.
He gave anthropology powerful concepts and invigorating theories. In a word,
he gave it propulsion. My purpose in this chapter is to show how this change
came about. In doing so I will draw not only on published writings, but also on
my personal experiences as a student, follower, and friend of Leslie White.[1]

Leslie Alvin White was born in Salida, Colorado, in 1900. His father, Alvin
Lincoln White, was a civil engineer who did location and construction work for
the railroads, and because of his work the family moved frequently. When Leslie
was five years old his parents were divorced, and his father was awarded custody
of the children—Leslie, his older sister, and his younger brother. Two years later,
because of ill health, Alvin White decided to give up the job he held then in
Kansas City and move to a farm near Greeley, Kansas. There they lived in a
house that, "as was the case of all houses in that community at that time . . . was
without running water, plumbing, or electric lights" (White n.d.: 3). One night
in 1910, Leslie's father took him outside and showed him Halley's comet, which
was then blazing across the sky; this event seems to have been a turning point in
his life. Leslie became very much interested in astronomy, and later read a book
entitled *Natural Philosophy* that his father had used in college. As a result, he
decided to become an astronomer or a physicist.

In 1914 the family moved to a farm near Zachary, Louisiana, where Leslie
finished high school at the age of sixteen. He would have enrolled in Louisiana
State University (LSU) immediately thereafter, but illness, and then in 1918 en-
listment in the United States Navy, delayed his entry into college. Of the effect
the war had on him, White wrote:

> The War changed my life purpose and outlook profoundly. I discovered somehow,
> during the War, that all I had been taught, formally and informally, about my soci-
> ety, my country, and related subjects, was a gross distortion of reality. I therefore
> determined, when I entered college, to find out why *peoples* behave as they do. My
> love for physics was not extinguished; it was merely pushed into the background. I
> majored in history and political science during my freshman and sophomore years
> at Louisiana State University, thinking they would answer my new and big ques-
> tions for me. They did not, and I turned to psychology, sociology and philosophy

during my junior and senior years at Columbia University, to which I had transferred. (quoted in Barnes 1960: xvi)

White was a student at LSU from 1919 to 1921 and at Columbia College from 1921 to 1923, when he received his bachelor's degree in psychology. He stayed on at Columbia to do graduate work in the same field under Robert Woodworth, receiving his M.A. in 1924. During his three years at Columbia, White did not take a single course in anthropology, despite the fact that Franz Boas was at the height of his fame there as a teacher. But at the same time that he was formally in residence at Columbia, White was taking courses at the New School for Social Research. There he took his first anthropology course, under Boas's student Alexander Goldenweiser, as well as courses from John B. Watson, the behaviorist psychologist; W. I. Thomas, the sociologist; and Thorstein Veblen, the economist.

After receiving his master's degree, White decided to go to the University of Chicago and enroll in the joint department of sociology and anthropology. About this move he wrote:

I still remained interested in what I then called "peoples" (rather than "culture"). Therefore, I went to the University of Chicago to study sociology. I quit sociology because I found that it seemed to me all theory and little fact. I jumped out of the sociological frying pan into the fire of anthropology only to find that the anthropologists had plenty of facts but no ideas. (quoted in Barnes 1960: xvii)

Just a year after transferring to Chicago, White published his first professional article, "Personality and Culture" (1925). This appears to have been the first article ever written bearing this title (Aberle 1960: 2). It is ironic that it should have been White who "pioneered" this field, since he came to abandon psychology as the master key to an understanding of human behavior. Indeed, he is often regarded as the archenemy of the personality-and-culture movement in anthropology. (He once remarked that those anthropologists who had been seduced by this approach were "selling their culturological birthright for a mess of psychological pottage" [1946: 86].)

It is clear from a book review White wrote of John Dewey's *Human Nature and Conduct* for Woodworth's course in social psychology in 1922 that he had found in Dewey the germ of the idea of culture as an external class of phenomena that exerted a powerful influence on human behavior. When considering a topic for his doctoral dissertation at Chicago, White first proposed to write a library thesis, highly theoretical and philosophical in nature, which foreshadowed a number of his later interests and views, including culturology. The thesis proposal was submitted to Benjamin Faris, chairman of the department and a sociologist, who rejected it as too theoretical and ambitious. (This rejection precipitated a dispute within the department, in which Faris was ranged against Fay-Cooper Cole, the senior anthropologist. The result was a split that ultimately led to the formation of separate departments of anthropology and sociology.)

His thesis topic rejected, White had to look elsewhere for material for his dissertation. The year earlier, 1925, he had gotten his first taste of fieldwork when he spent a few weeks among the Menomini and Winnebago in Wisconsin. This experience, he later wrote, "made a firm and lasting impression on me" (1973: v). But his first real fieldwork came in 1926 in Acoma Pueblo, New Mexico. White described the circumstances leading up to this field trip:

> After having taken courses for six consecutive quarters at Chicago I became restive, and Professor Sapir "prescribed" a field trip. He wrote to Dr. Elsie Clews Parsons, who was then in Egypt, to inquire if I might receive financial support from the Southwest Society (i.e., Dr. E. C. P.). She replied that financial support would be forthcoming, but said that I should not go to Acoma until she had briefed me fully with regard to the difficulties confronting a would-be ethnographer among the Pueblo Indians of New Mexico. But I was too restless to await my indoctrination and set out on my own before Dr. Parsons returned to the United States. During my first few weeks in the field, I received rather severe letters from her, chiding me for rashness in going into the field ignorant and unprepared. (1973: v)

In those days it was difficult to do fieldwork openly among the eastern Pueblos, and when Boas learned of White's field plans, he was concerned lest he be unable to obtain informants at Acoma. Boas wrote to Sapir solicitously that "it would seem very undesirable that a young man on his first expedition should fail to get any material" and passed on Parsons's advice that in such an event he should try working among the Pima (White 1973: v–vi). Nevertheless, White wrote his Ph.D. dissertation, "Medicine Societies of the Southwest," in 1927, based on his year of fieldwork at Acoma.

In 1927, degree in hand, White began his teaching career as an instructor in anthropology at the University of Buffalo. At the time, he was still a Boasian in outlook, at least as far as cultural evolution was concerned. Although he had never taken a course under Boas, he had been taught by Goldenweiser and Sapir and had read and absorbed Robert H. Lowie's antievolutionary manifesto, *Primitive Society* (1920). He had not yet read anything by Lewis Henry Morgan or the other classical evolutionists, having been discouraged from doing so by his teachers, who represented their work as "obsolete" (Barnes 1960: xxv). However, an experience White had while teaching at Buffalo began to change his attitude toward cultural evolutionism:

> I taught my students anti-evolutionism. But I had some very intelligent and alert students in my courses. They had never heard that the theory of evolution—so fundamental in biology—was out of place in ethnology. They challenged me on this issue. I repeated all the reasons the Boasians offered for rejecting the theory of cultural evolution. My teaching may have been acceptable to some of my students, but certainly not to all. They pushed me into a corner. Before long I . . . realized that I could not defend the doctrines of anti-evolutionism; then I realized that I could no longer hold them; they were untenable. (White 1987: 13)

Not far from Buffalo was the Tonawanda Indian Reservation where Morgan had studied the Seneca Iroquois. This prompted White to read Morgan, first his *League of the Iroquois* (1851) and then *Ancient Society* (1877). And as he did so he found that Morgan was not as benighted or archaic as he had been painted and that much of the evolutionism presented in *Ancient Society* was still valid and fruitful. Over the years, White continued to study Morgan's work and eventually edited some of his letters and journals, as well as the definitive edition of *Ancient Society* (see White 1937, 1940b, 1942b, 1944, 1951, 1957, 1959d, 1964). At the time of his death, he was undoubtedly the leading Morgan scholar in the world.

According to Harry Elmer Barnes, another important influence that led White to reassess the merits of cultural evolutionism

was that of a young colleague, the brilliant and learned philosopher Marvin Farber, who had joined the staff of the University of Buffalo the year before Dr. White came there. Farber had taken some anthropology as a student at Harvard and in extensive foreign study thereafter and was especially interested in the subject of evolution in general. He did much to undermine Dr. White's already fading confidence in the extreme anti-evolutionary arguments advanced by Lowie in *Primitive Society*. (Barnes 1960: xxv)

Still another factor in White's acceptance of evolutionism was his visit to Russia in the summer of 1929. This experience exposed him to the writings of Karl Marx and Friedrich Engels, who themselves had been very much interested in Morgan's work, especially as it bore on the transformation of primitive society into civil society. As a result of his trip to Russia and the reading it led him to do, White became convinced that socialism would ultimately prevail in Western society. The following year, 1930, at the annual meeting of the American Association for the Advancement of Science, he presented a paper entitled "An Anthropological Appraisal of the Russian Revolution" in which he predicted the collapse of the capitalist system and the eventual triumph of socialism. The paper received worldwide attention, including front-page coverage by the *New York Times* and *Pravda*. Some weeks later, in another article in *Pravda*, Maxim Gorki took favorable notice of White's remarks. Years later, recalling this incident, White remarked, "This didn't endear me to anyone in the United States except the Communists." He was asked to meet with the dean at the University of Michigan, where he had been teaching less than a year, and was told of the letters, phone calls, and telegrams the university had received demanding he be fired. "The dean told me I was indiscreet, and didn't predict long tenure for me" (Weiner 1969: 4).

While White never cited his indebtedness to Marx in print, he was certainly influenced by him. He once told me he had read the first chapter of *Capital* sixteen times and learned something from it each time. In the present era of Marxist chic, when young anthropologists vie with one another in quoting

Marx, it may be difficult for some to understand White's failure to acknowledge this influence. But one must remember that until relatively recently, citing Marx with approval might jeopardize an American scholar's academic career, as in fact White had already learned. White expressed heretical views so freely during his lifetime, and felt the sting of reproach so often, that one can hardly accuse him of academic timidity. On the contrary, his career was marked by the outspoken espousal of unpopular ideas.[2]

What White found most fruitful in Marxism was the concept of historical materialism—the idea that technological and economic factors play the primary role in molding a society. He took up this notion wholeheartedly and expressed it many times in his writings. Another Marxist idea he found useful was that major cultural changes occur through the accumulation of small, quantitative increments that lead, once a certain point is reached, to a qualitative transformation. However, it is important to note that White made no use at all of the dialectical method, making him, in Stanley Diamond's view, "a mechanical or mechanistic, as opposed to a dialectical materialist." Diamond concluded that White, "although obviously influenced by Marx, is not a Marxist in the traditional sense at all" (1974: 341).[3]

Among White's other intellectual debts were, as already mentioned, that to Morgan. He absorbed Morgan's evolutionism, his appreciation of the role of property in determining social relations, and his deep interest in kinship systems. From E. B. Tylor, White derived the concept of culture and the idea of a science of culture, as well as Tylor's more limited evolutionism.[4] From Herbert Spencer, White adopted the notion of evolution as consisting essentially of differentiation of structure and specialization of function. He also seems to have derived from him the idea of society as a system (see White 1959a, chs. 7 and 8). White's critical views of the Great Man theory of history also stem from Spencer, who vigorously attacked this theory, especially in *The Study of Sociology* (1873), which White said was his favorite of Spencer's work. "But above all," he once wrote to me, "from Herbert Spencer I learned how to think."

From Émile Durkheim, whose work he greatly admired and whom he considered a culturologist, White derived the ideas of a science of culture, cultural determinism, and the functional approach in general. This acceptance of functionalism may have been strengthened later by his reading of Bronislaw Malinowski and A. R. Radcliffe-Brown (see White 1947a: 183). White used to say in class that what was sound and illuminating in functionalism had been absorbed into the intellectual bloodstream of anthropology, and he was no doubt speaking for himself as well as for the profession at large. Certainly his article "History, Evolutionism, and Functionalism" (1945a) portrayed functionalism as equally valid with evolutionism.

Thus, White had several major intellectual debts. But he rendered no mentor full allegiance. He was not a disciple. He was not wedded to anyone else's system. Rather, he was an independent thinker concerned with building his own system. And though in doing so he took disparate elements from various sources, he articulated them into a unique and distinctive end product. His total philosophy, eclectic in its origins, was, once assembled, solid, unified, and integrated.

In 1930 White began teaching at the University of Michigan, replacing Steward, who had moved to the University of Utah. In 1932 he was promoted to associate professor and was made acting chairman of the department. However, largely because of the controversy that surrounded him at Michigan, promotion to full professor was delayed until 1943, and he was not made chairman (without the "acting") until 1945. He remained chairman until 1957; in the twenty-five years he headed the department he built up its strength from one full-time anthropologist to twenty and turned it into one of the most distinguished departments in the world.[5] In 1970, after forty years of teaching at Michigan, White retired. Later he found a second home at the University of California at Santa Barbara, where he was among former students and colleagues: Elman Service, Albert Spaulding, Thomas Harding, and the mathematician and his close friend, Raymond L. Wilder. Still trying to complete a manuscript, "Modern Capitalist Culture," which he had begun more than twenty years earlier, White died of a heart attack in 1975.

If that much-overused term "charisma" ever applied to a teacher, it did to Leslie White. Rather than personal, though, his charisma was intellectual. Students were drawn not so much to the man as to his ideas. As a lecturer, White did not have a smooth and polished delivery, but that did not matter. He was able to command attention as no other lecturer I have ever heard. There was an intensity in his manner, an incisiveness in his ideas, and a force to his personality that arrested the listener. His lectures before large undergraduate classes at Michigan were charged with electricity. Always there was an air of expectancy in those classes as students waited for lightning to strike. According to a former student, William Masters:

> At Michigan, Leslie White came to teach two kinds of courses. The first consisted of the immensely popular offerings with titles such as "The Evolution of Culture" and "The Mind of Primitive Man." Students from every walk of campus life flocked to these lectures and formed a large, if sometimes tense, audience. . . . [Some of the Michigan faculty]—notably heaven-storming romantics out of literature, converted Thomists out of philosophy, and the moodier type of analyst out of psychology—bridled at certain arguments in White's brand of anthropology. So they told their students, and the students, very naturally, attempted to carry the war to the floor of White's classroom. These students were in for a painful surprise. Over the years, White developed [a] lightning-witted acidity. . . . A student, equipped with a loaded question that he thought would demolish White . . . was outmanned, outgunned, and usually outflanked. Some of them probably still carry the scars. (quoted in Barnes 1960: xxiii)

"The Mind of Primitive Man" was a course White had first taught at Buffalo and had brought with him to Michigan. It was his largest undergraduate course; although it was not required, the enrollment in it often exceeded 300. It was the most heretical course offered on campus. Despite the fact that White trampled underfoot the students' most cherished values, sparing neither God nor soul nor freedom of the will, most of them enjoyed the course tremendously.

One day in class White remarked, offhandedly, that there was nothing original in the course. I was dumbfounded. As far as I was concerned, everything in it was original. Moreover, as an eager young disciple, I *wanted* everything to be original. It took me years to learn that White was right. In one way or another, every idea he had expressed in that class had been expressed by someone else before. But I have never found anyone who said these things so clearly, forcefully, and convincingly as he.

White never suppressed his opinions in the classroom, regardless of the consequences. This led to a certain amount of ill feeling when word of White's latest pronouncement filtered back to some other members of the faculty. For example, he used to refer to philosophy as "intellectual thumb-sucking," a remark that did not sit well with William Frankena, one of the leading philosophers on campus.

White's unequivocal rejection of theism, while routine to professional anthropologists, was not so readily accepted in the university community. Indeed, it brought him into repeated and bitter conflict with the clergy in Ann Arbor and drew down on him the full force of *odium theologicum*. The Catholic Church assigned nuns to enroll in "The Mind of Primitive Man" and take stenographic notes so there would be a verbatim transcript of White's remarks to use against him. On one occasion, Catholic and Lutheran clergymen together drew up an eight-page indictment that they took to the university president, demanding that White be fired. "They said I was guilty of robbing young people of their faith and ideals," White later recalled (Weiner 1969: 4). The tradition of academic freedom was strong enough at Michigan to prevent White's dismissal, but the long delay in his promotion suggests that clerical opposition to him impeded the progress of his career.

The biggest uproar resulted from a paper entitled "Anthropological Approaches to Religion," which White read at the annual meeting of the American Anthropological Association (AAA) in 1957. Ruth Benedict had once written: "Man is a creature of such freedom of action that he can . . . at any stage of technological development create his gods in the most diverse forms" (1948: 589). White disagreed with this assertion, and his paper was designed to show that a society's religious system was not idiosyncratic at all but reflected its socioeconomic system. He pointed out that the notion "the Lord is my Shepherd" reflected a pastoral economy. He argued that a society subsisting on wild food, with no knowledge of monarchy, could hardly have a conception of "Great

God, our King" or speak of "Christ, our Royal Master." "Contrariwise," he continued, "a monarchical cultural system is not likely to have a bear . . . for a god."
A few months earlier the Russians had placed the first Sputnik into orbit, and
White concluded his paper by saying, "A cultural system that can launch earth
satellites can dispense with gods entirely."

The next day, the *New York Times* carried a full-column story of the meetings, mentioning a number of the papers presented. In the middle of the article was a paragraph about White's paper, which quoted the above lines without
comment. The Detroit papers, with a ready eye for an issue they could sensa-
tionalize, picked up the story from the *Times*. They called various clergymen in
the state, asking them to comment on the fateful line. The clergy were only too
happy to oblige and denounced White for his irreligion. The Episcopal bishop
of Michigan accused White of "playing into the hands of people who would undermine the spiritual heritage of the Western world" (*Detroit News*, December
28, 1957). The *Michigan Catholic* of January 2, 1958, headlined a front-page
editorial, "How Long Will UM Let White Deride God?" Once again, pressure
was mounted to dismiss White, but discomfited though the university administration was, it again held firm. In a reply to his critics, which White prepared
for private circulation, he commented wryly:

> One wonders . . . at the vehemence of the clergy. If a puny anthropologist should
> in fact "deride God," does He need a protective clergyman to defend Him? Did
> the reaction of the clergy, their unwillingness to countenance a free competition of
> ideas, express a sense of insecurity on their part? Or, was it, perhaps, . . . the
> prospect . . . of technological unemployment?

In his graduate courses, White was very different than in his undergraduate
classes. With graduate students, most of whom already accepted his views, he
was relaxed and at times even jovial. Lewis Binford recalled his first graduate
class with White:

> Leslie White—the dragon slayer of Boasianism, the terror in debate, the irascible
> "deviant" who insisted that science was not a popularity poll—was my teacher.
> Every student had to take his History of Anthropology. I had pictured a large man
> with a strong voice, stern face, and cold, forbidding exterior. I walked into class,
> seating myself . . . directly in front of the teacher's desk. All the students were in
> their places before class began. . . . A small man with a shy smile and an arm full
> of papers came into the room. He placed the papers on the desk, shuffled them,
> and looked up, quietly saying, "My name is Leslie White."
> He looked more like a postmaster in a small Midwestern town than the dragon
> slayer I had pictured. He took out his note cards and began lecturing. His mind
> worked . . . [with a] sharp, sophisticated wit and a devastating sarcasm, all pre-
> sented in a gentle voice. . . . He would offer an empirical generalization regarding
> some position or bias alleged to have characterized Boas and proceed to read fif-
> teen quotes documenting the validity of his generalization. . . . His logic was made

explicit, his interpretations were put out for criticism, and he supplied you with the criteria and rules for criticism. (Binford 1972: 6–7)

Being a graduate student under White at Michigan in the early 1950s was exciting and exhilarating. We students had the feeling that we were being armed with powerful intellectual tools with which to go out and conquer the world for evolution and culturology. And in the early 1950s much of the world remained to be conquered. Most of it, in fact, was in enemy hands. At anthropology meetings it was Michigan against the field, and we would engage in prolonged and intense discussions with graduate students from other schools, especially Columbia, Chicago, and Northwestern. We never doubted for a moment that our views (White's views), then held by only a tiny minority, would ultimately triumph. I must add that we did this entirely on our own. We were never sent out to fight for White's theories. On the contrary, White disliked discipleship and never encouraged it. He attracted students very readily, but never tried to found a "Whitean School."

I turn now to the contributions of Leslie White to the science of anthropology. Chief among these was the resuscitation of cultural evolutionism. It must be difficult for younger students today to imagine that there was a time in American anthropology when cultural evolutionism was rejected and denounced. But such a rejection there was, and the results of it were crippling to anthropology. As White wrote, "It is particularly unfortunate that [Boas] and his disciples have rejected the theory of cultural evolution so vigorously and so thoroughly, for it has tended to deprive ethnology of one of science's most fundamental and vitalizing conceptions" (1947a: 192). However, he did not believe that this rejection could continue indefinitely, and he wrote, "The time will come, we may confidently expect, when the theory of evolution will again prevail in the science of culture as it has in the biological and the physical sciences" (1943: 356). Single-handedly at first, White led the struggle to restore evolutionism to ethnology.

The opening salvo in this battle, scarcely heard at the time, was fired in the early 1930s. Bernhard J. Stern's *Lewis Henry Morgan, Social Evolutionist* had just been published, and in it Stern had written that "cultures, no matter how primitive, are too complex and the forms of combinations of social institutions too variable to fit into any definite social evolutionary scheme" (1931: 135). In reviewing the book, White took exception to this statement, saying: "Mr. Stern, like many preceding critics, points out errors of Morgan's procedure, and then throws overboard the concept of evolutionary development of culture. This is quite unwarranted, in the reviewer's opinion. Mr. Morgan's shortcomings in the seventies do not invalidate a concept of cultural evolution in 1931" (1931: 483).

The ensuing struggle to rehabilitate cultural evolutionism that White undertook was long and difficult. Late in his life, he wrote:

The ethnologist who held to the theory of evolution found neither friend nor refuge on the anthropological landscape. For years I was virtually alone in my advocacy of cultural evolutionism. To make matters worse, I came to the defense of Lewis H. Morgan; I felt that he had been treated very unfairly by Boas and his disciples . . . and labored to restore him to the place of dignity, honor, and great scientific achievement that he had enjoyed during his lifetime. . . . I was ridiculed and scoffed at. Everyone knew that evolutionism was dead; my non-conformist behavior was regarded as an aberration. . . . (White 1987: 14)[6]

In his attempt to reestablish evolutionism, White met not merely intellectual opposition but personal derision. He recalled one such instance:

In 1939 . . . I presented a paper at the annual meeting of the American Anthropological Association held at the University of Chicago in which I spoke out in a forthright manner in support of evolutionist theory in ethnology. When I had finished, Ralph Linton, the chairman of the session, remarked that I ought to be given the courtesy extended to suspected horse thieves and shady gamblers in the days of the Wild West, namely, to allow them to get out of town before sundown. (White 1987: 14)[7]

In time, of course, Steward and V. Gordon Childe came to be regarded as allies of White in this struggle, and their prestige and influence no doubt helped evolutionism appear less the personal crotchet of one man. But the roles played by Steward and Childe in the fight for evolutionism remained limited and qualified. Steward himself wrote: "For many years Leslie White stood virtually alone in his uncompromising support of the 19th century cultural evolutionists and in opposition to the followers of Franz Boas" (1960: 144).

In rehabilitating the concept of evolution White had to refute the various arguments raised against it by members of the Boas school. Lowie had argued, for example, that the facts of diffusion negated evolution, and White replied that one had to distinguish between the culture history of a people and the evolution of culture as a whole. Among the Boasians the feeling prevailed, born out of an exaggerated cultural relativism, that cultures are incommensurable, as Ruth Benedict put it. Thus they could not be rated objectively, let alone rank-ordered numerically. To this White answered that Boas and his students failed to distinguish between "arbitrary" and "subjective." All standards of measurement are arbitrary, he said, but not necessarily subjective. There were indeed objective ways in which cultures could be compared, such as the amount of energy harnessed, and on this basis they could not only be compared, but also ranked in numerical order. And to the argument, How can one speak of evolutionary regularities when, among the Australian aborigines, a simple technology is coupled with a complex social organization? White replied that one must not confuse a certain intricacy in kinship systems with overall complexity of social structure.

White's first major affirmation in print of the validity of cultural evolutionism appeared in "Science is *Sciencing*" in 1938. He reaffirmed it the following year in his article "A Problem in Kinship Terminology." However, the first article that he devoted entirely to evolution and its causes was "Energy and the Evolution of Culture," published in the *American Anthropologist* in 1943. In it White for the first time proposed what has since been called "White's Law," namely, that culture evolves as the amount of energy harnessed per capita per year increases.

The campaign to rehabilitate cultural evolutionism within anthropology was hard and slow. White published a succession of articles (1945a, 1945b, 1947a, 1947b, 1947c) in which he pressed the issue vigorously, but it took fifteen years or so following the publication of "Energy and the Evolution of Culture" before it could be said that evolutionism in ethnology had fought its way back to respectability. We can take 1959, the year of the Darwin centennial, as marking the final triumph. The hundredth anniversary of the publication of *The Origin of Species* was celebrated by a major symposium at the University of Chicago in which a galaxy of internationally known scientists participated, as well as by a series of lectures by distinguished anthropologists at the Anthropological Society of Washington. White read papers at both meetings, and both were later published (1959b, 1960b). The same year saw the publication of White's volume *The Evolution of Culture* (1959a). And the following year, writing in the foreword to Sahlins and Service's *Evolution and Culture*, White felt able to proclaim that "antievolutionism has run its course and once more the theory of evolution is on the march" (1960a: vii).

Naturally, White was pleased to see cultural evolutionism restored to a place of honor in anthropology. But he once observed to me that now that evolutionism had become not only respectable but fashionable, evolutionists seemed to be coming out of the woodwork. And he went on to say that anthropologists he had once regarded as adversaries on this issue were now talking as if they had been evolutionists all along. As usual, White was leery of bandwagons. Noting the common tendency for Johnny-come-latelies to try to take over a movement, he commented, "Now that cultural evolutionism has become orthodox, I hope I won't be excommunicated."

In discussing modern evolutionism, especially as expounded by White, a number of anthropologists have referred to it as "neoevolutionism." White bridled at this term. In the preface to *The Evolution of Culture* he wrote:

let it be said, and with emphasis, that the theory set forth here cannot properly be called "neo-evolutionism." . . . Neo-evolutionism is a misleading term: it has been used to imply that the theory of evolution today is somehow different from the theory of eighty years ago. We reject any such notion. The *theory* of evolution set forth in this work does not differ one whit in principle from that expressed in Tylor's *Anthropology* in 1881. (1959a: ix)

In class, White often poked fun at "neoevolutionism," saying there was no such thing, any more than there was "neowhiskey." On his sixtieth birthday a party was held for him at the Sahlins home, and while Marshall was taking his guests' orders for drinks he turned to White and said, "Leslie, how about some neowhiskey?"[8]

Apart from rehabilitating evolutionism, White's most important contribution to anthropology was his clarification of the concept of culture. His article "The Concept of Culture," published in the *American Anthropologist* in 1959, is in my opinion the most acute analysis of the concept that has ever appeared. Kroeber and Kluckhohn's monograph *Culture* (1952) was essentially a catalogue of definitions, with only a tentative attempt to arrive at a consensus definition—which in any case would likely not have proved satisfactory to anyone. The definition of culture that was probably most common at the time was that culture is learned behavior. But animals as far down the phylogenetic scale as cockroaches can learn; I think most anthropologists would demand a more restrictive definition than to grant cockroaches culture. Into the miasma of conflicting and inadequate definitions, White introduced his own classic one: "Culture is a class of phenomena, comprising objects, acts, ideas, and attitudes that are dependent upon the use of symbols." White held that there was a qualitative difference between the mind of man and that of all other animals, including the higher primates, and he believed that this difference was based on the uniquely human capacity to invent symbols by bestowing meaning on things in which meaning did not inhere.

A milestone in the discussion of the basis of culture was White's article "The Symbol: The Origin and Basis of Human Behavior," first published in 1940. White had submitted it to the *American Sociological Review*, then to the *American Journal of Sociology*, both of whose editors rejected it. Finally the article was accepted by the journal *Philosophy of Science*.[9] The proposition it set forth was simple: "All culture . . . depends upon the symbol. It was the exercise of the symbolic faculty that brought culture into existence and it is the use of symbols that makes the perpetuation of culture possible. Without the symbol there would be no culture, and man would be merely an animal, not a human being" (1940a: 460).

In addition to characterizing the concept of culture, White proposed that the science that studied culture as a distinct and autonomous class of phenomena should have a special name, "culturology." The word, as well as the concept, met great resistance (White 1969: xxxv). Objections were raised that "culturology" was a barbarism, that it grated on the ear, that it combined Greek and Latin roots, and so on. C. W. M. Hart, for example, found it "a label . . . horrible to look at and as horrible to hear" (1950: 88). (The same objections greeted the introduction of the term "sociology" into the English language [Carneiro 1974: 549].) Nevertheless, White had the satisfaction of seeing the term included in *Webster's New International Dictionary* in 1959. White developed the notion of culturology most fully in his book *The Science of Culture*, which appeared in 1949. (While the volume was in press, he discovered that in coining the term he had been anticipated by the German chemist and philosopher Wilhelm Ostwald, who had used it [*Kulturologie*] in 1909 [White 1969: xxxv]. This discovery was exhilarating for White.)

The idea underlying culturology has been resisted and decried fully as much as the term itself. Indeed, culturology is by far the least accepted part of White's philosophy. It was opposed in the same way that Kroeber's "Superorganic" had been in 1917; namely, for those whose professional endeavors focused on the thoughts and feelings and actions of individuals *as such*, leaving the human being out of the equation explaining culture seemed unwarranted and even perverse. White dealt with these objections repeatedly (see, especially, "Culturological vs. Psychological Determinants of Human Behavior" and "Cultural Determinants of Mind," both chapters in White 1949a). Opposition to culturology comes from new sources nowadays. Chief among them are those ecologically oriented anthropologists who are closely associated with the field of animal ecology. Culture, for them, is simply the behavior of a particular animal species, *Homo sapiens*. They tend to regard human behavior as no different in kind from the behavior of other animals—or at least they propose to study it *as if* it were no different.[10] To those who see no qualitative difference in, say, the mode of hunting of a band of Pygmies and a troop of baboons, White might have asked: How would a baboon proceed to give the left hindquarter of every animal he killed to his mother-in-law while at the same time embarrassedly avoiding her glance?

However, there is a more fundamental question to be raised about White's view of the study of culture, one not so easily dispelled. Is there an inconsistency or contradiction between White's culturology and his cultural materialism? Can he hold that cultural phenomena are to be explained solely in terms of other cultural phenomena and at the same time argue that raw materials and energy sources, things whose existence is external to culture, are the prime movers of cultural development?

For White, traits often come into existence as a response to problems of adaptation and survival. Thus, in accounting for the origin of the incest taboo, White accepts Tylor's argument that it arose by human societies reacting adaptively to the choice between "marrying out or being killed out." But if culture traits arise in response to the exigencies of life, how can we say that they are explainable solely in terms of themselves? If the availability of raw materials and energy sources, and their incorporation into a culture, play a determining role in the way culture develops, must we not say that external environmental factors, no less than the interplay of existing culture traits, have shaped that culture? And if so, what happens to the autonomy of culture?

That White himself had become aware of this dilemma and felt that he had to resolve it is evident from certain passages in his last major published work,

The Concept of Cultural Systems (1975). Here White remarks that thinking about cultural systems while writing this volume made him realize that the idea that "the function of culture is to serve the needs of man" now seemed as invalid as it had been "obvious" to him before. On the other hand, he says, the statement, "'culture is a thing, or process, *sui generis*' means just what it says; and 'culture is to be explained in terms of culture' still holds." He adds that he was led "to see culture in a new light. No longer was it viewed as a handmaiden of Homo sapiens, to preserve and comfort him, but as a sector of reality in its own right whose behavior was governed by laws of its own" (1975: xi). And finally, in the concluding chapter of the book, he repeats: "We no longer think of culture as designed to serve the needs of man; culture goes on its own way in accordance with laws of its own" (1975: 159).[11]

White thus felt the weight of the inconsistency and tried to resolve it. But was his resolution satisfactory? Is not culture, first and foremost, something that man interposes between himself and the external world in an effort to secure his survival? And does it not have to fill that role before it can fill any other? Before it can take on "a life of its own" does it not have to ensure the life of its carriers? Is not culture, then, irresistibly concerned with the practical necessity of adapting man to his environment? And if this is so, can culturology dispense with ecology? Must it not in fact embrace it as an indispensable ally? And finally, cannot culturology grant a major causal role to those aspects of the environment affecting subsistence, security, and survival and still retain a large measure of validity?

White was well aware of the importance of the environment, but he kept it at bay theoretically while propounding culturology. This he did by saying that the environment, although significant in forming particular societies, could be averaged out when dealing with "culture as a whole" and therefore canceled from the equation used to account for evolutionary developments at large. This way of dealing with the issue never satisfied Steward, who was always very much concerned with the environmental side of cultural ecology. In his review of *The Science of Culture*, Steward wrote:

> Cultural differences are in part a function of the environmental variable, which White will not admit into the formula of causality. . . . Evidently shunning the stigma of "environmental determinism," he refuses to see that any given cultural heritage would have to be adapted to local habitats and that the processes of adaptation, the cultural ecology, would be creative ones. (1950b: 209)

This criticism seems to me somewhat overstated. White would surely agree with Steward that environment partly determines individual cultures: The Plains shaped the Sioux and the Arctic shaped the Eskimo. No one can doubt that. The real issue is: Can White legitimately rule out the environment in laying out the evolution of culture as a whole?

Before we can answer this question we first need to ask, just what is "culture as a whole"? Is it the sum total of all particular cultures, or at least of most of them? If so, since the environment is always operative on particular cultures, and operative in widely different ways, doesn't it necessarily affect "culture as a whole"? In that case, can we really hold it constant and cancel it out of the equation? The answer would seem to depend on the problem at hand. If we are trying to account for the existence of such traits as the couvade or teknonymy or the mother-in-law taboo, the effect of environment would appear to be negligible. Thus, in such instances, we could probably cancel it out. But what about other problems? What if our problem were, say, to account for the origin of the state? I have argued that environment was not neutral with regard to state formation (Carneiro 1970). One type of environment favored it, another type hindered it. Can we then say that in attacking the problem of state formation the environment is really cancelable? Not without vitiating our best explanation of the process. Should not culturology consider entering into a treaty of peace and mutual assistance with ecology?

I believe it is erroneous to think of White as lying outside of cultural ecology. In my opinion, when everything is considered, he can be found to be very much in the ecological camp. Steward is generally credited with being the father of cultural ecology, and there is no intent here to minimize his contributions to this field.[12] However, if judged by the number of students actually stimulated to pursue work along cultural-ecological lines and the positive accomplishment of these students, White need not take second place to anyone. White's students have been in the forefront of the development of a systematic, ecological approach in both archaeology and ethnology.

In White's days as a teacher, before he ever thought there might be a contradiction between culturology and cultural materialism, he taught them both, and his students absorbed them both. He constantly stressed the importance of the material conditions of existence, including the environment, and emphasized the function of culture as an adaptive mechanism in coping with these conditions. His students saw in this a clear invitation to try to account for particular social systems through the interplay of particular environmental, technological, and economic factors. A number of us tried to do just that. For example, Sahlins's Ph.D. thesis (published in 1958) was an attempt to do so for Polynesia, just as my dissertation undertook to do the same for a tribal village in central Brazil. And one can hardly fail to cite Binford, who made clear his great intellectual debt to White and who, in turn, has been enormously influential in bringing White's evolutionism and cultural materialism to bear on archaeology, thereby helping to create the "new archaeology."[13]

Closely related to White's advocacy of the autonomy of culture was his espousal of cultural determinism. According to this view, what one believes and how one behaves—no matter how much they may seem to come from the most intimate recesses of one's personality—are actually the products or reflections of one's culture. "Human behavior," wrote White, "is but the response of a primate who can symbol to this extrasomatic continuum called culture" (1949b: 379). White was a strict determinist. He denied there was such a thing as free will, maintaining it was merely an illusion (1948a). And he not only asserted that human behavior was determined by culture, he stressed that among these cultural determinants the material ones were paramount. Thus he minimized the role of ideas, values, and purpose, regarding them simply as epiphenomena of the material determinants. For White, the culture process was *impelled* by forces rather than being *drawn* by ideas.

This point of view was unpalatable, even anathema, to many. As White himself attested, a number of persons found the philosophy of cultural determinism "exceedingly repugnant" (1969: xxi). Today, thirty years after the publication of *The Science of Culture*, the issue is by no means dead. Even among anthropologists there are those who still deny cultural determinism outright or at least seek to restrict its application. And if cultural determinism was opposed within the ranks of anthropology, whose members had been thoroughly exposed to the concept of culture, one can well imagine that this philosophy would have been resisted all the more outside of the profession. This was true not only among literary, humanistic, and lay audiences, but among practitioners of other sciences as well.

Some who reject cultural determinism find solace and sustenance in the alternative philosophy that assures them that their fate is in their own hands. This is, of course, an ancient philosophy, and as White wrote, "primitive philosophies had other functions than explanatory [ones]; they sustained man with illusions, they provided him with courage, comfort, consolation, and confidence." However, the scientific status of a philosophy is not to be gauged by how much it inspires, consoles, or assuages, but by how well it explains events. On this score White's culturological and deterministic treatment of such problems as the rise of monotheism or the invention of the steam engine is much more discerning and convincing than an explanation based on the "iconoclasm" of Ikhnaton or the "genius" of James Watt (1949a: 190–281).

As noted above, critics of White sometimes assailed him as a fatalist (generally failing, however, to distinguish between fatalism and determinism). White, however, took pains to contrast what was determined and expectable in culture with what was, from a culturological point of view, adventitious. That is to say, he distinguished between the *culture process* and *history*. The culture process was a stream of interacting cultural elements whose general direction was clear and whose course could not be deflected by the intervention of even the most forceful or gifted individual. History, on the other hand, was a fabric in which the idiosyncratic and the fortuitous could leave their mark.

White's most pointed expression of the role of historical accident occurred at the meeting of the AAA at which he gave his controversial paper on religion. The paper was highly deterministic, emphasizing how the economic and social system of a society determined its religious system. After the formal presentation, someone in the audience asked White if he didn't believe in contingency in history. Without hesitating, White replied: "Yes, I believe in contingency in history. If a certain Corsican girl had not left her scarf on the beach one night two hundred years ago and gone back to retrieve it, the whole course of European history could have been different."

White was a formidable polemicist. Through the years he fought a number of battles in print, most notably with Lowie over cultural evolution (White 1943, 1944, 1945b, 1947b, 1947c; Lowie 1946a, 1946b). Much as we students enjoyed reading his spirited refutations of his opponents, some of us came to feel that White devoted too much of his time to them. He had been too long and unrelenting in his destruction of Boas (e.g., White 1963, 1966). The old antievolutionist had been killed and his corpse interred; there seemed no need to dig up the body and pummel it again.[14] We would much rather have seen Leslie pursue his own researches. We dearly wanted him to complete his history of ethnological theory, his biography of Morgan, and his manual of culturology—works that he had conceived and talked of more than twenty years before he died, but which he never came close to executing.[15]

On rare occasions, White seems to have recognized and regretted the trammels that his crusade against antievolutionism had placed on him. In his foreword to Sahlins and Service's *Evolution and Culture*, he remarked that in responding to the propositions advanced by the Boasian antievolutionists, he was restricted in his scope and perspective; he had to develop a type of theory in opposition to specific criticisms and attacks. But, he added:

> these younger anthropologists have been free from such handicaps. They were not reared in the atmosphere of antievolutionism; they accepted cultural evolutionism from the very start and have therefore been relatively free from the restrictions of polemics; they have been free to explore the implications of the theory of evolution as it applied to culture and to develop its many and fruitful possibilities. (1960a: xi)

Of White's other contributions I can list only a few. He contributed to a solution of the vexing problem of the Crow and Omaha systems of kinship terminology (1939). He resurrected Tylor's solution to the problem of the origin of the incest taboo, buttressed it with further argument and evidence, and gave it much wider currency (1948b). His treatments of invention, of the culture process, of the individual and culture, and of the Great Man theory are all noteworthy elucidations of these problems. His article "The Expansion of the Scope of Science" (1947d) presents the first major theory of the filiation of the sciences since the classic treatments of this problem by Auguste Comte and by Spencer in the nineteenth century.

Some persons, familiar only with White's contributions to theory, have tended to regard him as an "armchair theorist" unacquainted with the chastening realities of fieldwork. Yet this was anything but true. Not only did White do fieldwork; he published separate monographs on five Keresan Indian Pueblos: Acoma (1932a, 1973), San Felipe (1932b), Santo Domingo (1935), Santa Ana (1942a), and Sia (1962). It is true, though, that he rarely cited his Pueblo data in his theoretical writings, maintaining that fieldwork and theorizing were separate and distinct activities. Indeed, his field monographs are descriptive treatises with no theoretical slant.[16]

It is not easy to summarize White's contribution to anthropology since it was so extensive and profound. But to my mind the essence of it was this: White entered anthropology at a time when the prevailing current of opinion stressed the diversity, idiosyncrasy, and incommensurability of cultures. Accordingly, cultures were dealt with descriptively, historically, and even artistically. Generalizing and theorizing were frowned upon and avoided; anthropology was idiographic rather than nomothetic. White reacted against this tradition. He knew what science was in its fullest sense, and he saw the need for something more than collecting and classifying facts. He felt the necessity to develop concepts and theories, to see culture as a unified process displaying regularities and revealing general trends. Thus, he began to try to reconstruct the evolution of culture and, in so doing, concerned himself not only with sequences and stages but with the dynamics of the process as well. Gradually, he hammered out and riveted together a coherent and powerful philosophy that could bring order and intelligibility to the multiplicity of cultures. And he was eloquent, forceful, and untiring in his attempts to show the profession that this was where the future of anthropology lay.

White never felt he had to conquer the world single-handedly, though. He saw his task as that of laying out a ground plan for others to follow and fill in the details. Once, when I asked him why he had never actually calculated the amount of energy harnessed per capita per year by any society, he replied, "That's for you to do." He saw himself, I think, as one who had forged the tools, and he was content to have his successors accomplish with them what he had left undone. And those of us who studied under White felt not only that we had been technically equipped for the task, but also that we had had instilled in us all the incentive needed to pursue it.

How will history treat Leslie White? It is the fate of many germinal thinkers to suffer a temporary eclipse in the years immediately following their death. As they cease to be "contemporary," an increasing portion of their work remains unread. At the same time, their contributions may be absorbed into the intellectual bloodstream of their science and no longer be remembered as their own. Or they may even be assigned to someone else. This fate may yet overtake White. Already there is some evidence of it. An example is the treatment White receives at the hands of Marvin Harris in *The Rise of Anthropological Theory* (1968), the book from which many students today derive their history of the science. Harris consistently belittles or ignores White's contributions. Yet the curious fact is that the three leitmotifs of Harris's book—evolutionism, cultural materialism, and the importance of energy—all were either introduced into anthropology by White or were most strongly championed by him.[17]

Ultimately, as with other thinkers, White will survive through his effect on those he taught, directly or indirectly. The magnitude of the influence on those who studied under him is perhaps difficult for others to comprehend. This influence was intellectual and professional rather than personal, but it was also more than that. Without being paternal, as was the case with Boas, it was nevertheless encompassing. It affected not only careers but lives as well.

In May 1975 I was with Napoleon Chagnon in a small mission station on the Upper Orinoco in the middle of Yanomamö territory. We had just left the Yanomamö villages we had been studying and had come to the mission on our way back to civilization. Some mail had accumulated for Chagnon, and the first letter he opened was from White. Despite his ill health, he had written to express interest in the progress of the field trip. After reading the letter, Chagnon opened one from his wife and learned that White had died. Chagnon told me the news. After a moment I said, "If it hadn't been for Leslie White, I wouldn't be here right now." And Chagnon replied, "Neither would I."

DISCUSSION

SPENCER TERKEL: I think it's clear from White's writings and also from his predecessors'—Spencer, Morgan, Tylor, and the Russian evolutionists—that this is a Lamarckian evolutionism. Could you talk about the relationship of White's evolutionism to the Darwinian concept of evolution?

CARNEIRO: I think White's evolutionism was first and foremost Spencerian. Spencer was convinced that Lamarck was right only in the sense that he saw that evolution explained things better than creation did. I don't see White's evolutionism in terms of Lamarck at all. I don't know that he ever read Lamarck; he certainly wasn't influenced by him. I also think you have to distinguish two aspects of evolution: one is the process itself, the nature of the process; and the other is the kind of dynamic that you introduce to account for the process. The nature of the process, as White sees it, is essentially one of increasing complexity, which is straightforwardly Spencerian. The motive force that pushes evolution ahead he sees, of course, as energy.

Darwin's evolutionism sees really any kind of change in the organism as being evolutionary; this is the basis of specific evolution. The Spencerian view—

White's view—is to accept as evolutionary only those changes that give rise to greater differentiation of structure and specialization of function.

ALEXANDER LESSER: I was impressed with your description of Leslie White's gentle personality and his pleasant relations with other people. One point you made brought back a question that has been in my mind. You remarked that many of you had come to feel that he should stop the belaboring attacks on Boas, and, nevertheless, he really didn't. There was a great deal in his attacks on Boas that was bitter and personal. I have been asked why many times, and I have never been able to answer. I have heard one theory, that White wanted to take a Ph.D. at Columbia and that Boas refused to entertain him as a student; I know this is false. There are all sorts of reasons why White's personal links with Columbia should have been friendly. For instance, White did most of his field research under the patronage of Elsie Clews Parsons, who was very close to Boas and did a great deal of financing for students at Columbia as well.

CARNEIRO: White never talked about this with me, but it's pretty evident that for ten or fifteen years White was a virtual outcast. He was espousing theories that Boas's students, and most American anthropologists, thought erroneous and wrongheaded; they belittled him and scorned him. The defensiveness and the ire aroused by being in a minority position and having abuse heaped on him for years took its toll on him. All I can say about the extended attack on Boas is: I don't condone it, and I can't explain it.

ERIC WOLF: You identified Leslie White as one of the ancestors of the ecological interest. It's true that a lot of the people who were influenced by White have been interested, in their work, in the relationship of technology, environment, and energy; it's also true that White wrote the preface to the Sahlins and Service book, in which general and specific evolution are discussed and in which a strong ecological influence appears. But in earlier statements White said that environment is a constant in the evolution of culture; that when we look at the evolution of culture in general, at the cultural process in general, the environment can be regarded as a constant. I have wondered whether there was a shift in his position at some point. At one time White and Steward locked horns; although they both talked evolution, they really talked past each other. But there may have been some accommodation between them, perhaps in the late 1950s.

CARNEIRO: I'm not aware that White ever changed his position on the effect of the environment. He did say, in speaking of the evolution of culture as a whole, that one could hold environment constant; I don't know that he ever modified this view. I also don't know of any evidence that Steward influenced him. What he's written about Steward has generally been critical, although in his courses we were encouraged to read Steward. We were made to feel that his ecological approach was a positive way of attacking problems. I don't see any interstimulation between the two that led to a modification of views.

I don't believe that one can hold environment constant in explaining culture process as a whole. For example, in looking at the rise of civilization, there are certain key environmental variables. But White used to put an equation on the board in which he used symbols for environment, for technology, for energy, and so on. The environment was one such factor which you had to take account of in explaining a specific situation. Certainly we students came away with the feeling that it was perfectly legitimate and valid and promising to apply the ecological approach and to introduce environmental factors. White rarely used the word "ecology," but we absorbed this point of view; it was implicit in the way he talked that this line of approach would be a rewarding one to follow.

SYDEL SILVERMAN: In Murphy's discussion of Steward he said he believed that an anthropologist's real teachers were the people he or she worked with and not his academic professors. Yet for all the ethnographic work that White pursued in the Southwest, there seems to be no link between his ethnography and his theory. Do you see any such link?

CARNEIRO: Not really, and White himself was aware of it. Barnes takes this point up in his Festschrift foreword. One would have to say that in expounding his theory White simply found better examples elsewhere than in the Southwest. He thought of this work in the Southwest as straightforward ethnography, not essentially different from that carried out by members of the Boas school— just recording what the native culture had been. When it came to theorizing, the entire panoply of the world's cultures was available to him, and he selected whatever suited his purposes.

MAY EBIHARA: In view of White's antipathy to Boas, it is rather curious that his undergraduate course was called "The Mind of Primitive Man."

CARNEIRO: I think I know where the name comes from. White had established a course by that title at the University of Buffalo and then brought it with him when he started to teach at Michigan. The name does not surprise me at all; remember that until the early 1930s he was still a Boasian. He had absorbed Boas's ideas from Goldenweiser and Sapir and had no reason not to borrow the title of the famous book by Boas for his course. It was a very varied course, and he changed the content quite considerably from one year to another.

ROBERT BETTEREL: I can remember him saying at the beginning of "The Mind of Primitive Man" that the content did not have anything to do with the title, that he had inherited the title a long time ago and it had become associated with him; so he just kept the title and shifted the content.

STANLEY NADEL: He also used to say that he gave true/false questions for exams; he didn't bother changing the questions from year to year, he merely changed the answers.

On the point about ecology, White always made a break very sharply between evolution and history; ecology fell under the rubric of history as being something specific. This was not the idea of specific evolution, which I don't think he subscribed to. His conception of evolution always began with technology, and never considered environment or ecology.

BETTEREL: Yes, he made a very definite distinction between history and evolution, and there was never much of a connection between the two. History was specific, adaptation was specific, ecology was specific. Evolution had to do with changes of a global sort, that had nothing to do with specific societies.

CARNEIRO: I think that explains why in his book *The Evolution of Culture* he doesn't try to cast, say, Andean civilization or Mesopotamian civilization into his framework, or bring into his discussion details of the actual history of these areas. That was uncongenial to what he wanted to do.

GERTRUDE DOLE: Even though White didn't stress ecology, or even focus on it, he did stress another distinction—that between culture in general and *a* culture or society. With respect to the latter, in *a* culture he saw the environment as being effective; that had to do with his concept of contingencies in the history of mankind. The evolution of culture referred to cultures in general, and in that context, environment could be held constant.

SILVERMAN: Was White's position on the qualitative difference between man and other animals ever modified as a result of the development of primate studies and the newer views of human evolution, which led many people to reject his rather dogmatic stance?

CARNEIRO: I don't know whether, in the last ten years or so of his life, he really kept up to date with the new studies. I have no indication that he ever did modify his views. I personally think that the evidence isn't all in.

BIOGRAPHICAL NOTE

Photo by Ruth Q. Liebowitz   c. 1990

ROBERT L. CARNEIRO was born in New York City in 1927 and grew up in the Riverdale section of the Bronx. His interest in the quantitative expression of facts goes back to his childhood; he "practically teethed on the *World Al-manac.*" After graduating from Horace Mann, a private boys' high school, Carneiro went to the University of Michigan. He planned to major in journalism, but after working on the campaign of an older student who was running for Congress, he opted for a major in political science. He soon became disenchanted with the field when he found it was not a science at all. He "champed at the bit at the excessive respect we were showing the political theories of thinkers who did not have the factual knowledge or necessary attitude to solve the problems they tackled." Enrolling in two anthropology courses with Leslie White, he discovered that *"here* was a discipline with the theoretical and factual arsenal to attack those questions which now seemed to [him] so important."

A graduation present from his father in 1949 took Carneiro on a trip around the world, after which he entered the family's newspaper-machinery export business. After five months he found that he was unfit for business and unhappy pursuing it, and he decided to return to Michigan for graduate work in anthropology. Taking all the courses in theory (taught mostly by White) and ethnography that the department had to offer, Carneiro "became a dedicated culturologist and evolutionist, and enjoyed arguing these approaches with anyone who would listen."

Wanting to do fieldwork with a primitive and isolated group as untouched as possible, Carneiro went to the Amazon Basin in 1953–1954. His dissertation, "Subsistence and Social Structure, An Ecological Study of the Kuikuru Indians," earned him the Ph.D. in 1957. The title, which may be the first use of the term *ecological* in a dissertation, reflects his early interest in cultural ecology, which he always thought was perfectly compatible with White's cultural materialism and evolutionism. Subsequently, Carneiro worked with two other Amazonian groups, the Amahuaca of eastern Peru (1960–1961) and the Yanomamö of southern Venezuela (1975). He proved to be an avid field ethnographer, who found there was no experience as rewarding as putting down on paper cultural data that no one else has ever recorded before

Carneiro taught at the University of Wisconsin (Madison) in 1956–1957. The following year he joined the American Museum of Natural History as an assistant curator of South American ethnology. He has been a curator since 1969, supervising the ethnographic section of the Hall of South American Peoples, as well as temporary exhibits such as "Baseball as America" (2002). He has also taught (in visiting appointments) at Hunter College, Columbia University, the University of California at Los Angeles, Pennsylvania State University, the University of Victoria, and Fordham University.

Carneiro's major theoretical interest is cultural evolution, which he joins to ecology. The most important intellectual influence on him, after White, has been Herbert Spencer, about whom he has written "resuscitative" articles. Carneiro has applied his ecological-evolutionary approach to such problems as the origin of the state (1970) and the social implications of slash-and-burn cultivation. He has a passion for facts—for quantified information and for formulas that express distilled facts in their logical relationship ("the most compact encapsulation of a regularity you can have"). But facts are of a piece with theory in Carneiro's anthropology, which has been guided by his belief that "the function of theory was to explain fact, and that the more one immersed oneself in facts, the better theory one could do."

Carneiro had a close association with White until his death, and he coedited a Festschrift for White (Dole and Carneiro 1960) and a volume of White's essays (Dillingham and Carneiro 1987). His recent publications include *The Muse of History and the Science of Culture* (2000) and *Evolutionism in Cultural Anthropology: A Critical History* (2003).

Robert Redfield in his office at the University of Chicago. University of Chicago Library

8

ROBERT REDFIELD

Eric R. Wolf
Nathaniel Tarn

Among Leslie White's fellow students in the joint department of sociology and anthropology at the University of Chicago during the 1920s was Robert Redfield. Anthropology there was still in the Boasian tradition, but the functionalist anthropology developing at the time was also influential—an influence that became pronounced after anthropology became a separate department and A. R. Radcliffe-Brown joined it (remaining from 1931 to 1937). Redfield spent his entire professional life in that department, beginning from his first teaching assignment in 1927; he became a professor in 1934. He was still an active teacher and scholar at the time of his death in 1958.

Redfield was one of the originators of the anthropology of complex societies. He was perhaps the first American anthropologist to do fieldwork in a peasant village, with his study in 1926 of Tepoztlán in Mexico. In part a holistic study in the spirit of the new functionalism, in part an application of the Chicago brand of urban sociology to the hinterlands beyond Mexico City, it marked the beginning of his enduring interest in folk (later called "peasant") societies and in the influence of urban society upon them. A pioneer of community studies, Redfield in the 1930s inspired a number of landmark studies of communities in modern nations. His folk–urban concept was enormously influential in both anthropology and sociology during the 1940s and 1950s. As the predominant theoretical framework for dealing with complex societies at the time that anthropology expanded its interests in that direction after World War II, it was not only applied to many areas of the world, but it also stimulated a critical literature that led to the development of alternative approaches. Redfield's later general works on the little community and on peasant society and culture became the first texts in the anthropological study of peasantry.

Redfield's interests focused on culture understood as meanings and values, and he saw social relations primarily as vehicles for the communication of ideas. Like Ruth Benedict on national character, he applied to complex societies the culture concept in its ideational and integrative sense—as conferring and organizing meaning—but his view of civilization was more differentiated and processual than Benedict's. His approach contrasted diametrically with Julian Steward's application of the culture concept to complex societies, which gave priority to "basic socio-economic institutions" and emphasized the differences among subcultures grounded in different productive processes. Redfield's work became the foundation for important symbolic studies of civilizations.

This chapter offers two perspectives on Robert Redfield. The first, by Eric R. Wolf, was presented at a conference in 1997, where it was offered as an appreciation and critique of Redfield's key role in the development of anthropological studies of peasants and of communities.[1] The second was written for the CUNY lecture series in 1976 by Nathaniel Tarn, a student of Redfield's who, after completing major research in Mesoamerica and in Southeast Asia, left anthropology. His paper differs in style and purpose from the others in this book, for he writes as both poet and anthropologist, considering Redfield from a distance of twenty years as a way of reflecting on the relationship between anthropologist and poet.[2]

When I entered graduate work in anthropology at Columbia University in 1946, Redfield's *Folk Culture of Yucatan* (1941) was one of the ten required books that one was expected to read from stem to stern, to learn by heart, and to take to heart. By the time I first went to Mexico in 1951, Redfield's folk–urban schematization was the major apple of intellectual contention among the rival anthropological patron–client sets of *indigenistas*, old-fashioned trait-counters, and developmental *socialistas*. Later, while serving as an underling at the University of Illinois at Urbana and occasionally journeying to Chicago to attend the famous Wednesday seminars, I had some personal contact with Redfield. I have thus learned much from Redfield, both in agreeing with him and, perhaps even more, in defining my differences from him.

Robert Redfield was born in 1897 in Chicago. His father was a successful lawyer, the grandson of an Englishman who settled in the Illinois countryside northwest of Chicago in the 1830s; his mother was the daughter of the Danish consul in Chicago. In his youth, Redfield typically spent the warm months of the year in the rural paternal "clan community" in Illinois. James Redfield has suggested that his father's conceptions of the "folk society" were shaped, even before he had any contact with the social sciences, by his experience of neighborly reciprocal relations there. Charles Leslie has also written that Redfield acquired there "a deep sense of the social changes that in a few generations had transformed a wilderness landscape, where pioneers encountered Indians, into an area of commercial farmlands adjoining the great industrial city" (Leslie 1968: 350). The colder six months, in contrast, were lived in the urban, "hyperrefined" ambience of his mother's Danish-speaking and Danish-traditionalizing kinfolk. One might discern in this cyclical alternation of residence between country and city a prefiguring of the folk–urban continuum.

A rather protected child, Redfield was first tutored at home. Then he attended the University of Chicago Laboratory School, where he developed literary interests, and he entered the University of Chicago in 1915. In 1917, however, he enlisted in an ambulance unit in support of the French army. After returning home, he briefly studied (and disliked) biology, and he eventually got a law degree and went to work in his father's firm. He married Margaret Park, the daughter of the sociologist Robert Park, and in 1923 the couple took a trip to Mexico. There they met the Chicago-trained anthropological archaeologist Manuel Gamio as well as the folklorist Frances Toor, both of whom had worked in Tepoztlán. This experience led Redfield to decide that he would be an anthropologist. He entered the newly revitalized anthropology program within the Department of Sociology and Anthropology at Chicago in 1924, and learned Boasian anthropology primarily from Fay-Cooper Cole, as well as sociology from Park.

American sociology had a late and inauspicious start around the turn of the century, with a strong drive to solve the "practical" problems of social disorganization and pathology. Park, however, belonged to a new generation of sociologists, who sought to find ways to combine general theories of society with empirical observation and interviewing. From the distance of a century this does not strike us as a very novel undertaking, but it was then in its uncertain infancy. Park (1864–1944), born on the Minnesota frontier, was first a journalist who specialized in human-interest stories drawn from various urban milieus. He then studied sociology at Harvard, and later with Georg Simmel and Wilhelm Windelband in Germany, and wrote his Ph.D. thesis on public opinion at Heidelberg in 1904. A decade later he joined Albion Small and W. I. Thomas at Chicago, and taught there until 1936. Thomas's role in American sociology is important because he coauthored with the Polish sociologist Florian Znaniecki the sociological landmark study *The Polish Peasant in Europe and America* (Thomas and Znaniecki 1958 [1918–1920]). Together, Thomas and Park, subsequently joined by Edward Burgess, developed the characteristic mode of inquiry of the Chicago school of sociology, aimed at comprehending the variations in social life within the urban settings and neighborhoods of a city. This orientation laid the basis for the required practicum for sociology students at Chicago in what was referred to as "the laboratory of the city."

Park, Redfield's sociological mentor as well as his father-in-law, took a Social Darwinist perspective on the competitive struggle for status among social groups, arguing that groups came to occupy different positions in the course of these struggles and that such differential positions in the struggle for status were correlated with differential positions in physical space. This perspective opened up a concern with race relations and, by implication, with questions of immigration, major issues at the time in the United States. (Park's own sympathies in these struggles lay with the competitively less successful groups, such as African Americans; he hoped that his science would contribute to their advancement in social position.) To pursue their interest in sociological mapping, Park and his student Roderick McKenzie baptized and developed the field of "human ecology." It yielded the Chicago ecological model of the city: the hub of the city was in an initial highly accessible, densely populated, and dominant central zone, which expanded outward concentrically to produce a succession of new zones of activities and settlements, each successive zone less dense and more marginal or peripheral than its predecessor.

Thus, when Redfield became a student in the Sociology and Anthropology Department, his burgeoning concern with Mexico first led him to carry out his practicum in the Mexican neighborhoods of Chicago. He drew from this the conclusion that there was a need to study the "conditions under which Mexicans in Chicago had been raised" in "semi-primitive village communities" in order to understand "the problems arising out of the growing Mexican immigration into the United States" (Stocking 1992: 303). It is current folklore that anthropologists at this time were entirely focused on the isolated rural community and paid no attention to the movements and experiences of migratory populations; but, in fact, Redfield's attention to problems of migration and immigration preceded his first community study in Mexico.

In 1926 Redfield and his family moved to Tepoztlán, on the reverse side of the mountains surrounding Mexico City. They lived in Tepoztlán for three and a half months, then sought sanctuary in Mexico City after a local battle between *Cristeros* and "Bolsheviks," and continued in "commuter fieldwork" for another four and a half months. After returning to Chicago, Redfield received a Ph.D. in 1928 for his "frankly sketchy synthesis" (Stocking 1992: 304) and then published a rewritten version as *Tepoztlán, A Mexican Village: A Study of Folklife* (1930).

This work pioneered a mode of study and representation that became, for several decades, a major genre of ethnological reporting. Theoretically, it did several things. It took the Chicago ecological approach to spatial distribution around a dominant center as an outcome of competition among populations: Mexico City was the dominant center, Tepoztlán an Indian village on its periphery, at the end of the line of transport from the capital. This ecological gradient corresponded to Clark Wissler's mapping of culture traits as spreading outward from a culture hub or center. Mexico City produced the traits of "civilization"; Tepoztlán received the diffused traits and mixed them with its own

cultural repertoire, in what later came to be known as a process of acculturation. But Redfield also converted the ecological gradient and the gradient in the
diffusion of culture traits into a gradient of a process of communication—"in
understanding culture process, the mode and character of the communication
should be the center of attention" (1962 [1930]: 148). Thus, Redfield also en-
visaged a gradient in the flow of cultural messages: from people in the big city
to the so-called *correctos* who lived around the central plaza of the village, at
the terminus of transport and communication. The *correctos*, in turn, communicated city ways to the *tontos*, the benighted folk in the rural neighborhoods.

Whether or not these characterizations were ethnographically correct (and
all evidence points to the fact that they represent very partial truths), this form
of treatment opened up the possibility of looking at people in cities and people
in the countryside as participants in a common field of relationships, however
that field was to be thought about and researched in practice. *Tepoztlán* was
thus one milestone on the road to acculturation studies, studies that did not envisage each culture as a closed universe, distinctive unto itself. It also shifted attention from asking native informants to reconstruct their cultures from
"memory" to studying living "Indians" in interaction with living "Mexicans" as
part of an embracing system, operating in the here and now. Thus, Redfield
played an important role, together with Melville Herskovits and Ralph Linton,
in legitimizing interests in "acculturation," which was thought of at the time as
the study of somehow inferior and not quite real "hybrid" cultures (see Beals
1953)—"mongrel" cultures, as Salman Rushdie might say.

Following his work in Tepoztlán, Redfield in 1930 became a research associate of the Carnegie Institution of Washington, D.C. In 1924 Carnegie had
launched a major program of investigation centered on the pre-Hispanic city of
Chichén Itzá, under the leadership of the archaeologist Sylvanus Morley. Under the auspices of this program, Redfield developed a project for comparative
field research in four communities in Yucatán. As he put it in the introduction
to *The Folk Culture of Yucatan*:

> The outstanding cultural contrast in Yucatan is that between the Spanish-modern
> area of the populous northwest, including the one large city of Merida, and the
> more Indian and rustic hinterland in the sparsely populated southeast. This book
> reports the results of a comparative study of four communities chosen to represent
> points along the line of this contrast: a village of tribal Indians, a peasant village, a
> town, and the city. (1941: xv)

City, town, peasant village, and tribal village were thus seen to "lie along the
northwest-southeast line of diminishing communications" (1941: 370, n. 3).
Mérida, the city, was intensively studied by Asael Hansen for three years. Dzitas, the town, a station on the railroad through which passengers and goods
were ferried to Chichén Itzá, was studied only tangentially by Margaret and
Robert Redfield, who did not live there. Chan Kom, the peasant village, was a

settlement largely formed by recent colonists connected with the socialist movement organized by Felipe Carrillo Puerto. It was studied by Mérida-born Alfonso Villa Rojas, who taught school there for four years, and by Redfield and Villa for four months in 1933 (Redfield and Villa Rojas 1934). Redfield revisited the village briefly in 1948 and reported on changes between 1931 and 1948 in *A Village that Chose Progress* (1950). Tusik, the village of "tribal" Indians, was located near the shrine center at Xcacal Guardia, where rebel Maya had set up an independent domain in their southeastward retreat during the War of the Castes in the mid-nineteenth century. It was studied by Villa for two periods, of about eight months in all, during 1935–1936.

The clearly different historical trajectories of these four communities might have prompted Redfield to undertake a study of their histories, but Redfield followed Park (as Park had followed Windelband) in distinguishing generalizing nomothetic science from particularistic ideographic inquiry. By then (1931) Radcliffe-Brown had arrived in Chicago and attracted a persuaded following, and Redfield cast his interests in Radcliffe-Brownian terms as "social anthropology"—"that kind of study of contemporary peoples which is guided by generalizing hypotheses as to society and cultural behavior and is related to the other generalizing social sciences" (1962 [1936]: 14). He wanted to deal with "singular propositions referring to a definite place and time of service only as they illustrate or contribute to general propositions as to the nature of classes of phenomena"; the scientist "deals with types, abstracted from particular experience" (1962 [1936]: 13). Redfield thus understood Mérida, Dzitas, Chan Kom, and Tusik as types illustrating such general propositions, typological way stations in a cultural process that led from communal isolation and social homogeneity to extremes of contact and social heterogeneity generated by the regional capital at Mérida. Tusik and Chan Kom, more isolated and homogeneous than Dzitas and Mérida, could, moreover, be "grouped to constitute a 'type' in opposition to the 'type' formed by assembling the opposite characters of the less isolated communities" (1941: 343). Thus, one might take a further step and make Tusik stand for primitive societies in general and Chan Kom for peasant societies in general—primitive and peasant societies will be more isolated and homogeneous, hence possessed also of a more highly organized body of understandings, more sacralized, and more oriented toward the collectivity. "When such societies undergo contact and communication with urbanized society (or at least with modern Western urbanized society), they tend to change in the direction of the opposite of these characters" (1941: 343).

The general propositions to be illustrated were synthesized by Redfield out of his reading of Henry Maine on the movement from status to contract; Ferdinand Tönnies on the movement from gemeinschaft to gesellschaft; Thomas and Znaniecki on changes from organization to disorganization; Lewis Henry Morgan on the movement from *societas* to the individualization and formal political constraints of *civitas*; Émile Durkheim on the movement from a mechanical division of labor to an organic division of labor; and Durkheim as well on the movement from sacrality to secularism. Common to these separate efforts was the attempt to portray the transformation of human society from one generalized type to another. Redfield saw these typological characterizations as mental instruments "abstracted from particular experience" (1962 [1936]: 13) that could be put in the service of a nomothetic science. Thus, for Redfield, the "folk society" was an "ideal type," "a mental construction," "an imagined entity, created only because through it we may hope to understand reality" (1941: 232–34). Then, comparison showed him that "the less isolated and more heterogeneous societies of the series of four in Yucatan are the ones which are more characterized by disorganization of culture, by secularization, and by individualization" (1941: 342). In this comparison, the features of isolation and homogeneity were taken to be the "independent variables," while "organization or disorganization of culture, secularization, and individualization are regarded as dependent variables." When societies become less isolated and more heterogeneous, "loss of isolation and increasing heterogeneity are causes of disorganization, secularization, and individualization" (1941: 344).

At issue, of course, is what such ideal types delineate and explicate, and what they omit as secondary or irrelevant. At the root of Redfield's employment of these typological schemata seem to lie two problematic sociological suppositions. One postulates a general movement of society toward quantitatively increasing and ever-more-intense social interactions. The other supposition, perhaps drawn from Herbert Spencer, envisions a general trend toward ever-increasing social differentiation. As interactions multiply and differentiate, so then do "understandings." Both of these suppositions also underlie much of what has been called "modernization theory," and in that sense Redfield can be counted as one of the pioneers of that problematic approach. What is striking, in retrospect, is that Redfield called this "social anthropology," but it is certainly not social anthropology in the Radcliffe-Brownian sense of stipulating the structure of social arrangements and assessing their jural implications. Instead, Redfield leaps over "society" altogether, in setting up a direct linkage between interactional effervescence on the one hand and cogitation in human minds on the other, but omits any questions about how social interaction might be grounded in material circumstances and material organization. By this short-circuiting of the "middle ground" of history, political economy, and social anthropology, Redfield deprived himself of the opportunity to deal analytically with peasantry and its many variants, leaving "the peasant" as an empty typological category halfway between tribe and city. There is certainly no Marxian or even Stewardian recognition in Redfield that humans must draw energy from the natural world in order to survive and that these transactions with nature structure human relations in quite specific, historically constituted ways. Thus, there is no discussion at all of the role of the maize and henequen plantations that shaped nineteenth-century Yucatán, if only as a background to the Maya frontier colonists in Chan

Kom who sought to escape from the grip of the haciendas, or to the presence of Maya rebels on the commercial frontier with Belize. There is also no recourse to Max Weber, who created typologies of the "economic ethics" of the world religions (Weber 1946 [1922–1923]). There is, furthermore, no recognition that material interchanges with nature, social relations, and even cognitive and emotional understandings involve power and differentials of power.

This becomes most obvious in the concluding chapter of *Folk Culture*, where Redfield addresses Sol Tax's findings in the midwestern highlands of Guatemala that Indian communities there were long-isolated and homogeneous, and yet were characterized by marked individual mobility and impersonal relationships, as well as by a considerable degree of secularization. Redfield offers as one possible explanation the conjectural history that these societies already possessed money and impersonal state controls before the Spanish Conquest and that both of these features were perhaps intensified by the Conquest and the development of local markets, so that the evaluation of success in monetary terms could have enhanced the trend toward secularization. Such leaps of the imagination parallel Redfield's leap from his social physics to explicating the quality of social relations and socially constituted minds, without any benefit of either a processual history of any of these social relations or an analysis of their respective political economies. Using money is not just a culture trait that universalizes and secularizes social relations—it is an instrument in the accumulation of capital and the mobilization of labor. Moreover, not all markets are alike: marketplaces in Highland Guatemala are part of a quite specific political-economic history, in which landholding and commerce by non-Indians (*ladinos*) were curtailed, while considerable autonomy was granted to indigenous communities and markets (see Smith 1984). Paying attention to Guatemalan and Yucatecan history, defined not as two sequences of unique events but as complex manifolds of specifiable processes, would have saved both Redfield and Tax from falling into the trap of hitching their culturalist analyses to overly abstract and generalized sociological categories and variables.

It is here that Julian Steward and those who followed his lead, including myself, strove to render the "middle ground" of society and its multiple domains and levels more amenable to analytic understanding. Redfield acknowledged as much when, in *The Little Community* (1955), he laid out ways of understanding the community as an ecological system and a social structure, each with its history or histories, and also took cognizance of efforts then underway to situate the actions and transactions within communities in relation to the multiple levels of the larger system of which they form a part. Redfield acknowledged Steward's use of the concept of multiple "sociocultural levels of integration" with reference to Puerto Rico (Steward 1950a), Betty Starr's "levels of communal relations" developed to understand the villages of Las Tuxtlas in Mexico (Starr 1954), and Borje Hanssen's use of the idea of multiple activity fields in his analysis of Swedish Scania (Hanssen 1953). To render a concept like "the peasant" analytically useful, one needs to specify the diverse economic, social, political, and ideological dimensions of peasanthood subsumed under that constructed concept. One must define the variable, historically constituted ways in which people typified as peasants derive and allocate their resources, enter into alliances or coalitions with others—or are drawn into them—and cope with the characteristics of the political domains that make demands on them.

After an effort to launch anthropological work in China came to naught, due to the Communist takeover in 1945, Redfield turned away increasingly from the study of people in villages to focus on civilization. He treated civilization both as a singular construct, "a formed thing of the mind," and in the plural, seeing civilizations either as cultural systems "in which the parts making up the whole are ideas or products of ideas in persisting relationships with one another" or as social systems, "typical arrangement of parts, in which the parts are kinds of people in characteristic relationships with one another" (1962 [1951]: 375–76). He began to teach courses about civilization at Chicago in 1951 and then to organize seminars, colloquia, and conferences on the study and comparison of civilizations. Many of these collective efforts were carried out in collaboration with Milton Singer, who began as a philosopher and assimilated to anthropology in his later days. These seminars and colloquia engaged problems of Chinese, Islamic, and Indian civilization; India indeed became a major field area for staff and graduate students from Chicago, beginning in the 1950s.

It was in thinking about the architecture of these great complexes that Redfield made a most fruitful contribution by raising the question of "the social organization of tradition" (1956: 40–59). In this he conceived of traditions within a civilization as consisting of two streams—the "great tradition of the reflective few," practiced in special sites by specialists, and "the little tradition of the largely unreflective many," which informed "the lives of the unlettered in their village communities." At the same time, these great and little traditions were seen as intertwined "in reciprocal communication, through centuries," by processes in which understandings are alternatively universalized and parochialized. India now became the region of ethnographic reference, and McKim Mariott furnished relevant case material from his study of the Jat-dominated village of Kishan Garhi in Uttar Pradesh (Mariott 1955). Little traditions may be caught up and amplified in the spread of a universalizing Great Tradition; alternatively, little traditions refashion elements of the Great Tradition, parochializing and adapting them to the local level. It is also significant whether the traditions expand and elaborate a shared "orthogenetic" pattern or whether they are responses to influences carried in or imposed from outside and then elaborated innovatively in their new habitat. Redfield and Singer distinguished between orthogenetic cities, in which patterns were carried forward by priests and literati and then spread through chains of traditionalizing practitioners, and heterogenetic cities, in which new patterns were spread by technical personnel, representatives of the "technical order," rather than by the orthogenetic representatives of the "moral order"

(Redfield 1962 [1954]: 326–50). Many of these interests and concerns have been pursued more recently, in rather different ethnographic contexts, by Fredrik Barth in his work on the boundary-processes defining the multiple traditions of an Omani town (1983) and on the construction of cosmologies among the Mountain Ok of New Guinea (1987).

Robert Redfield thus played an important role in moving anthropologists away from a concern with supposedly autonomous, pristine, and isolated groups toward an engagement with wider and more complex fields of interaction. This interest led him to a study of folk and peasant societies in interrelation with cities, a move that focused attention on the interchanges and communicative transactions among rural and urban facets of larger societal wholes. In the process he legitimized the study of acculturation and of culturally hybrid populations, thus opening up perspectives that still inform our efforts. Out of this came, as well, Redfield's productive emphasis on the social organization of tradition and on the communicative processes that articulated the "great" traditions of civilization with the "little" traditions of local folk. What he did not do was to place his concern with the communication of "understandings" in relation to a sociologically informed political economy or to social-anthropological analysis of the competition among religious and political regimes. Some of this work is now being carried forward by new cohorts of investigators.

ERIC R. WOLF

This performance has been, and will be until it ends, a sundance for me, with the sun dark. Because there is no language in which it can be written, which will satisfy both you and me. The anthropologist's discourse moves toward knowledge, the poet's moves outward from knowledge. The anthropologist records but knows no meaning until the part recorded fits into a whole. The poet starts from whole, spending the rest of his life, or his poem, mining whole for parts. The anthropologist predicts, the poet prophesies. The poet knows what he wants from the beginnings, he knows *before*; he has precognition, and he takes the rest of the poem to find it out. The anthropologist does not or should not know what he wants until the end but by that time he knows it. How shall you and I, and the you in I, talk together? How *dialogue* in Don Roberto's favorite sense of communication?

The Redfield I deal with today sets sail from *The Primitive World and Its Transformations* (PWT, 1953) and the tide runs at its highest perhaps under what, if he had lived in this metaphor, he might have called his "little" *Little Community* (LC, 1955). In this book, after examining his debts to Maine, de

Coulanges, Morgan, Tönnies, and Durkheim and after his acknowledgment that "no very great claims to originality may be made by those of us who have made use of and developed these ideas in the twentieth century," Redfield defines his own progress as follows:

> My own efforts went to develop an imagined or ideal-typical folk-society in considerable detail of characterization and to make use of the conception in describing, in more general and abstract terms than is usual in studies of changing primitive society, some comparisons among tribal, peasant, and urban communities in Yucatan. More recently [he is talking of the late forties and early fifties] I have become interested in the characterization of the over-all transformations of human living from precivilized to modern times, as guided by the conception of the folk society, and in the examination of the types of urban societies as they affect the folk societies and give rise to new forms of society. (1955: 143)

A few flashes from this: Redfield is interested not in tribes but in peasant villages; not in the ethnographic present but in the tenses of change; not in the social isolate but in the part-society turned like a sunflower toward a large whole; not in society itself all that much but in the structure of culture, sensed as a spider's web with a spider at the center.

PWT is his first "cogitational" work; LC follows it in short order in 1955. In this latter work, Redfield is at his most secure in the uses of models. He writes, "The intellectual forms for describing communities hover over the writer of many an ethnographic account" (1955: 164), but it is he that is the windhover or falcon here and we have a strong and exhilarating sense of a mind in movement. It is in this work that his abiding interest in ideal-type constructs and his holistic approach to culture come together most convincingly. Here the text dances so, and Redfield hovers so above it, that he can play off one model against another according to the greater or lesser precision of focus, the wider or narrower width of frame that he desires. The sense of discourse is everywhere present, as it is in PWT; anthropology is made of words that are *said* or *heard* in dialogue before they are thought about: "If we try to *say* something about the important qualities of a people, we have not many choices as to the manner in which we *say* it. We can attempt to *say* something that includes all aspects of that mode of life; we can *mention* all the principal customs and institutions of that society. Then we find ourselves describing at length" (1953: 84; italics mine). Or, in what is for us so often the equivalent of *hearing*: "in the accounts of these I *read* how the associations fulfill personal needs or societal functions that help to integrate society. Or, if we *read* . . . [X, Y, and Z] have shown us how the Plains Indian soldier societies . . ." (1953: 122; italics mine). He will speak of the "major principle of composition" which governs the presentation of this or that model (1955: 56); he makes frequent reference to anthropological uses of "metaphor" or "suggestive analogy" (1955: 74–75); he has a fascinating aside on the role that "portraiture" plays both in works of literature and in ethnographies (1955: 161); he is constantly using dramatic metaphors, such as the "every world-view is a stage set" of PWT (1953: 86, 91, 93; see also 1955: 28, 102). This reaches something like apotheosis in his comparison of a "written account of a community" with the community itself in LC (1955: 150). All of this, in my readings, imparts a curious innocence to the text; it is as if it were rolling up its sleeves like a conjurer and showing exactly what is or is not there: "Trust me" the text says, "it is morning here, we are just beginning."

And indeed, the analyses are extraordinarily broad and generous. As many have said, Redfield did not write polemically: he preferred to bring in as many views as he could and find out what one could learn from them. If he sometimes seems to slip into the wings, leaving the conflicting views in dialogue one with another, without really having told us what he thinks about the issue, or if he will often invoke a model modesty ("a sketchy review" [1953: 27]; "the vagueness of all universal characterizations" [1953: 93]; "a background of even off hand characterization" [1953: 96]; "a study far beyond my competence" [1953: 58]; "it is only the first paragraphs . . . with which I dare concern myself" [1953: 113]; not to mention the sometimes overfamiliar use of the word "little" in LC at large), the result can only charm you the more as you feel style, indeed, becoming—in Alfred North Whitehead's phrase quoted by Charles Leslie concerning Redfield—"the ultimate morality of the mind" (Leslie 1976: 160). And it does not concern you overmuch if he often seems to retreat from a difficult position into the details of ethnography; after all, isn't that where one always feels safest in any book?

In LC, the little community is seen in the first and last chapters as "a whole" and "whole and parts" (to quote the titles). In between, it is examined as "an ecological system," a "social structure," a "typical biography," a "kind of person," an "outlook on life" (or worldview), a "history," a "community within communities," and a "combination of opposites." Note, in passing, that if we conflate (as a detailed thematic study would lead us to do) the "kind of person" model and the "typical biography" model, the "worldview" model stands exactly in the center of the book.

At this point, I want to stay with the models or "forms of thought" Redfield uses, rather than their content. Early in LC, he envisages that, of the various models set up, some are going to have to become parts of other models that are more holistic. He never makes it completely clear how this is to happen, and there is considerable play between the proffered hope of this integration and his own denial of its possibility: "The systems, so far as here suggested, do not connect themselves one to another by any rule or principle that I can see . . . [and] . . . I do not pursue further the problem of relating these systems to one another and the very difficult problem of representing the whole community by an ordering of part-systems" (1955: 24). Indeed, we discover soon enough that certain models are going to inhibit others as well as enhance each other. A general movement away from the social toward the cultural, however, is clear. Again and again, Radcliffe-Brownian ecological and social-structure models, as reported by E. E. Evans-Pritchard, Raymond Firth, or Meyer Fortes, prove themselves too narrow and leave no place for the mind. Ecology is not made of fields and plants alone as such: "The human environment is in large part mental" (1955: 30). "'Market' means both a state of mind and a place to trade" (1956: 30); social structure only becomes interesting as a set of norms and expectations or a "set of ethical paradigms, an exemplary; an ideal system of demands that men can follow" (1955: 47). A number of suggestions concerning his shift of interest here interweave with each other. One is that the narrow frame is scientific whereas the wider frame is going to have to belong to the humanities, indeed, specifically to the arts (1955: 16, 70). Another is that this shift is one from anthropology to what we might have to call a meta-anthropology: First we think about the facts, "And then we turn to the form of thought we have used in thinking about [them] so, and we think about this thought" (1955: 16).

A curious paradox in Redfield has to do with the stress he places on all that is *individual* at the heart of every discussion of the *collective*. Of course, behind this stand Ruth Benedict and Margaret Mead and even, perhaps, Paul Radin, but the stress permeates the work. At the very moment when he first asks what it means to consider a little community as a *whole*, he gives the answer: "It means that a band of hunters or a long-established village is unified, as is a personality, and has its own character, as does a personality" (1955: 9). In another image, he states: "The face of a living person is such an immediately apprehended whole" (1955: 17). Even when he is comparing the views of various anthropologists he feels that "we shall go forward more safely if we follow, for a time, the guidance of some one of these men" (1955: 33). Matter of substance or of rhetoric? I have never stopped feeling that this was a deep-seated inhibitor of the comparativist he sought to be in social science.

The connection of this stress with what I take to be the basic axis of Redfieldian concern cannot be missed. The axis of the shift from narrow to wide focus, science to humanities, anthropology to meta-anthropology, is the concept of worldview; worldview, in turn, is the paramount locus of a yet more important shift, perhaps, from the "outside view" to the "inside view." This first appears in LC where Redfield calls for "concepts to describe the little community which are not so exterior to [the] villager's mind as is the concept of ecological system" (1955: 32). This must separate initially two facets of the inner/outer binary, one ethnographic, one anthropological. The first is connected to the central fact about his fieldwork based on the bridge between the little community he knows and the wider world, external to it, which culminates in the urban metropolis. The second facet appears when Redfield discusses the problem of entering the human mind and the tools we have had for doing so since Freud (1955: 64).

I hinted earlier at Redfield's apparent difficulties in his two chapters "Typical Biography" and "Kind of Person" in sorting out (a) the biographical from the modal personality approaches and (b) both of these, but especially the second, from "ethos" and "values." He tries to follow Alfred Kroeber—as so often—on the flying trapeze of "getting into metaphors that personify culture as if it has a will and purpose of its own" (1955: 69). After worrying at the scientific validity of all this, he ends, nonetheless, with the individual: "World-view, temperament or group personality, and ethos are (remarked Milton Singer) all on the self axis. All represent the shift of description from products of culture to psychological characterization" (1955: 79).

The concern with ethos, unresolved in these chapters, continues in the chapter "The Little Community as an Outlook on Life," though we have in the meantime established that "value system" is "more of an inside view" than an outside one (1955: 75). Discussing worldview as the overall outlook on the universe around them held by a little community looking out at it, Redfield, already aware of the possible centripetal collapse of his discipline as exemplified by the silence of Frank Cushing, declares: "This tension between the inside view and the outside view, this obligation to manage correctly the relationship between them, is the *central problem* in studies of culture and personality" (1955: 82; italics mine). We are now close to a statement on Redfield's part of the full complexity of the situation:

> It is because we have moved from conceptions developed from a consideration of institutions and institutionalized relationships between kinds of persons to conceptions that lie on the axis of the self, that the management of the relationship between inside and outside views has become so difficult and subtle. There is the inside view of what a person is. There is that view of what he ought to be, his own inside view. There is our outside view of what the person there is. (What we think he ought to be is, by the declared rules of science, excluded from our subject matter.) And there are our formulations made in terms admissible to science, of these three things. All this without adding the relations among what people think they are or should be and what the outsider finds them to be or the development and explanation of these things! (1955: 85)

In the following pages, Redfield manages to sort out the relative positions of group personality, ethos, and worldview; to ask what would happen if one "attempted to maintain the inside view over the whole range of the native's life without a preliminary commitment to value" (1955: 86); and to see a danger in this question. He then brings us very quickly back to the recognition that the normative and the cognitive cannot be separated from one another *anywhere* outside *our* minds, although this is bought at the price of a category slippage in which cognitive, affective, and normative collapse into and become aspects of worldview. Meantime, after stressing that "it is *their* order, *their* categories, *their* emphasis [i.e. the natives'] upon this part rather than that which the student listens for" (1955: 88), Redfield returns to the "horns of the ethnographical dilemma" (1955: 92). What the outsider, that is, the anthropologist, is doing, since any attempt to present the inner view directly *in its own terms* would be unsuccessful, is *translating* the inside view to his fellows on the outside: "If we use only his terms [the native's] and forms of thought we merely become natives like those we study, speaking and thinking as he does—imagining for a moment this possibility could be achieved—and no communication to outsider would result . . . and that way lies a permanent solipsism of the cultures" (1955: 92).

The solution for Redfield seems to lie in an "alternation of talking and listening," that is to say, in a dialogue about "the common human" (1955: 93–94), and it is with this reassurance that the worldview chapter ends.

The person standing outside the little community and the outside mind looking into it are one and the same. For what I cannot fail to notice twenty years later—with astonishment at how few could notice it then—is that there is someone missing in this dialogue and that is the informant himself. Redfield's stress on the inside view should have brought him, as much as any anthropologist, to the realization that this could one day mean the informant himself becoming the anthropologist, insisting that translation be a two-way process and that he should be in on the dialogue. Further, it might have dawned on him, not merely that there was a danger of solipsism if the outsider ceased to anthropologize, but that the insider could call an end to anthropology by refusing to entertain this purely imaginary peripheral status of his periphery. As Eric Wolf, among many others, has pointed out in the interval, what is left out is the question of power. Is this the reason why Redfield might feel uncomfortable with the concept of ethos in LC and that we find ethos has no separate chapter in this key methodology by one of anthropology's greatest ethicists? It would be good to think so, despite his open acceptance of double standards in the matter of cultural relativism at the end of PWT. Could this also be some sort of reason for the constant, nervous return to the "axis of the self"? The scientist-judge, with his impeccable moral stance, corresponding to the impeccable informant meditating, albeit slowly (1963: 34), on his worldview and his ethos within his little community: these two individuals who are, when all is said, Redfield's two favorite objects of study, are they not masks for the collectives on both sides which can then be relegated to the abstractions of social structure and the like? Or collapsed upon themselves in the true solipsism that is going on here: when the culture in "culture and personality" collapses into personality alone? Is it not difficult to trust today a view in which history itself becomes merely one more of the forms of thought with which to look at any community, little or big? Might it not be, if the outsider to the little community happens also to be its only translator, that the very folk–urban continuum itself becomes questionable as one of the tools with which the center may have blinded us to the rights of the peripheries? The ultimate confusion may well be, at a late point in LC, the good-hearted equation of the discourse and its subject: "A written account of a community is something like the community itself: to understand it one needs to take the inside view of it. Of the published study, the inside view is the author's view. With what ends in mind did he make the study?" (1955: 150).

For, of course, it is still the outsider who is the author here, and shall we then spend too much time on the inside of the outside? Perhaps not. Perhaps it is more important to look at the outside of the inside. Redfield, at least, had the courage to trot out the monster that revealed him for what he himself was, for without discussing the outside, we could not have had the outsider, or even the beginnings of the suggestion that the insider could complain. It is not so much Don Roberto who is in question here, but rather the profession and the culture in which his book is embedded. I deliberately oscillate here between a view of style that implies the individual track a text's author makes, when he steers the writing working through him, upon that writing—and another view of style in which the world, social or cultural, surrounding the author impresses that track in a variety of codes as the writing comes into being, through the author indeed, but independently of authorial intention. "Anthropological discourse" as I use it here is such a sociocultural style. Redfield's innocence arises out of his sense as a writer of the gap between personal style and sociocultural style and his re-fusal to allow the first to be devoured by the second. He remains innocent by refusing the mask that the second style implies, that is to say, he is "sincere." But here "sincerity" (sometimes a literary device) involves a price. The price is an uneasy conscience of what is speaking through one nevertheless, in that other, second, style: the classical liberal discomfort to which Redfield has given a more elegant expression than anyone else. A more complete analysis of all his writing would doubtless reveal this more clearly. It would be hard to do the same with the jargon-ridden pages of many of his contemporaries, or immedi-ate followers, for they wear the iron mask and it is elsewhere than in the style that one must hunt for dragons.

At the very opening of LC, Redfield refers to massive cultural units that are of interest to me:

> Each person, each stable human settlement with an organized way of life, each his-torical people, *even each art or body of literature* associated with such people, has a sort of integrity which is recognized both by common sense and by much schol-arship, humanistic or anthropological. . . . But the discussion here will be with ref-erence to small communities only. The generalization of the problems to other kinds of human wholes is a further and much more difficult problem. (1955: 2; ital-ics mine)

Redfield constantly referred to art and aesthetics (he told a certain student of his that, because of his aesthetic bent, he was sending him to a place—Lake Atitlán, Guatemala—where he would bless his mentor every morning on open-ing the wooden shutters), but it is not my impression that he ever did much more than salute them from afar. It is possible that his "aesthetic expectations" were satisfied entirely by his own holistic approach. It is also my impression that Redfield is interested in *Literate* Man rather than in *Literary* Man: the text he reads is ultimately a political, not an aesthetic text. Yet Literary Man goes back a long way in civilization, does he not—not to mention the little oral-tradition poems?

I want to end this assay with a quick, glancing take on Redfield's use of the terms *literati* and *intelligentsia* as a means of extending this concern. In a rich, long article, "Robert Redfield's Development of a Social Anthropology of Civilizations," Milton Singer (1976) sees his subject moving, around 1949, out of the study of cultures seen from "the bottom up" and into that of civilizations seen from "the top down." In this enterprise, Redfield asked for the cooperation of Orientalists and other students of major civilizations. Many of us now wonder whether the primitive isolate wasn't a convenient figment of anthropological imagination, as well as whether it is not *state* rather than *city* that matters in elite control of peasantries. However this may be, Redfield's ever-growing insistence on peasants for his view of people as no longer isolated from the world around them but embedded in situations great segments of which were determined by urban leaders, led him to study acculturation as something more like what someone has called "transculturation." That is, he wished to find out what aspects of town culture were at work in the lives and, especially, in the minds of peasant villagers and also what part of the latter's folk culture was at work in the lives and minds of the urban elite. An attempt to deal with such major civilizations as Islam, Hinduism, and Confucianism (rather, I think, than China, India, Arabia, etc. per se), required the addition to his conceptual apparatus of a concept that would come to grips with the eons over which he saw civilizations enduring.

I am not at all sure of being happy with Redfield's concept of "historic structure" as Singer depicts it, but, in fairness, Redfield had little time in which to develop it. I also feel Redfield continued to underestimate the work of humanists. It is not that he was unaware of this work: Sometimes Redfield seemed to know of models more complex than he was using but declined to change his middle-level approach (I was about to say middlebrow) for reasons best known to himself. However this may be, it is part of Redfield's positive achievement that he was prepared, against much criticism and for what he saw as the universal good, to make this effort. The guiding "form of thought" was that of "great and little traditions." Here, Redfield and Singer looked at how ideas at large in the folk society might be systematized so as to grow into what they came to call indigenous primary civilizations, reacting back upon the folk as a set of intellectual and moral standards ideologically corresponding to the politico-economic rule of the elite over the peasants. In contrast stand secondary civilizations involving cases in which "a folk society, precivilized, peasant or partly urbanized, is further urbanized by contact with peoples of widely different cultures from that of its own members" (Redfield and Singer 1954: 61). At the level of cities, we have a basic distinction "between the *carrying forward into systematic and reflective dimensions an old culture* and *the creating of original modes of thought that have authority beyond or in conflict with old cultures and civilizations.* We might speak of the orthogenetic cultural role of cities as contrasted with the heterogenetic cultural role" (Redfield and Singer 1954: 58; italics in original). This latter stage might also include feedback to the periphery, whose moral orders, disturbed by heterogeneity, would be reorganized. Redfield, as some have suggested, may have been overoptimistic about the degree of trauma involved for the periphery. Others saw the trauma as deep and enduring. At the level of personnel, finally, the primary-orthogenetic complex seems to involve mainly V. Gordon Childe's *literati* who use literacy to evolve or continue the local sacred tradition, while the secondary-heterogenetic type seems to involve mainly Arnold Toynbee's *intelligentsia* who use literacy to mediate between the external urban world and the inner folk world (see as far back as Redfield 1953: 44).

Note that we are back once more to the *in* and the *out*. A long analysis of the matter would, I believe, bring out yet more of the ambivalences I have discussed before. Such a study would involve a close look at the relation of *cosmology* to *worldview* in the development of Redfield's thought from PWT onward (involving somewhat unrelated contentions that cosmology can be both an inner elaboration of a worldview by an indigenous philosopher *and* the elaboration of such a worldview by an outside observer, i.e., an anthropologist). It would then involve the same kind of study of the terms *literati* and *intelligentsia*, revolving, for me, around the fact that the *literati* are not only insiders, but when they move out of the little community to elaborate the orthogenetic city, they are also mediators between rulers and ruled (see Redfield and Singer 1954). In later writings, these terms begin to carry too much weight and are clearly very vulnerable. By 1957, Redfield seems to be supplanting them by the term *intellectual*, which—it is not too clear—may be inclusive of them both (1960: 358). In any event, the confusions between these binaries again involve political issues revolving around the question of ruler and ruled. Of greater concern to me here is his associating "originally creative artists" and philosophers with civilization, while mere "proto-artists and proto-intellectuals" are linked with the periphery (1960: 359). It would not be too difficult to trace in Redfield a condescension toward primitives perhaps greater than he would have wished to reveal, given his "double standard" of cultural relativism.

I am somewhat dismayed, in glancing back at Redfield's later work, with the distance that had grown up between his social and cultural anthropology. It worries me that I cannot find the exact link Redfield intends to make between peasant and Toynbee's internal and external proletariats: What is the link—is a proletarian merely an angry peasant or what? It worries me, thinking about the relation of all this to our culture, that in all the later work I find only one reference to suburbanites (1953: 52). I find only two references to mass culture (1955: 147; Redfield and Singer 1954: 70). It is clear that Redfield sees himself as never getting near our own situation. When he does, he finds his concepts stalling on him: "It may be that for a rapidly changing and heterogeneous civilized people the notion of world view is quite unmanageable" (1962: 398). Most worrisome of all is that I can find only one, elusive, reference to class (1953: 42), just before the first discussion of *literati* and *intelligentsia* as it happens. So what do we have finally? The folk on the one hand, the elite on the other, and nothing in the middle? But is any equivalent to the middle classes really that late in civilization? Not only do we get very little attempt to distinguish between political, economic, religious, and aesthetic leadership and the like, but in addition we have a conceptual desert between folk and elite. It may be that once social anthropology has got you it will never let you go, but I find it hard to buy a cultural anthropology at such a price!

And it is a pity because I am so sure that it is not only the sociology of literacy that has not yet been written (1953: 36), but also the sociology of the literary. "The precivilized hunter or villager is preliterate," Redfield had said a few lines before, "the peasant is illiterate." What exactly is modern consumer man? I am concerned, in our own culture—and for me and my like it is a question of *bare* survival—with the fate of the arts. What I see, briefly, is a rapidly dwindling folk anywhere in the world and also here in these States; an elite that is far more concerned with power and money than with culture; and an immense, constantly growing, stupefied, and consumerized middle range whose concern with culture is almost purely oriented in terms of status acquisition. The war between poet and critic pales into insignificance beside the role of the media in defining what culture it is that this middle range is going to acquire next. I need concepts today to raise the almost forgotten issue of "taste" and to deal with a host of problems involving taste in the production and consumption of art objects. These might range, without sticking to literature, from, say, the study of the passage from function to decoration (so called) in such a humble "folk-art" object as the duck-hunting decoy, via the study of how "gift-shop," "kitsch," or "airport art" arises and is dealt with by places such as the one I live in (New Hope, Pennsylvania) all the way across to Skagway, Alaska, to a full sociology of readership, televisionship, or other forms of art consumption that we suffer through in our time. You will doubtless gather from this that I am an unreformed normativist in aesthetics; in this perhaps I would have gained some degree of approval from Don Roberto.

I doubt this has made you into poets yet or has turned me back into an anthropologist. But we have made the trip now and have made it in Robert Redfield's company. It is a tribute to him, I think, that this could be. There are not many of his profession with whom we could have made it. Perhaps it is because while respecting the handmaiden science far more than we sometimes think he did, he knew that the "true gods within the temple" are "understanding and her apotheosis, wisdom" (1955: 168; see Tarn 1976).

NATHANIEL TARN

BIOGRAPHICAL NOTE

Photo by Janet Rodney; courtesy of Department of
Special Collections, Stanford University Libraries
1990

For biographical note on ERIC R. WOLF, see chapter 2.

NATHANIEL TARN was born in Paris in 1928. He moved with his family to Belgium when he was seven and then, at the outbreak of war, he was sent to England. There he studied at Cambridge University, taking a B.A. in English and history in 1948. That year he went back to Paris, where he happened to see a movie in which the young hero visits the Musée de l'Homme. Tarn went there the next day, was overwhelmed, and three days later enrolled in university studies in anthropology. He worked first with Marcel Griaule, then with Claude Lévi-Strauss and Paul Lévi, a Southeast Asianist.

In the early 1950s Tarn went to the University of Chicago under a Fulbright grant and studied with Fred Eggan, Sol Tax, Robert Redfield, and others. Redfield included him in a project called "Comparison of Total Cultures" and in 1952 sent him to Guatemala to do a study of worldview. The following year Tarn returned to England and became a graduate student at the London School of Economics under Raymond Firth, Isaac Schapera, and Maurice Freedman. He found British social anthropology narrow in the range of its interests, but he learned a great deal about field techniques and as much "scientific objectivity" as he ever imbibed (which he still considers a good basis to start from). While at the LSE he wrote a thesis on his Mesoamerican research, receiving his Ph.D. from Chicago in 1957. In 1958 he went to Burma on a Rockefeller Foundation grant to study the social organization of Buddhist in-

stitutions. In the course of this fieldwork he became interested in what he referred to as "Messianic Buddhism" and wrote the first articles on this topic in
the areal literature. After Burma he returned to London to take up a lectureship in South East Asian Anthropology at the School of Oriental and African
Studies (SOAS), a post he held until 1967.

Tarn's first book of poetry, *Old Savage/Young City*, was published in 1964.
Three years later, he decided "he could no longer conciliate the mental sets expected of him as an anthropologist and those he wished to achieve as a poet."
He resigned from SOAS and joined the publishing house of Jonathan Cape
Ltd., where he founded and edited a multidisciplinary series of texts and a poetry press. Subsequently, he published over twenty books of his own poetry, as
well as translations of Latin American and French poetry, and essays in literary
and cultural criticism.

From 1969 to 1971 Tarn held visiting professorships, first in English at the
State University of New York at Buffalo and then in Romance languages at
Princeton University. Deciding at this time to move permanently to the United
States, he joined the faculty of Rutgers University, where he was a professor of
poetry, comparative literature, and anthropology. He took early retirement
from Rutgers in 1984.

Tarn's anthropological interests reemerged in 1975 when he served as a con-
sultant to native arts groups in Alaska. In 1979 (partly as a result of the arrival
at Rutgers of the Mayanist Norman Hammond) he returned to Guatemala to
do a restudy of Atitlán, the community where he had carried out his original
fieldwork. A part of this work was published as *Scandals in the House of Birds:
Shamans and Priests on Lake Atitlán* (Tarn and Prechtel 1998). Since his retirement he has traveled extensively in the Himalayan region and in Russia,
where he plans to teach American poetry at the Saint Petersburg State University. He has continued to publish his poetry, most recently his volume *Selected
Poems: 1950–2000* (Tarn 2002).

Tarn's interests within anthropology have centered on religion, especially on
the effort to elucidate complex symbolic systems, and his approach blends
structuralism with ethnohistory. (Most of his anthropology has been published
under the heteronym of E. Michael Mendelson.) For many years, he has been
exploring the relationships between anthropology and literature, partly as a
member of the Ethnopoetics group (which publishes the journal *Alcheringa*)
since its inception in 1970. "Torn all his life between a recording angel and a
creative angel," he has looked for the possibility of a new genre lying between
anthropology and literature, one in which "scientific procedure and poetic
process are experienced as two arms of the same body." Nathaniel Tarn lives in
Santa Fe, New Mexico.

Margaret Mead with her signature walking stick at a Burg Wartenstein conference, 1973. Wenner-Gren Foundation for Anthropological Research, Inc.

9

MARGARET MEAD

Rhoda Metraux
Sydel Silverman

No anthropologist, with the possible exception of Franz Boas in his day, has had a more prominent place in public life—and has been more identified with anthropology in the public image—than Margaret Mead. A student of Boas, a younger colleague of Ruth Benedict, and a contemporary of several figures in this book who received their Ph.D.s around the same time as she did (Leslie White and Robert Redfield at Chicago, Julian Steward at Berkeley, Raymond Firth at the London School of Economics, and Alexander Lesser at Columbia), Mead's life spanned much of the history of anthropology in the twentieth century.

Mead was born the year that Alfred Kroeber completed his studies under Boas and left for California, just at the time that the American Anthropological Association (AAA) was created. When she died in 1978, her discipline was marking a break with its past in several waves of "reinventions." First, in the early 1970s, as part of the upheavals engendered by the Vietnam War, the feminist movement, and the entry of new minority and indigenous voices into the academy, there was a critical thrust demanding a more political and socially responsive anthropology (e.g., Hymes 1969; Asad 1973). Then, beginning in the late 1970s and culminating in the 1980s, from the ranks of interpretive anthropology (see Geertz 1973) and an emergent postmodernism, there came a questioning of the entire ethnographic enterprise (Marcus and Fischer 1986; Clifford and Marcus 1986). At about the same time, a reassertion of biological determinism in the sciences and in public discourse yielded a version of neo-Darwinism in anthropology. Mead was (or would have been, had she lived longer) uncomfortable with, if not deeply opposed to, each of these developments.

A towering figure among her anthropological colleagues, the many scientists and intellectuals from other fields with whom she collaborated, and the larger American public, Mead was also a target of much criticism. Many anthropologists considered her not to have been a serious scholar because of her simplified translations of anthropology to her public audiences, although those same anthropologists welcomed the messages she carried and the renown that she brought to their discipline. Others— mostly outside of academia but also within it—blamed her for what they saw as her pernicious influence on society. Neither charge was entirely fair: She was an accomplished ethnographer who produced an enormous corpus of scholarly writing on her research, and her public impact was hardly as draconian as purported. New controversies swirled around her after her death, until a more balanced picture of her contributions came into play as the centennial of her death was marked.

In this chapter, Margaret Mead is considered from two perspectives. A biographical sketch by her close friend and collaborator, Rhoda Metraux, written for a special issue of the *American Anthropologist* shortly after Mead's death, is reprinted here.[1] It is followed by a retrospective view of Mead by the editor of this volume, which was originally presented to a mixed audience of anthropologists, other academics, and the general public in conjunction with the Mead centenary.[2] This piece, written by one who knew Mead but was not close to her, reflects upon the significance of her contributions for anthropologists, and others, today.

Thinking back over her life, Margaret Mead wrote:

> I went to Samoa—as, later, I went to the other societies on which I have worked— to find out more about human beings, human beings like ourselves in everything except their culture. . . . But how many social scientists are there, today, who are trying to think out ways in which primitive peoples, where they still exist, can become our partners and co-workers in the search for knowledge that may, in the end, save their children and ours? (1972: 293–94)

Was this an optimist's question—or challenge? Margaret Mead had the gift of confidence. She deeply believed that we, human beings, have the capacity and the cultural expectations necessary to keep our human enterprise going, even now when we have also the technical power to destroy ourselves and the world. Very early she committed herself—with zest and humor, imagination and respect for hard facts, and above all continuing disciplined work—to the task of adding to the necessary knowledge and, somewhat later, of persuading other people, at every level, to act on behalf of this enterprise. She had confidence and very few illusions, an almost uncanny combination. It won her enormous admiring audiences—and many detractors.

In general, her purposes were direct and readily intelligible. But her enjoyment of diversity was so great, her fund of observations so rich, and her network of professional and personal relations so densely woven that it is very difficult to present a brief biographical statement that mirrors the reality. This essay serves to remind us of sequences.

The plain facts of Mead's life are familiar. Her audiences, her colleagues, her friends, her students, her children, and her informants in the field, as they came to know her, all delighted in her accounts of her childhood, her anecdotes of other times and places. Yet she never lived in the past. She drew on her own life as a precious resource. She used her past to illuminate the present, for herself and others, and in this way to light up the future—the possible future.

Her significant memory images never dulled. They remained lively and precise, so that certain ones are now as present to me—a longtime listener—as are my own eidetic images. This precise access to her life experiences was extraordinarily immediate and free flowing, combining always in new ways, and her easy movement through time gave many people the curious impression that she crossed generation lines and belonged simultaneously (for some) to the youngest and (to others) to the oldest living generation. However, she placed herself unequivocally within her own generation, whose lives, spanning the twentieth century, have been subjected to almost unequaled change and the necessity for drastic adaptation. Although, over time, she spoke to a great many people very frankly about a great many things, a kind of mythology is already beginning to take over. This is perhaps inevitable. But we can try to keep the record straight.

Margaret Mead was born on December 16, 1901, the eldest child of Emily Fogg and Edward Sherwood Mead. All her life she enjoyed knowing that she was the first infant delivered in a new, modern hospital in Philadelphia. Richard, her brother, was born in 1904; though he was paired with her, he was frail and accident-prone—not the companion she had hoped for. Katherine, the next child, died in infancy in 1906. So there was a real gap between the elder and the younger living children, Elizabeth, born in 1909, and Priscilla, born in 1911.

Margaret Mead was brought up in a household of educators. Emily Mead had been a teacher before her marriage and, while Margaret was a small child, studied Italian immigrant families in Hammonton, New Jersey, in preparation for a master's degree in sociology; Margaret carried the study a step further in her own master's thesis in psychology (1924). Edward Mead was a professor at the Wharton School of Finance and Commerce of the University of Pennsylvania, and very early introduced his daughter to academia in all its complexity and narrow politics. But the most important person in her early life was her father's mother, Martha Ramsay Mead, who had long been a widow and lived in her son's home from the time of his marriage until her death in 1927. She had been a teacher and a school principal and had progressive, if somewhat unusual, ideas about the education of small children.

Grandma was Margaret's first and, until she went to Barnard, probably her only important teacher. As she explained, "between the ages of five and seventeen I spent two years in kindergarten, one year—but only half-days—in the fourth grade and six years in high school" (1972: 71). At home she learned algebra, before arithmetic, and botany in the fields around the farm where the family lived, at least part of the year, in Holicong, Bucks County, Pennsylvania, from 1911. She also learned always to finish a task and, when only ten years old, to take adult responsibility for her small sisters when her mother was away from home due to illness. Grandma became her conscience, but a conscience in which trust was matched with trust. She was also at the center of Margaret's audience when, a young field-worker, Margaret wrote letters home from Samoa; she said that her grandmother was "the one person whom I wanted most to understand what my work was about and the one it would be hardest to convince that I had chosen well in becoming an anthropologist" (1977: 8).

Early in her childhood Margaret discovered a need for privacy—to be herself and alone. In every house to which the family moved, she found herself an upstairs room, often an attic, of which her museum office—in the sixth-floor storage area of the southwest tower—was a replica. Much later, trains and planes, hotel rooms, and the quiet hours before dawn gave her the privacy that meant a kind of freedom.

In the same period, when she was eleven, she began her deeply religious life within the formal beauty of the Protestant Episcopal Church. She chose her own godmothers and was baptized in the old church in Holicong, where she was later married to Luther Cressman; as she wished, she is now buried in the churchyard. Much later she worked devotedly on committees of the World Council of Churches. But although she spoke and wrote on topics related to religion, all her life her faith was implicit and part of the privacy she cherished and guarded.

Her father teased her painfully about her religious decision. In spite of this she felt that the Mead children were treated as persons with the full right to make their own choices. In her family the price of autonomy was not rebellion but finding a way. As an adult, Margaret had almost no tolerance for arbitrary restrictions of autonomy. Yet she had little empathy with rebellion. There had to be another way.

Her first college, DePauw, was not of her choosing, and she was totally unprepared for the treatment meted out to her as an outsider, an Easterner, who did not fit in any way into the style and prejudices of sorority life. It was her first, her only real, rejection, something she never forgot or forgave. And she made one important discovery—how difficult it is in our society to organize those who have in common only the fact of rejection.

The following year she transferred to Barnard College, and, one may well say, the die was cast. At Barnard, she lived in a dormitory apartment with a group of sophisticated and talented young women, who shared the sense of excitement and expectancy—the exhilaration—of the 1920s. It was her first young-adult taste of friendship and intimacy by choice within a group.

In college Mead weighed the possibilities of half a dozen careers. Out of a curious modesty she made the choice for which she was most eminently suited. Describing her reasoning, she wrote: "I wanted to make a contribution. It seemed to me then—as it still does—that science is an activity in which . . . any individual, by finding his own level, can make a true contribution. So I chose science—and to me that meant one of the social sciences. My problem then was which of the social sciences?" (1972: 111).

Her first choice was psychology. But, even while she was writing her master's essay, she had made her final choice of anthropology. She herself has described how she came to make that choice—through her growing friendship with Ruth Benedict and the enthusiasm Franz Boas roused.

When Benedict said to her that "Professor Boas and I have nothing to offer but an opportunity to do work that matters" (quoted in Mead 1972: 114), she saw that as a responsibility that could not be avoided. Long ago she had learned to take responsibility, and there it was—for her to accept and carry out. Equally important, I believe, is the fact that Boas valued women highly, recognized talent where he saw it, and backed choices made out of strength. Mead remembered that Boas spent time with his less talented students, so the more talented had to work on their own; she remembered his opposition to her initial plan to work in the remote, isolated Tuamotu Archipelago, but he backed her more modest demand to go to American Samoa against those who thought she was too frail to go anywhere in the field. He feared she might break down not if she went into the field but if she were prevented from doing the work she wanted to do (1959: 288).

So, in 1925, when she had completed her graduate training and had written a library dissertation, *An Inquiry into the Question of Cultural Stability in Polynesia* (1928a), she set out for Samoa—the only field trip in her life in which she worked as an anthropologist alone. Her voluminous letters home kept her in balance, but when she left Samoa her need for intellectual companionship was almost overwhelming.

I have given a disproportionate amount of space to an account of Mead's early years because she herself suggested the themes that connected the early to the later years of her life. Certainly, there is congruence between her view of herself as a child and as a mature woman. From time to time, men in particular have emphasized her aggressiveness, as they saw it. Yet she was not an aggressive woman. She demanded much of others, as she demanded much of herself. But she had little patience with mistaken estimates of one's own capacities.

Margaret Mead herself felt that there was a change point in her life in the years immediately following World War II. In fact, one may discern not two but four phases in her professional life. What was begun in one continues in those that follow; what changes is the emphasis as experience and events alter the choices that can—or must—be made. When the atomic bomb burst over Hiroshima, Mead set aside an unfinished manuscript on the postwar world. We regret the loss. But she felt the world had changed: "We had entered a new age" (1972: 271).

The first phase is *the period between 1925 and 1939*—the period of intense preoccupation with fieldwork. In the brief span of fourteen years, she made five field trips and studied eight peoples: Samoa (1925–1926), where she worked alone but lived with an American naval family, on Tau; Manus (1928–1929), with her second husband, Reo Fortune; Omaha (summer 1930), with Reo Fortune; New Guinea—Arapesh, Mundugumor, and Tchambuli (1931–1933)— with Reo Fortune; Bali (1936–1938, 1939) and New Guinea—the Iatmul of Tambunam (1938)—with her third husband, Gregory Bateson. In between she worked with collections at the American Museum of Natural History, where she was assistant curator of ethnology, and visited museums in Europe to see the old and famous collections in her Pacific area. As a scholar, she achieved a brilliant mastery of the areas she had chosen for her own and published nine major monographs and books (and uncounted articles) on her research and fieldwork. From the beginning she worked in a new and untried field of anthropology that has since been known, generally, as "culture-and-personality." Together with Bateson, she made a dramatic change in methodology through the use of photography. And from working alone and then with one other fieldworker in a close collaboration, she and Gregory developed working relationships with other field-workers, having different talents and skills, who were also engaged in research in Bali.

The second phase includes *the period between 1939 and perhaps 1948,* when, opening the way for so many of us, she applied her knowledge to the very specific applied problems of the war and post-war years in the United States and, increasingly, abroad. As executive secretary of the Committee on Food Habits, National Research Council, she had already grasped how essential interdisciplinary thinking was in approaching these problems, and she succeeded in turning her distinguished and diverse committee into a productive working group that drew on still other research. She continued to publish—an innovative study of Bali, with Bateson (Bateson and Mead 1942); her own first essay on American culture (1965 [1942]); and a number of articles on contemporary problems. Later, in the 1960s, she came to feel that those publications had not reached a younger audience now come of age, and she agreed to republish a set of papers as *Anthropology: A Human Science* (1964).

In the preface of this volume she wrote: "We have reached a period in history in which every discipline is needed . . . in our attempt to deal responsibly with an endangered world" (1964: iv). She was certainly not alone in reaching this conclusion in the war and postwar years, during which interdisciplinary work became a necessity and, briefly, a fashion. But few succeeded in the venture as did those who worked with Mead at this time. During a third phase, more or less *between 1948 and 1953*, we experimented with an open, though carefully controlled, form of interdisciplinary research in Columbia University Research in Contemporary Cultures, for which Benedict had obtained the initial grant from the Office of Naval Research. Its realization, after Benedict's death in 1948, depended in large measure on Mead's coordinating abilities. This was the first in a series of projects that grew out of the applied work on contemporary cultures during the war and became variously known as studies of culture at a distance and studies of national culture or national character. The initial study was comparative in its total design, as research was carried out simultaneously on seven cultures (Mead and Metraux 1953; Mead and Wolfenstein 1955).

It is difficult to say, even now, just why this form of research was so very short-lived, but the willingness of anthropologists and others to take on further projects died away, funds dried up, and the demand for the kind of information by governments dropped off more or less simultaneously.

Finally, *the twenty-five years between 1953 and 1978* became a medley in which all of Mead's talents and interests were intricately interrelated. They were her principal teaching years in the most diverse settings. They were the years during which she became a renowned public speaker with audiences the world over; the years during which she took part in high-level discussion and study groups, served on innumerable committees and commissions, and held high office in scientific organizations; the years during which she finally became a full curator at the museum (in 1964); the years during which she received twenty-seven honorary degrees as well as many awards.

In these years Mead looked for a publishing medium through which an anthropological approach to contemporary problems might reach a very wide audience. It was suggested that she write a newspaper column somewhat like that written by Eleanor Roosevelt. The idea did not appeal to her; these columns would necessarily be very brief and would require an unremitting volume of daily research. Somewhat later, following a very successful interview with Margaret Truman in *Redbook*, she was invited to contribute a monthly column to that magazine, a publishing relationship that continued for seventeen years.

What was more significant in her own eyes was the continuation of her innovative scientific work. In 1953 she returned to Manus, together with

Theodore Schwartz and his wife, now Lenora Foerstal, to undertake recording the immense changes that began during the war and have continued as the Manus people have made their way into the contemporary world. Thereafter she returned five times—in a continuing effort to grasp the intricate process of change—to follow research that was being done by others.

In 1967 and again in 1971, she traveled with me to Tambunam, on the Sepik River, where she had worked with Bateson in 1938, in order to bridge the years and help me initiate another study of the process of change in a very different setting. In 1957 and 1977 she made return trips to Bali, and in 1973 she spent some weeks with a group of Mountain Arapesh who had been scattered and were recently reunited in an experimental oil-palm resettlement on New Britain. From one point of view, these visits were much too short for any coordinated work. But in each situation, with her capacity for intense observation and her prodigious memory, there were details that only she could illuminate for others about past and present.

During these years, as well, Mead and a very young team that she brought together herself worked on preparation of the hall she had been brought to the museum to organize when she came, in 1926. The Hall of the Peoples of the Pacific finally opened in May 1971. By 1975, owing to the reorganization of museum space, the hall was closed; she herself approved the plans for the new hall. [Ed. note: the hall opened in 1984.]

In 1978, as her strength ebbed, Margaret made an immense and valiant effort to meet her obligations; she even dreamed of traveling to Manus once more. It was too late. But, characteristically, her last conversation was related to fieldwork. Five nights before her death she began to plan how we would spend the coming winter analyzing Bateson's Iatmul films in great detail. Her mind moved as swiftly and played as lightly with ideas as on the morning, long ago, when we first talked in her office.

She died quietly on the early morning of November 15.

RHODA METRAUX

It is fitting that we commemorate the centenary of Margaret Mead's birth, in view of her larger-than-life presence in anthropology and in American society for over fifty years. But it does not serve us to rewrite her life and work in celebratory terms. What I wish to do, rather, is to think back on the trajectory that Mead followed, from her first foray to Samoa in 1925 at the age of twenty-three until her death in 1978, and to ask what messages we may draw from it today. I propose to focus on three aspects of Mead's career: her championing of culture as an antidote to biological determinism and American ethnocentrism, drawing especially on her studies of seven cultures in Oceania; her pioneering of new approaches in anthropology and her visions of its future; and her advocacy of a public role for anthropology, a role that she assumed as her personal mantle.

To understand Mead's career, it is necessary to go back to Franz Boas, her mentor, who established the department at Columbia at about the time that Mead was born. As Boas struggled against the prevailing theorizing of his day, which viewed primitive cultures in terms of evolutionary schemes, and against a typological and racialist tradition in physical anthropology, he counterposed against these the notions of *culture* as an independent realm, separate from race (and from language), and of *cultures* as historically situated contexts for learned human behavior. These concerns, of course, had political implications, and Boas brought his views into the public arena. For example, his own study of the bodily changes in the children of immigrants, in comparison to their parents (1911a), spoke directly to the capacity of the then-surging numbers of immigrants to the United States to become assimilated Americans, and he used his research to challenge anti-immigration policies. Boas imbued in his students a belief in the importance of their anthropological expertise and the necessity of communicating it to the public. This project took on new urgency with the rise of Nazism in the 1930s and the undiminished destructive force of American-style racism, even as national energies focused on World War II.

Eric Wolf (1969b), in attempting to relate major phases in the history of American anthropology to periods in the development of American society, labeled the years from the last decade of the nineteenth century to the onset of World War II as a period of (intermittent) liberal reform in the United States. The dominant themes of this period were an assertion of the claims of society as a whole against the rights of the untrammeled individualistic entrepreneur and a sponsorship of the mobility of groups not hitherto represented in the social and political arena. The corresponding emphasis in anthropology was on cultural plurality and relativity, human malleability, and a view of individual cultures as organic wholes and moral paradigms. Boas, of course, was the main spokesman of this kind of anthropology, which had its manifestation first in historical particularism and then in the culture-and-personality schools that came to the fore in the 1930s.

Boas's research program for his discipline emphasized empirical study of the diverse cultures of the world, especially through fieldwork. His approach encompassed both historical strategies, which began with methods for tracing culture traits but increasingly called attention to the internal patterning of cultures, and psychological interests in the individual in culture. These two aspects also represented an epistemological contrast: between the historical and the scientific. Although Boas himself combined and shifted between these aspects, the generation of his students after World War I emphasized the second.

Mead was part of that second generation. Boas seems to have mellowed by that time. This cohort of his students included a substantial number of women (some of them beginning as his secretary); he chose their research topics and found funds for their fieldwork, although none of these women achieved regular academic positions during his lifetime. Ruth Benedict, who went on to produce the most extreme example of Boas's integrationist thread, her *Patterns of Culture* (1934), became his administrative right hand, although she was passed over for his chair in favor of Ralph Linton.

After Mead moved from DePauw University to Barnard in her second year of college, she took courses with Boas, but it was Benedict to whom she became closest intellectually and personally. Mead took her M.A. in psychology with a thesis on Italian immigrant families in New Jersey (completing the study begun by her mother). Then—with Benedict's offer, on Boas's behalf, of "only work that mattered"—she embraced anthropology, writing a library dissertation on Polynesia (1928a).

Mead's maiden field trip to Samoa was in the spirit of Boas's scientific side. She had decided that she wanted to do fieldwork in Polynesia, and Boas agreed reluctantly, selecting for her a research topic he thought was consistent with her age and persona: the relative strength of biological puberty and cultural patterns of adolescence. Given the Boasian belief in cultures as diverse contexts for human development and behavior, the study would question the general assumption in the United States at the time that adolescence was inevitably stormy because of biological, hormonal givens. In fact, Mead made no effort to study "relative strengths" of biological and cultural factors; she thought, rather, that if she found a single negative case, it would disprove what was taken to be a universal. The study was also a pursuit of Boas's psychological interests, an attempt (as he said in the preface to *Coming of Age in Samoa* [1928b]) "to enter the mental life of a group in a primitive society." Mead's work opened up several new niches for anthropology, including new interests in the Pacific and several topics not heretofore central to the discipline. Moreover, once she acceded to her publisher's suggestion that she popularize her book by adding a chapter on implications for American society, it also became a touchstone for what would soon become her special public role as a commentator on American culture from the perspective of a trained observer of the exotic. *Coming of Age* was the initial basis for her popular fame and for much of the later criticism of her fieldwork; less attention has been paid to her parallel technical account, *Social Organization of Manua* (1930a), which has been lauded for its ethnographic range and the probity of its analysis.

Mead's subsequent field studies in Oceania during the 1930s followed the same pattern of dual publication: a popular book that carried her message of cultural diversity and applied her research with primitives to issues in contemporary life, and records of her data and analysis for the use of specialists. Thus, Samoa was followed by Manus in the Admiralty Islands, which resulted in both *Growing Up in New Guinea: A Comparative Study of Primitive Education* (1930b) and a detailed monograph on kinship (1934). She went to Manus (with Reo Fortune) to study the presumed "animistic thought" of primitive children but found that the idea was erroneous, and instead she focused on how children's mode of thought changes as they grow into adulthood. She used these findings to speak, in her popular book, to the current American educational system and to offer recommendations for changing it.

Her next field trip (again with Fortune) was to the Mountain Arapesh in New Guinea. It yielded five monographs on material culture, supernaturalism, socioeconomic life, and other aspects of her ethnography. It is best known, however, as the first of her cases in *Sex and Temperament in Three Primitive Societies* (1935). Mead's central problem was to study "the different ways in which cultures patterned the expected behavior of males and females" (1972: 196). She continued this interest in her fieldwork in Mundugumor and then in Tchambuli (Chambri), both in the Sepik River area in New Guinea. These constitute the other cases in *Sex and Temperament*. The comparison of the three cases enabled her to make broad statements about the plasticity of human sex roles and the diverse ways in which biological differences are molded into culturally appropriate behaviors and temperaments of men and women. This book became enormously popular and influential in the United States.

In Bali, with Gregory Bateson, Mead focused especially on child rearing, which she linked to cultural patterns of various kinds. This work, along with that in Iatmul (on the Sepik in New Guinea), left a vast and unequaled photographic record (see Bateson and Mead 1942 for Bali), although Mead did not publish a full ethnographic account of either culture.

In reviewing Mead's Oceania ethnography, it is well to note how different her accounts are from the Boasian tradition out of which she emerged, even from her own doctoral dissertation on Polynesian culture traits and their diffusion. As Nancy McDowell (1980) has argued, Mead introduced a vivid sense of dynamic processes, of living people with their individual personality differences manipulating cultural norms as much as conforming to them, liberally laced with her own intuitive generalizations. In this, Mead ushered in a new style of ethnography and of ethnographic writing.

Mead's insistence upon culture and upon what cultural diversity has to teach modern society was cruelly distorted by Derek Freeman (1983, 1999) and other latter-day critics, who accused her of launching a long period of permissiveness in child rearing (in this she was presumably abetted by Dr. Benjamin Spock, her friend and family pediatrician) and associated societal ills from the sexual revolution to the antiwar movement. (Many of her admirers also attributed this influence to her, *crediting* her for it.) Neither Boas nor any of his students, including Mead, believed in "absolute cultural determinism," as Freeman charged. Boas's anthropology was premised on the interaction of biological and cultural phenomena (and he championed four-field anthropology partly on that basis), but he and his students were also continually battling against racial determinism, especially beliefs that the "races" had different mental capacities. Their weapon was a cultural determinism which argued that behavior and mentality were products of learning within specific cultural settings. Mead in Samoa was simply not concerned with studying the relative strengths of biology and culture, despite the formal phrasing of her research problem. Her point, along with other anthropologists of her time, was the fundamental lesson of cultural variability.

In fact, Mead herself was much inclined to bring biology into her explications of cultural patterns. *Male and Female: A Study of the Sexes in a Changing World* brought to a popular postwar audience the problem, "How are men and women to think about their maleness and their femaleness in this twentieth century, in which so many of our old ideas must be made anew?" (1949: 13). Here Mead argued that every question involving human beings must consider both biology and culture and that "our full humanity" is "rooted in our biological ancestry that we dare not flout" (1949: 26). When she was criticized for trying to "have it both ways" (both cultural and biological explanations of sex differences), she responded that "we not only can have it both ways, but many more than both ways" (Sanday 1980: 340). This position later put her at odds with the feminist movement—Betty Friedan charged her with laying the cornerstone of the "feminine mystique"—although after her death feminists claimed her for their ranks.

Nevertheless, Mead's message about the role of culture in human affairs is one that anthropologists have had to return to again and again throughout the second half of the twentieth century, and it is no less relevant in a time when foreign policy is guided by a banal language of good and evil and when similar simplistic notions are made to define ethnically marked peoples. Cultural relativism never meant a bland denial of enduring values or of principled political stances, least of all as Mead intended it. It has always meant a quest for knowledge of cultural contexts and cultural causality. As Mead argued, to understand cultural processes in their own terms as a first step in that quest is not to condone or to excuse, but to fail to take that step is a formula for disaster.

This aspect of Mead remains vital for the present in a particular way, in view of the challenge of a "biology is destiny" wave that has been overtaking our public discourse in recent years. This development, which was only beginning at the time of her death (if we take the publication of Edward O. Wilson's *Sociobiology* in 1975 as the opening gun), was the context in which Freeman launched his postmortem attack on Mead in 1983. Although he framed his argument around the charge that she was "hoaxed" by her Samoan informants (a charge he expanded in his later book [1999]), his agenda was in fact to discredit her culturalist stance. With the cultural dimension demolished, Freeman insinuated, the explanation of Samoan behavior would have to be (by default) rooted in biology. Moreover, through his equating of culture versus biology with positive versus negative human qualities, he underscored disagreeable qualities of Samoan life discounted in Mead's supposedly idyllic depiction. In fact, whatever limits there were to Mead's ethnography Freeman's assault neither identified nor corrected.

More importantly, Mead's insistence on the significance of culture, in all its complexity, for any understanding of human behavior speaks directly to the biological, genetic, and other new reductionisms that have become common not only in academic circles but also in the media and in policy discussions. Most prominent among these is the view that all of human behavior is the product of natural selection governed by Darwinian principles of reproductive competition. Like Mead's generation in their own struggles against racialist theories, most anthropologists today acknowledge the evolutionary basis of human behavioral patterns but take strong issue with the erasure of cultural variability and of social and historical context in this approach. For example, when evolutionary psychologists designate specific items of behavior as universal and locate their origins in the conditions of the evolutionary past, the items identified are often neither neutral nor self-evident; rather, they are taken from our own or some other known culture and are defined in culturally framed ways. As Mead argued tirelessly (beginning with Samoa), for an item to be considered a universal it would have to apply to all known times and places, not just to isolated instances selected from here and there. Moreover, she would have insisted, because cultures are internally patterned they cannot be treated merely as lists of discrete items.

In the course of the 1990s, as the mapping of the human genome and other developments in genetics progressed, the earlier versions of biological determinism increasingly became genetic determinism. It is now "the gene" that is explanatory. Yet recent research of anthropologists has underlined the extent to which genetic "information" is shaped by and interwoven with social practices and cultural interpretations, which throws into question the use of notions of genetics as all-purpose explanations and problem solvers (e.g., Goodman et al. 2003). More than ever we need to remember what Mead and many other anthropologists labored long and hard to discover and affirm—the complexity of cultural phenomena that can only be severely violated if they are reduced to some presumably more "basic" level.

Mead was in many ways a pioneer. First and foremost was her approach to methodology. She saw other cultures as irreplaceable natural laboratories for science, and she was scrupulous about detailed recording, about keeping data in a form that made them usable by other scientists, and about stating explicitly the methods she used and the circumstances under which her data were collected. (In her field methods seminar at Columbia, she warned students that they needed to keep their notes in a form that—"if you died tomorrow"—they would be accessible to others.) She embraced new technologies as they emerged and saw them as tools as well as topics for anthropological research. A prime example was her early, elaborate use of photography and film as methods for field research, especially in Bali and Iatmul with Bateson. She was among the first to use psychological tests in the field, such as the Rorschach test and children's drawings. She also experimented with innovative ways of presenting her data and methods in monographs (McDowell 1980: 293).

Mead quickly grasped the implications of new developments in science and in other fields, such as the beginning of the atomic age, the invention of computers, and the emergence of cybernetics and systems theory. Each such development drew her into interdisciplinary collaborations, which involved her in numerous working committees, conferences, and joint publications; whatever the concrete results of these efforts, they gave social science (including anthropology) a voice in discussions of the vital issues of the day. Through her participation in such activities, Mead repeatedly defined new areas for anthropological interest, including such now-trendy topics as the built environment and science studies. She was in many ways anthropology's futurist: she wrote and spoke about the future of the family, of cities, of work and leisure, of education, of war and peace, and other themes that she believed anthropology could address. In her foreshadowing of directions that her discipline would take she was more right than wrong, even if others pursued these directions in ways different from those she anticipated.

I witnessed her reaction to one major development of our time. In the fall of 1957 I took one of her heavily enrolled courses in the General Studies Division at Columbia. One evening she asked the class: What was the most important thing that happened to you this week? Different people ventured responses: I found an apartment; I got a new job; I broke up with my boyfriend. After hearing us all out, Mead said: No, the most important thing that happened to you this week was that Sputnik went up. For most of us, there was a disconnect between what happened "to us" and what was unarguably the most important thing that happened to the world. Not for Mead. Her view was not only that we were all profoundly affected, now living in a changed world, but that anthropology was uniquely equipped to understand it; her first reaction to Sputnik was that every space flight from then on should carry an anthropologist. She never doubted that this could be done or that anthropology would yield special insights into our new world.

Mead was above all a pioneer in her commitment to a public role for anthropology—the third aspect of her work that I want to consider. She advocated
anthropology's "going public" at a time when many would have been happy to
be left alone to their academic pursuits. Throughout her career, she took two
routes—often simultaneously—to bring her messages about culture and the anthropological perspective to the public. One was through her engagement with
scientific projects, organizations, and networks, building alliances with other
scientists and intellectuals to speak to the large concerns of the time and to try
to influence public policy. The second route was her individual entrepreneur-
ship, using especially the popular media (magazines, lectures to diverse audiences, radio, then television), a pattern that goes back to her early years when
she was feted as the girl scientist among the savages.

As World War II loomed, she immersed herself in this public role. Unlike
in the wartimes of the latter twentieth century, anthropologists, like others
in America and the allied countries, eagerly enlisted in the common cause.
The problem anthropologists had was not any doubts or dissension about the
war effort but the fact that no one in government paid much attention to
them. But Mead, for one, had extraordinary confidence in the potential of
anthropology to point to directions for national policy. She also had extraordinary naïveté.

Her frame of mind can be detected from a letter she wrote to Eleanor Roosevelt in August 1939 (cited in Yans-McLaughlin 1986: 194–95). Identifying
herself "as a professional anthropologist" who was speaking in light of her "field
experience of simpler social systems" and referring to the conjectures of some
psychiatrists about "Hitler's peculiar psychological make-up," she claims that
we can "enlist Hitler actively on the side of peace" and "halt [his] present march
towards destruction." What Mrs. Roosevelt needed to do was to urge her husband to "divert [Hitler] from an undesirable course towards a desirable one" by
putting his past acts "into a moral setting" and persuading him that he, "by
virtue of his great constructive efforts to build up his own country, had the
chance now" for greater glory, by building the peace of all Europe. (A month
later, Hitler overran Poland.)

This pattern of direct approaches to presidents (or their wives) was to continue throughout her life. It reached its height in her contacts with Jimmy
Carter, to whom she offered advice based on her reading of his personality and
of his regional culture. Both in personal encounters and in letters to "Dear
Jimmy," she held forth on numerous issues facing his administration and even
analyzed his style of leadership with diagrams (for which he graciously thanked
her) (Dillon 1980: 320–24).

Her first organizational effort to engage World War II came in 1939 with her
involvement, along with several psychologists and other behavioral scientists, in
the Committee for National Morale, a private organization whose purpose was

to prepare social scientists to analyze population morale and advise the government on how to advance it. In 1942 she shifted her focus to a Committee on Food Habits of the National Research Council, becoming its executive secretary. In that capacity she initiated multidisciplinary research geared to policies to change the food habits of Americans and to feed our allies; the research yielded recommendations if not actual influences on government policy (Mabee 1987: 3–5).

The best-known aspect of Mead's contribution to the war effort was her prominent place within a group of anthropologists who used their skills to provide cultural analyses of our enemies and allies. What became the "national character" approach began with the four anthropologists on the Committee for National Morale, working closely with Benedict and Geoffrey Gorer, and was further advanced when Mead, along with Bateson, Lawrence K. Frank, and Edwin R. Embree formed the Council for Intercultural Relations in 1941 (Mead 1959: 351). Drawing on the personality-and-culture movement of the 1930s and developing methods for studying cultures no longer directly accessible, they extended the notion of "cultural character structure" to depictions of the Japanese, German, Russian, British, and peoples of other nations. Mead herself wrote (in 1942) one of the first books in this vein, on the American character, *And Keep Your Powder Dry*, which was intended to aid the morale of the American public (1965 [1942]). These studies were designed to predict the behavior of particular groups, and as Mead later recounted, they had a variety of political purposes: to implement specific governmental programs, to facilitate relationships with allies and partisan groups in occupied countries, to help estimate enemy strengths and weaknesses, and to recommend and provide rationales for policies (Mead and Metraux 1953: 397). Mead credited the national-character work, specifically Benedict's research on the Japanese for the Office of War Information, with having a direct impact on the American government's decision to retain the Japanese emperor as a figurehead at the end of the war. Others have found little evidence of this widely accepted claim and believe that Alexander Leighton was closer to the reality in observing that government policymakers used social science the way a drunk uses a lamppost, for support rather than light (Mabee 1987: 10).

After the war Benedict and Mead expanded this effort into a large-scale project, the Columbia University Research in Contemporary Cultures, under a grant from the U.S. Office of Naval Research. The project was organized around research groups that focused on seven different cultures, which would be studied "at a distance," from New York City. When Benedict died in 1948 Mead became the project coordinator. Mead's hope was to expand the range of cultures included, and as always, her ambition was as grand as her sweep, but the project found little resonance with policymakers and it fell into obscurity.

During the postwar years of rapid change throughout the world, Mead initiated and encouraged studies of cultural continuities and change, revisiting areas where she had done fieldwork before the war (usually in the company of younger scholars now working there) and commenting from her anthropological perspective on changes in other societies, including her own. In the standoffs of the Cold War, she remained firm in the conviction that cross-cultural communication held the key to peace. Throughout this time she was a prominent public presence, pursuing both routes to bringing anthropology to national (and international) consciousness and policy. (Wilton Dillon has described her as "a multinational enterprise . . . acting on a series of world stages" [1980: 332].) She used her fame and personal contacts in the political arena, such as by testifying before Congress, and was active in numerous organizations of scientists addressing public issues. Despite the chastening experiences of Hiroshima and Nagasaki and the chilling effect of McCarthyism on many of her professional colleagues, her confidence in the power of anthropology was not diminished.

This was the period of her life when I knew Margaret Mead, when I was a student at Columbia during the late 1950s and early 1960s. Her primary base was still at the American Museum of Natural History. I first met her, as had countless others before and since, by climbing the stairs to her tower office with a letter of introduction from someone in her vast network of acquaintances to ask her for career advice, which she gave generously. She taught part-time in the Columbia anthropology department, whether by her choice or theirs we did not know; she held the title of adjunct professor but never had a regular appointment there. My cohort was advised by more advanced graduate students to avoid working too closely with her; if you became her student you would have her attention and loyalty, but other professors would not take you seriously. Still, we took her courses, and we learned some useful things from her: how to pay attention, with an anthropological ear, to the world beyond the university; how to take field notes (and mail them home regularly); how to remember people's names (as a result of which I still remember the name of one student in our seminar unknown to me before or since); how to identify the cultural background of informants she brought in to demonstrate interviewing techniques (my guesses were always wildly wrong); and other wisdom, both valuable and dubious.

The revolutions of the 1960s and 1970s and the divisions of the Vietnam era shattered the illusions of anthropologists not only—like others—of national unity but also of the unity of anthropology. In this intradisciplinary strife, Mead often found herself opposed and embattled. She never gave up the ideal, born of World War II, of an anthropology in service to the national cause, even when there was reason to question the cause.

Within the AAA, matters came to a head in 1970 when charges were made public that a number of anthropologists were implicated in counterinsurgency research in Thailand. Mead was appointed to head a committee to investigate the charges, as well as the countercharges that the Ethics Committee of the Association had acted improperly in questioning the activities of colleagues. Its official name was "Ad Hoc Committee to Evaluate the Controversy Concerning Anthropological Activities in Thailand," but it was always referred to as the Mead Committee. Mead was the "obvious choice" for this role because of the respect she commanded—according to George Foster, then president-elect of the AAA, she was a "mother-goddess" in her relationship to the tribe of anthropologists (Wakin 1992: 201).

The Mead Committee report in essence chastised the Ethics Committee while downplaying the original charges. The report concluded that the anthropological research now treated under the label of "counterinsurgency" referred to "much the same activities that were called 'community development' at an earlier time. . . . [It is] well within the traditional canons of acceptable behavior for the applied anthropologist, and is counterinsurgent only for present funding purposes; a decade ago it might have been 'mental health'" (Wakin 1992: 205). At the next meeting of the AAA, the membership roundly rejected Mead's report in a humiliating repudiation of this epic figure. In a final chapter of the story, Mead had all the documents of her committee's investigations destroyed (this despite her long insistence on the preservation of research records for the use of other scholars). Referring to the behavior of those who had opposed acceptance of the report, she wrote to the executive director of the AAA in 1972: "After the continuing display of irresponsibility, the committee decided to destroy the files. This was done" (Wakin 1992: 230).

Despite, or because of, her public role, there was always a distinct ambivalence in the relationship between Mead and the anthropological profession. She was dismissed by many as a popularizer; E. E. Evans-Pritchard's characterization of the Samoa book as "the rustling-of-the-wind-in-the-palm-trees" kind of anthropology was widely repeated by her own compatriots. (Ironically, Freeman's attack led to a posthumous reappraisal and defense of her scholarship by some who had been critical of it.) Some of this ambivalence surely came from envy of her fame, but many anthropologists despaired of her too-ready generalizations, for she would speak unhesitatingly—often authoritatively but sometimes pushing beyond her knowledge with shrewd guesswork—and offer anthropologically informed opinions on practically any subject put to her. At the same time, she was the conscience and the scold of the profession, both for those who agreed with her and those who did not, those who found her analyses compelling and those who considered them trivial. In a real sense, she guarded the borders between anthropology and the public; to a large extent, she succeeded both in raising the stature of the discipline in the world and in keeping her colleagues in line. For years after her death, anthropologists lamented that there was now no one else to speak for them to their publics.

Mead's commitment to engaging public issues and applying her science to them left a legacy for anthropologists who came after her. But it must be said that her vigor and outspokenness in public pronouncements went along with a certain timidity where controversial political matters were at stake. She avoided giving offense—for the sake, she would have said, of wielding influence in the longer term—and she preferred working behind the scenes rather than direct confrontation. I had a taste of this when, in 1976, I contacted her for help in a crisis facing the anthropology programs in the City University of New York. She refused my request to intervene and instead chastised me, saying, "Be an anthropologist!" (the most stinging reprimand an anthropologist could receive). I later learned that she had in fact made the calls I had asked for, and they were effective.

Using Mead's own accounts to look back over her life as a public anthropologist (or an anthropologist in public), I believe one can see a remarkable consistency in what she thought she was about, although she adapted her purpose to the needs of different times. She began her work as an ethnographer with a scientific goal—to construct a systematic picture of how human culture works—and with an avowedly scientific methodology, taking primitive societies as her laboratory. But she always had another purpose in mind for this work: to provide a scientific basis for building a better world (1965: 14). Her interests, she later said, had always turned on the relevance of the study of primitive peoples to our understanding of our own customary behavior and our attempts to change it, and for that reason she had always ended her books on peoples of the South Seas with a discussion of how the results could be applied to modern societies (1965: xxvii).

But she thought of a "better world" from her distinctively American perspective, and she never pretended to scientific detachment in the messages she brought to her public. She wrote that her 1942 account of the American national character was "frankly and completely partisan" (1965: xi), and she regretted that contemporary anthropological studies of the United States (the Middletown, Yankee City, and Deep South books) were critical of ("indicted") American culture. Her own book ended with an expression of faith that Americans have the tools necessary to develop a new world order, one that would allow the realization of human potentials (1965 [1942]: 252). Moreover, her optimism about America was not just wartime patriotism. Her introduction to *New Lives for Old* says:

> This book is set firmly against such pessimism [about our ability to meet the challenges of the world of the 1950s]. It is based on the belief that American civilization is not simply the last flower to bloom on the outmoded tree of European history . . . but something new and different. . . . This book is based on the belief that Americans have something to contribute to a changing world which is precious. . . . This

precious quality . . . is a belief that men can learn and change . . . quickly, happily, without violence, without madness, without coercion, and of their own free will. (1966 [1956]: 31)

Another aspect of Mead's consistency was her view of the role of government and of a citizenry's relationship to it. This view was set firmly in place during the World War II period, as Dillon has suggested (1980: 335). Although she was not a champion of big or intrusive government—on the contrary, her ideal was "small is beautiful," and she believed that individuals and small groups had the power to change the world—she thought it was the responsibility of anthropologists, as citizens and scientists, to support government policies and work to enlighten and improve them. No doubt her unchanged convictions in this regard were the source of her misreading of anthropologists' positions on the Thailand affair and her dismay at the AAA membership's reaction to her role in it.

Underlying what I have described as Mead's consistency as an anthropologist in public was the fact that, in Dillon's words (1980: 337), she "was free of conflict between her roles as fastidious fieldworker and as improver of the self-knowledge of her countrymen by sharing anthropology with governments and various publics." Yet the relationship between those two roles took different forms as times changed. She described some of that process herself in her introduction to *New Lives for Old*.

During the early years of her intensive ethnography, a sense of the Boasian scientific mission dominated. This was the first time, she said, that the scientific world of the West was ready to use constructively knowledge of the so-soon-to-vanish living behavior of people not yet within any of the great streams of civilization. Anthropologists could now go beyond armchair ruminations and set up problems to answer—not by turning human beings into experimental animals, but by scientifically controlled observations of the living stuff of history. And the payoff would be that we could add enormously to our knowledge of human potentialities (1966: 35). Where to go to do this work was a judgment about what was the logical next step in our developing science (1966: 36).

Priorities changed, however, when the immediate threat was Nazism and fascism; now the need was to choose problems that could confront the threat. For Mead, the most pressing problem was how individuals become members of a culture, regardless of their racial inheritance or the culture of their ancestors. This meant a focus on the study of personality in culture, character formation, and the relationship of cultural character to institutions. The emphasis in this had to be on human plasticity (1966: 37). The study target also shifted, from primitives to modern nations. The postwar, post-Hiroshima, world—a time of emergency for humankind—presented new challenges. Mead saw the key problem then as how change occurred in a single generation, the problem that took her back to Manus in 1953 (1966: 38).

After this revisit, she did no further fieldwork but concentrated on the second of her roles, as an "improver" of the self-knowledge of her countrymen—and increasingly of an international public as well. Yet she did so cloaked in the mystique and the knowledge that came out of her life as a field-worker. It is said that she sometimes consulted her New Guinea field notes before going into a committee meeting on some current social problem or testifying before Congress, just as her pronouncements in the media about American culture drew continually on her storehouse of ethnographic examples.

Much has changed in anthropology and in the world since Mead first "went public." Her ready prescriptions for her own society based upon her fieldwork among the primitives came to be seen—not surprisingly—as simplistic, although we can appreciate the validity of her underlying message. Her national-character contributions to the war effort have long been criticized for their ready collapsing of internal complexities and historical contingencies into thumbnail accounts of nationwide uniformities. The Cold War world of aligned nation-states and a passive Third World has passed, and anthropology has turned its efforts toward grasping processes of transnationalism, globalization, political mobilization, and cultural reconstitution. No one would have been less surprised by these changes in her discipline than Mead, and she herself anticipated some of them, but there is little in her work that offers analytical guidance for such a reshaping of anthropology.

The publics to whom anthropology speaks today are different from those of Mead's time. Undergraduate classes that used to learn about cultural diversity by being introduced to the exotic peoples of the world now often include some of those exotics, and students may themselves practice and believe in the odd customs their anthropology professors exhibited for culture shock or pedagogical titillation. Another of anthropology's publics, those with whom and for whom anthropologists work beyond the walls of academia, has also changed. Applied anthropology goes back to Mead's own time, and indeed she was one of its architects. But today more than ever in the past, anthropologists are employed by organizations of various kinds that set the terms of what the anthropologist will do and how his or her work will be used. This situation poses contradictions that defy Mead's confident prescriptions for using anthropology for the enlightenment of nonprofessionals. Still another public is the citizenry to which anthropologists belong and to which they may wish to contribute their expertise—for example, when anthropologists find themselves among the few people who know anything about the strange and distant places that suddenly become the fare of daily news. For Mead, this role was unproblematic, but it becomes more complicated when the anthropologist has deep criticisms of government policies. Mead would have advised caution in expressing criticism for the sake of ultimately being able to exert influence, but some would find this strategy naïve and futile. Finally, there is "the public" at large. This is a different lot than those who read Mead's columns in *Redbook* or listened to her expound on late-night

television about cultural differences in gender definition or child rearing. Today's public is both more sophisticated and more misguided than was Mead's. It
is doubtful that her assertions and admonitions would be as convincing as they
once seemed.

Each of these new publics represents challenges for the anthropologist. Margaret Mead would have seized the challenges with gusto, and she would probably have turned a blind eye to the contradictions and dilemmas they pose,
exhorting her colleagues to "just get to work." Hers was a presence that belongs
to another time, and it is one that has no real successor in anthropology today.

SYDEL SILVERMAN

BIOGRAPHICAL NOTE

Courtesy of Daniel Metraux   *c. 1970*

RHODA METRAUX was born in 1914 in Brooklyn, New York. She attended Vassar College, where she received a B.A. in English literature in 1934, and went
on to Columbia University to study anthropology. In the early 1940s she carried
out fieldwork in Haiti, in collaboration with her then-husband Alfred Metraux;
in Mexico, on a study of responses to wartime food shortages; and in Argentina.
She returned to Haiti in 1948–1949 to work on a UNESCO project in fundamental education, which formed the basis for her Ph.D. dissertation at Columbia," "Kith and Kin: A Study of Creole Social Structure in Marbial, Haiti" (1951).

During the war Metraux served on the planning staff of the Office of Strategic Services, studying problems of German civilian and Japanese armed-forces

morale. Having also worked closely with Margaret Mead on the Committee on Food Habits, she was intimately involved in the project initiated by Mead with Ruth Benedict, the Columbia University Research in Contemporary Cultures, which continued from 1947 to 1953. In this project, Metraux applied the methods of qualitative analysis of verbal materials she had developed in her earlier work, combining them now with interview data and historical sources to construct depictions of cultures that were not accessible through fieldwork. Metraux, whose particular area of expertise was French culture, was co-editor of two of the volumes to result from the project, *The Study of Culture at a Distance* (Mead and Metraux 1953) and *Themes in French Culture* (Metraux and Mead 1954). In 1952–1953 she directed a project on German national character, which was the basis for three chapters on German children that she contributed to *Childhood in Contemporary Cultures* (Mead and Wolfenstein 1955).

When these projects ended, Metraux became director of the Montserrat (British West Indies) Anthropological Expedition. She then served as associate director of a study of "the factor of allopsychic orientation in mental health" funded by the National Institutes of Health, in which she applied the methods she had earlier developed for work on verbal and visual materials to the analysis of sensory modalities. She returned to Montserrat in 1966, when she embarked on a project to compare the cultural structure of imagery there with Manus and Iatmul of Papua New Guinea, peoples that had been studied by Mead and her collaborators in the 1930s. In several trips to Iatmul (some in Mead's company), she looked at continuity and change since Mead's original study and recorded traditional music.

Rhoda Metraux, an active researcher and lecturer on anthropological contributions to psychology and psychiatry, education, and the health sciences, maintained her institutional base at the American Museum of Natural History. She now lives in retirement in Vermont.

BIOGRAPHICAL NOTE

Photo by June Finfer   1998

SYDEL SILVERMAN was born in Chicago in 1933, the youngest of seven children of a rabbi (himself descended from a line of rabbinical scholars) and an uneducated but powerfully intelligent, independent mother. Both parents had emigrated from Lithuania as young adults. Sydel Finfer grew up on the West Side of Chicago; had a brief stint as a pre-med at the University of Illinois; then, after two years of college, entered the M.A. program of the Committee on Human Development at the University of Chicago. By the time the M.A. was awarded in 1957, she had spent a year in Europe with her artist-husband (Mel Silverman) and had moved to New York. There she found that her interdisciplinary master's degree (along with her typing skills) qualified her for jobs as a secretary for, among others, Louis Finkelstein, chancellor of the Jewish Theological Seminary, and the architect Frederick Kiesler. She then decided to return to graduate school.

Wanting to gain expertise in a single discipline, Silverman opted for anthropology (the most interdisciplinary field she could find that still carried a disciplinary label) and enrolled at Columbia, the only real choice for doctoral study in New York at the time. The department required training in the four fields of anthropology, and the students took (or audited) courses all across the spectrum of the discipline. Marvin Harris and Morton Fried gave the cultural anthropology a strong materialist emphasis, but Silverman also studied with Conrad Arensberg, Charles Wagley, Harold Conklin, Joseph Greenberg (who taught a famous theory course), the linguist Uriel Weinreich, Margaret Mead, and others. Arensberg was her major influence, especially in his theoretical approach to complex societies, including Europe. Europe was still suspect as a place for anthropological fieldwork, but Arensberg showed it to be an ethnographically promising area and encouraged students to consider it for their dissertation research. Silverman was attracted to Italy from her earlier travels there, and she quickly discovered that Central Italy was a distinctive, yet virtually unstudied, region; moreover, its agrarian economy resonated with the then-predominant concern with peasantry in the emerging anthropology of complex societies.

Silverman did fieldwork in Umbria in 1960–1961 and wrote her dissertation on the traditional *mezzadria* share-farming system and its implications for social stratification and town-country relations. When she returned to Italy in 1968 and then in the 1970s (with her second husband, Eric Wolf), the *mezzadria* had been abolished and the Central Italian countryside transformed. The dramatic change led her into historical research on the area, which she joined to her earlier ethnography in her book *Three Bells of Civilization: The Life of an Italian Hill Town* (1975). Delving into history, in turn, drew her attention to the political context of urban festivals such as the Palio of Siena (e.g., 1979), which had been analyzed primarily as symbolic expressions, and she embarked in the early 1980s upon a comparative study of such competitive festivals throughout Central and Northern Italy. During this period, she also became increasingly interested in the history of anthropology.

After receiving her Ph.D. in 1963, Silverman began teaching part-time at Queens College, where her colleagues included Hortense Powdermaker and fellow Mediterraneanist Ernestine Friedl. That job grew into a tenure-track position and ultimately a professorship as the City University of New York enjoyed a major expansion during the 1960s. She served as chairman of the Queens anthropology department (1970–1973) and then, in 1975, moved to the Graduate Center as executive officer of the CUNY Ph.D. Program in Anthropology. Except for a year as acting dean of the Graduate School (1982–1983), she held that position until the end of 1986, when she became president of the Wenner-Gren Foundation for Anthropological Research (1987–1999).

At Wenner-Gren, Silverman strove to combine the support of basic research in anthropology with initiatives to enhance anthropology as an integrative, comparative, international discipline. Her most significant achievements toward that end were in the twenty-five international symposia that she oversaw, described in her book *The Beast on the Table: Conferencing with Anthropologists* (2002). Through the symposium program, she also sponsored new international organizations, including the European Association of Social Anthropologists and the Pan-African Association of Anthropologists. In addition, consistent with her own interests in the history of anthropology, she initiated a long-term effort to conserve anthropology's own documents through the creation of the Council for the Preservation of Anthropological Records, CoPAR (see Silverman and Parezo 1995).

Sydel Silverman now works as an anthropologist-at-large from her home in Irvington, New York.

NOTES

CHAPTER I

1. Stocking has summarized how Boas changed the concept of culture from that of Tylor's time to its modern usage, incorporating the elements of historicity, plurality, integration, behavioral determinism, and relativity (1968a: 200).

2. The author's title for the paper on which this chapter is based was "Franz Boas and the Modernization of Anthropology." It was presented, with some variations in content, at the University of Pennsylvania (1973), Yale University (1973), Calgary University (1974), Cornell University (1974), Barnard College (1975), Hofstra University (1975), and McMaster University (1975). The author acknowledges the kindness of the American Philosophical Society (APS) for use of materials from the Boas collection.

3. Boas's comments on this occasion are reported in the *American Anthropologist* 9 (1907): 646–47.

4. Marian W. Smith was trained at Columbia and was an active anthropologist for years in the United States before she went abroad, where later she became secretary of the Royal Anthropological Institute of Great Britain and Ireland. She was well experienced in both American anthropology and British social anthropology.

5. All quotations in this paragraph are from Boas's "Diary from Baffinland" (APS, 2).

6. This quotation is from "Proceedings of the American Ethnological Society" in the *American Anthropologist* 23 (1921): 514.

CHAPTER 2

1. I've always thought this was something of a blessing, since it enabled him to write in the middle of a pandemonium of children and grandchildren without ever

hearing them. It also served him in conversation. He would locate certain people on his deaf side and smile reassuringly as they would explain their position, making them feel they had their day in court. Then Kroeber would emerge with his ideas quite unchanged.

2. The social historian Carl Schorske has written a sensitive and illuminating piece (1962) on similar responses among Viennese intellectuals before World War I.

3. This article also invited a response from Radcliffe-Brown, who was at one with Kroeber in chastising Malinowski for making reference to "human needs" as having something to do with culture. Radcliffe-Brown and Kroeber both detested the idea that such utilitarianism should ever have raised its head in anthropology.

4. The same can be said of Leslie White.

CHAPTER 3

1. This chapter draws on material included in my essay on Radin in the *International Encyclopedia of the Social Sciences* 13 (1968): 300–303.

I was neither a student nor a disciple of Radin, merely a colleague and friend who came to respect, and tried to understand, him and his work. The first time I met him was at Columbia in 1948. He had come to give one of the famous and, quite literally, seminal Wednesday seminars, having been particularly invited in order to respond to Leslie White's crusade against Boas, which had then reached its height. I had been assigned as White's graduate assistant that summer, and I was rather interested in what Radin had to say. He attacked White for his undiscriminating attacks on Boas, which were, and continued to be, intemperate, if not fanatical. At the same time, Radin analyzed White as a mechanical materialist, while subtly situating himself in the Marxist tradition; although this was never declaimed, it was strongly implied in his own work. The result was delightful, humorous, and devastating.

I saw him over the years from time to time and then established a closer collegial and personal relationship with him when he accepted our invitation to come to Brandeis in 1957, two years before his death.

2. His lack of careerist continuity and bureaucratic responsibility was held against him by many anthropologists. One even managed to strike a pejorative tone in the obituary he prepared.

3. Perhaps appropriately, he recorded Winnebago medicine rites in a hotel room in a midwestern city, since his informant, who had developed into an aboriginal anthropologist of sorts, was risking his life and possibly Radin's by imparting sacred information.

CHAPTER 4

1. This chapter covers some of the same ground as my introductions to the symposium *Man and Culture* (Firth 1957) and to the translation of his field diaries, but focuses more specifically on Malinowski's theories. I am indebted to Phyllis Kaberry, Audrey Richards, and other colleagues for help at various times in preparing this memoir. I have also been encouraged by audiences at the New York Academy of Sci-

ences (1971) and the departments of anthropology at Chicago (1971), Cambridge (1973), and Berkeley and Davis (1974) to rewrite what was originally a lecture not intended for publication. I have given few biographical details of Malinowski here. These will be found in my article on Malinowski in the *Encyclopaedia Britannica* (15th ed., 1974) and that by Rhoda Metraux in the *International Encyclopedia of the Social Sciences* 9 (1968): 541–49. A full biographical study, using family correspondence and much other unpublished material, is being prepared by his daughter, Helena Wayne Malinowska.

2. Significant reviews of *A Diary in the Strict Sense of the Term* (1967), as by Anthony Forge (*New Society*, August 17, 1967), Clifford Geertz (*The New York Review of Books*, September 14, 1967), Audrey Richards (*Cambridge Review*, January 19, 1968), and George Stocking (*Journal of History of Behavioral Sciences* 4, April 1968), have brought out the relevance of Malinowski's reactions to the field situation.

3. I am indebted for information and an example of this stamp to Matthew Ciolek. Malinowski's portrait, flanked by a Trobriand yam house, also appears on a ten-cent stamp of the Territory of Papua and New Guinea, issued on August 19, 1970, as part of a celebration of the forty-second congress of the Australian and New Zealand Association for the Advancement of Science, held in Port Moresby.

4. See *Sex and Repression in Savage Society* (1927a: 113, 143, passim). H. A. Powell, in a detailed review of Trobriand evidence and Malinowski's interpretation of it, supports the orthodox Freudian position, using the telling argument that in Kiriwina such formal authority as is wielded over a small boy is exercised by his father, who is also his sexual rival with the mother. But the matter is complex and much depends on the weight placed on the personal affective as against jural components in the relationships (Powell 1969: 184–86). Michel Panoff, on the other hand, is impressed by Malinowski's model of the dynamics of a matrilineal family, in which he showed how the Melanesian facts corresponded to a logical transformation of the Freudian model in the different setting (Panoff 1972: 80–81; cf. Lombard 1972: 74–79).

5. These passages come from "A Glimpse of Malinowski in Retrospect" in the *Journal of the Anthropological Society of Oxford* 5 (1974): 104–8. I am indebted to Phyllis Kaberry for permission to reproduce them.

6. President Kenyatta has placed his acknowledgment on record in the preface to his book *Facing Mt. Kenya* (London: Martin Secker & Warburg, 1938, xvii). Malinowski wrote an introduction to this work.

7. Reprinted as chapter 9 of Gluckman 1963 (235–43). The review was published in slightly different form at two earlier dates.

8. Thurnwald 1921: 16, quoted in Malinowski 1926b: 24n. The page reference indicated by Malinowski is incorrect.

9. See foreword to Uberoi 1962. The foreword is by Max Gluckman and I. G. Cunnison, but I have attributed the most characteristic expressions to Gluckman alone. Cunnison and Gluckman later published a comment on their foreword (*American Anthropologist* 65 [1963]: 1135) emphasizing the accuracy of Malinowski's rich material and its "honest comprehensiveness." A brief account of a visit to the Trobriands in 1947 by the government anthropologist to the Territory of Papua and New Guinea gives vivid confirmation of Malinowski's description of the ritual respect paid to the Tabalu chief of Omarakana (see Charles Julius, "Malinowski's Trobriand Islands," *Journal of the Public*

Service of the Territory of Papua and New Guinea 2 (1960): 5–13, 57–64. This report does not appear in Uberoi's bibliography, nor does the analysis of ownership rights by Rudiger Schott, "Die Eigentumsrechte der Trobriand-Insulaner in Nordwest-Melanesien," *Anthropos* 53 (1958): 88–132.

10. An interesting sidelight on the influence of Malinowski in a literary field is given by René Étiemblé, who cites Malinowski on the definition and function of myth, noting with approval Malinowski's "excellent critique" of nature mythology and of the constructions of the historical school (Étiemblé 1961: 43, 407).

CHAPTER 5

1. This chapter grew out of a lecture I was invited to deliver at the Graduate Center of the City University of New York in 1976. I am indebted to Jacqueline Mintz and Sydel Silverman for very useful suggestions and editorial comments on earlier drafts.

2. Modell (1975, 1978) developed her interpretation of Benedict's work along parallel lines. We discovered our similar views when I sent her the transcript of the original lecture from which this chapter has been adapted. Modell later published a revised version of her dissertation (1983).

3. I confess that my memory of the matter is somewhat different. While the pamphlet was indeed denounced in Congress, one of the objections voiced by Congressman Andrew May of Kentucky was that Ad Reinhardt's cartoon showing Adam and Eve on page 4 depicted Adam with a navel. The real reasons why the pamphlet was denounced, of course, had to do with the position taken by the authors on the concept of race itself and on the equality of the races.

4. In retrospect, it strikes me that, whatever their attacks on anthropology, very few of our critics of the 1940s were offering alternative models for the study of humankind. Anthropology might have been considered romantic, irrelevant, unscientific, egalitarian— but hardly anyone thought at the time that humans were only complex computers, smart apes, genetic printouts, turf-conscious hippopotamuses, or terrestrial dolphins. The cries of outrage that once greeted the heresy that humankind was not unique apparently now greet the assertion that, in other regards, it is.

5. The Office of War Information, according to Margaret Mead (1959: 352).

CHAPTER 6

1. This chapter is based on a lecture delivered at the Graduate Center of the City University of New York. Although the present version departs from the original talk, it owes much to questions and comments from members of the audience. I am also indebted to Morton Fried, Sydel Silverman, and Eric Wolf for their reviews of the manuscript, and to Brian Ferguson for his continuing support and motivation.

2. Kroeber was a visiting professor at Columbia from 1948 to 1952.

3. A fuller coverage of Steward's career is given in my introduction to the volume *Evolution and Ecology* (Murphy 1977). That essay also presents a systematic overview of the totality of Steward's work.

CHAPTER 7

1. For reading an earlier draft of this chapter and giving me the benefit of their perceptive criticisms, I am indebted to Barbara Bode, Sydel Silverman, Mary Ann Harrell, Gertrude E. Dole, Elman R. Service, Christian E. Guksch, and Beth Dillingham. To Dillingham, coexecutor with me of Leslie White's literary works, I am especially grateful for making available to me the fruits of her extensive gleanings of White's letters and papers. The White materials have been deposited in the Bentley Historical Library, University of Michigan, Ann Arbor.

2. Morris Opler, in a disingenuous attempt to discredit White by exposing the Marxist roots of his historical materialism, wrote in 1961: "It is curious that our neo-evolutionists constantly acknowledge their debt to Darwin, Tylor, and Morgan and never have a word to say about the relation of their ideas to those of Marx, Engels, Bukharin, Plekhanov, Labriola, Suvorov, Lenin, Stalin, et al. Yet it is patent that their formulations are a great deal closer to those of Bukharin and, indeed, to those of any thoroughgoing materialist than they can ever be to those of Tylor or Morgan" (Opler 1961: 18). The irony of Opler's paper is that it purports to be a critique not of White at all, but of Betty Meggers. Indeed, in the eighteen pages of the article there is not a single mention of White by name.

3. This point has been made by others. Morton Fried, for example, remarked of White that "throughout his life, if anything characterized his work, it was the absence of the dialectic" (1976: 600); see also Harris (1968: 637). At least one Soviet anthropologist, S. N. Artanovskii, has pointed out the ways in which White falls short of being a true Marxist, and has described him as "a prisoner of various anti-Marxist evolutionary theories" (1964–1965: 26).

4. However, he appears to have been introduced to it by his older contemporaries Kroeber and Lowie: "I discovered the science [of culture] retrospectively, so to speak, from Kroeber's 'The Superorganic' (1917); Lowie's *Culture and Ethnology* (1917); then Tylor's first chapter of *Primitive Culture* (1871): 'The Science of Culture'" (White 1987).

5. As Service wrote: "although the oldest and by far the most eminent of the Michigan department's faculty, [White] was not the highest paid, having never 'played an offer'" (1976: 616n).

6. Robert F. Murphy has written that "the efforts of Leslie White . . . to revive the work of Morgan must rate as one of the most courageous intellectual stands ever taken by an anthropologist" (1977: 28). As for White's "nonconformist behavior," White told me that on one occasion Ruth Benedict had psychoanalyzed him to his face, as if his deviation from the established views of the profession must reflect some underlying personality disorder.

7. According to Esther Goldfrank, a number of Boas's friends and former students who were at the meeting "quickly rose to his defense." Boas himself was also in attendance, but: "The eighty-year-old dean of American anthropology alone seemed unmoved. When the session ended, he left the room surrounded by those closest to him, his silence louder than any biting retort" (Goldfrank 1978: 153). However, White salvaged some satisfaction from the occasion: He recalled that "later A. V. Kidder congratulated me upon my paper and said, in effect, that the Boas school 'had a good licking coming to them—and I hope you'll give it to them!'" (White 1987).

8. I do not know of a single student of White who calls what he is doing "neoevolutionism." Thus Melville Jacobs (1964: 29) is quite mistaken when he writes that followers of White "speak of themselves proudly as neo-evolutionists."

9. The article has been reprinted no fewer than nineteen times. If the reprinting of his articles is a measure of the stature of a scientist, then surely White towers in his profession, for a number of his articles have been reprinted half a dozen times or more. [Ed. note: these estimates of reprintings are only as of 1980].

10. The most explicit statement of this point of view is probably to be found in Vayda (1965: 4); see also Vayda and Rappaport (1968: 492–94).

11. Why did White recant his earlier view? Apparently because he became increasingly impressed with the cruelties that cultural systems, especially modern ones, have inflicted on the human species. As he expressed it: "Although they have provided man with food and the fire with which to cook it, huts and houses to protect him from the elements, games and dances to entertain him, gods and myths to beguile him, they have also slaughtered millions of men, women, and children in warfare, tortured and killed them in inquisitions, or burned them to death as witches. They have initiated or aggravated great plagues by urban congestion and unsanitary practices. The cultural systems brought into being and perpetuated by the Agricultural Revolution reduced the majority of mankind to slavery and serfdom, condemning them to a life of labor, privation, and piety." (1975: 10)

12. While he disliked Steward's brand of evolutionism, White, I think, respected him. One day in 1950 I happened to walk into White's office shortly after he had read the critical review by Steward of *The Science of Culture* (Steward 1950b). This review had followed on the heels of another critical one by C. W. M. Hart. White remarked that it didn't really bother him when a "Lilliputian" like Hart failed to understand the book, but he couldn't help being disappointed when someone of Steward's stature failed to do so.

13. The initial reluctance of archaeology to accept White stemmed from an ingrained antievolutionism, which characterized archaeology no less than ethnology. Thus, Gordon Willey and Jeremy Sabloff have written, "In the mid 1950s, when Willey and Phillips published their scheme for New World prehistory [in which they were careful to avoid speaking of evolutionary stages], cultural evolutionism was still largely proscribed in American anthropological circles" (1974: 178).

14. Moreover, there were new foes of White's philosophy abroad in the land against whom he might better have directed his arguments. But White, who later in life told me he hardly ever had time to read anymore, was unable to keep up with the latest developments in anthropology.

15. Among the things he did live to bring to publishable form were "The Fuel Revolution" and "Modern Capitalist Culture" (which were still in manuscript at the time of his death). Originally, these were to be the second and third parts of a single volume to be called "The Evolution of Culture." However, when he presented a manuscript of more than 1,000 pages to his publishers, they balked at its length. White then removed the second and third parts and had the first part published alone as *The Evolution of Culture* (1959a).

16. Elvin Hatch has even gone so far as to state, "White's Pueblo studies, even the latest, give little evidence of the theoretical side of his thought; they could have been written by any one of a number of Boasians who were dogmatic antievolutionists" (1973: 130).

17. Harris's unwillingness to give White any of the credit due him is seen again in his *Cultural Materialism* (1979). One wonders why it is that, in a book devoted entirely to cultural materialism, the only mention Harris can bring himself to make of White is to relegate him to the camp of the idealists for his "insistence that culture is a realm of symbols" (1979: 236).

CHAPTER 8

1. The paper was presented at the Conference on Anthropology and the Mediterranean, Laboratoire d'Ethnologie Mediterranee et Comparative, CNRS, in Aix-en-Provence, May 12–18, 1997, and published as "The Role of Robert Redfield: Communities, Peasants, Traditions" in *Anthropology and the Mediterranean,* ed. by Dionigi Albera, Anton Blok, and Christian Bromberger, 85–97 (Paris: Maisonneuve et Larose). It has been revised slightly by the editor of the present collection.

2. Tarn's original paper, for which his title was "The Literate and the Literary: Notes on the Anthropological Discourse of Robert Redfield," can be found in its entirety in the first edition of this book. It has been abridged by the editor for inclusion in this edition.

CHAPTER 9

1. Extracted from Rhoda Metraux, "Margaret Mead: A Biographical Sketch." *American Anthropologist* 82 (1980): 262–69; abridged by the editor. Reprinted by permission.

2. The lecture on which this section of the chapter is based was entitled "Margaret Mead in Retrospect: Some Lessons for our Time," presented at the Binghamton University Art Museum, Binghamton, New York, on December 6, 2001, as part of "A Commemoration of the Centenary of Margaret Mead's Birth."

REFERENCES

Aberle, David F. 1960. "The Influence of Linguistics on Early Culture and Personality Theory." In *Essays in the Science of Culture in Honor of Leslie A. White*, edited by Gertrude E. Dole and Robert L. Carneiro, 1–29. New York: Crowell.

APS (American Philosophical Society), Boas Archives. Philadelphia.
  1. Vita. Ms. post-gymnasium.
  2. Diary from Baffinland.
  3. Letter from Franz Boas to Ernst Boas, August 6, 1914.
  4. Letter from Max Yergan to Helene Boas Yampolsky.

Artanovskii, S. N. 1964–1965. "The Marxist Doctrine of Social Progress and the 'Cultural Evolution' of Leslie White." *Soviet Anthropology and Archaeology* 3: 21–30.

Asad, Talal, ed. 1973. *Anthropology and the Colonial Encounter.* London: Ithaca Press.

Barnes, Harry E. 1960. Foreword to *Essays in the Science of Culture in Honor of Leslie A. White*, edited by Gertrude E. Dole and Robert L. Carneiro, xi–xlvi. New York: Crowell.

Barth, Fredrik. 1983. *Sohar: Culture and Society in an Omani Town.* Baltimore, Md.: Johns Hopkins University Press.

———. 1987. *Cosmologies in the Making: A Generative Approach to Cultural Variation in Inner New Guinea.* Cambridge: Cambridge University Press.

Bateson, Gregory, and Margaret Mead. 1942. *Balinese Character: A Photographic Analysis.* Special Publications of the New York Academy of Sciences, vol. 2. New York: New York Academy of Sciences.

Beals, Ralph. 1953. "Acculturation." In *Anthropology Today*, edited by A. L. Kroeber, 621–41. Chicago: University of Chicago Press.

———. 1968. "Alfred L. Kroeber." In *International Encyclopedia of the Social Sciences* 8: 454–64.

Benedict, Ruth. 1934. *Patterns of Culture*. Boston and New York: Houghton Mifflin.

———. 1936. "Marital Property Rights in Bilateral Society." *American Anthropologist* 38: 368–73.

———. 1940. *Race, Science, and Politics*. New York: Modern Age.

———. 1941. "Race Problems in America." *Annals of the American Academy of Political and Social Sciences* 216: 73–78.

———. 1942. "Victory over Discrimination and Hate: Differences vs. Superiorities." *Frontiers of Democracy* 9: 81–82.

———. 1946a. *The Chrysanthemum and the Sword*. Boston: Houghton Mifflin.

———. 1946b. "The Study of Cultural Patterns in European Nations." *Transactions of the New York Academy of Sciences* 8 (8): 274–79.

———. 1947. (manuscript) "Postwar Race Prejudice." In *An Anthropologist at Work: Writings of Ruth Benedict*, by Margaret Mead, 361–68. Boston: Houghton Mifflin, 1959.

———. 1948. "Anthropology and the Humanities." *American Anthropologist* 50: 585–93.

Benedict, Ruth, and Gene Weltfish. 1943. *The Races of Mankind*. Public Affairs Pamphlet 85. New York: Public Affairs Committee.

Binford, Lewis R. 1972. *An Archaeological Perspective*. New York: Seminar Press.

Boas, Franz. 1897. "The Social Organization and the Secret Societies of the Kwakiutl Indians. Based on Personal Observations and on Notes Made by Mr. George Hunt." Annual Report of the National Museum, 1895, 311–738. Washington, D.C.: Government Printing Office.

———. 1899. "The Cephalic Index." *American Anthropologist* 1: 448–61.

———. 1901. *Kathlamet Texts*. Smithsonian Institution, Bureau of American Ethnology, Bulletin 26. Washington, D.C.: Government Printing Office.

———. 1910. "The Real Race Problem." *The Crisis* 1: 22–25. National Association for the Advancement of Colored People.

———. 1911a. *Changes in Bodily Form of Descendants of Immigrants*. Reports of the Immigration Commission. Senate Document 208, 61st Congress, Second Session. Washington, D.C.: Government Printing Office. (Reprinted in 1912 by Columbia University Press, New York.)

———. 1911b. *The Mind of Primitive Man*. New York: Macmillan.

———. 1927. *Primitive Art*. Oslo: H. Aschehoug.

———. 1928. *Anthropology and Modern Life*. New York: Norton.

———. 1930. "Anthropology." *Encyclopedia of the Social Sciences* 2: 73–110.

———. 1938a. "An Anthropologist's Credo." *Nation* 147: 201–4.

———. 1938b. Introduction to *General Anthropology,* edited by Franz Boas, 1–6. Boston: Heath.

———. 1940. *Race, Language, and Culture*. New York: Macmillan.

———. 1945. *Race and Democratic Society*. New York: Augustin.

Carneiro, Robert L. 1970. "A Theory of the Origin of the State." *Science* 169: 733–38.

———. 1974. "Herbert Spencer's *The Study of Sociology* and the Rise of Social Science in America." Proceedings of the American Philosophical Society 118: 540–54.

———. 2000. *The Muse of History and the Science of Culture*. New York: Kluwer Academic/Plenum Publishers.

———. 2003. *Evolutionism in Cultural Anthropology*. Boulder, Colo.: Westview Press.

Clifford, James, and George Marcus, eds. 1986. *Writing Culture: The Poetics and Politics of Ethnography*. Berkeley: University of California Press.

Codere, Helen. 1966. Introduction to *Franz Boas, Kwakiutl Ethnography*, edited by Helen Codere, xi–xxxii. Chicago: University of Chicago Press.

Cole, Douglas. 1999. *Franz Boas: The Early Years, 1858–1906*. Vancouver: Douglas & McIntyre; Seattle: University of Washington Press.

Darnell, Regna. 1990. *Edward Sapir: Linguist, Anthropologist, Humanist*. Berkeley: University of California Press.

———. 2001. *Invisible Genealogies: A History of Americanist Anthropology*. Lincoln: University of Nebraska Press.

Dewey, John. 1932. "Human Nature." *Encyclopedia of the Social Sciences* 7: 531–36.

Diamond, Stanley. 1974. *In Search of the Primitive: A Critique of Civilization*. New Brunswick, N.J.: Transaction Books.

Diamond, Stanley, ed. 1960. *Culture in History: Essays in Honor of Paul Radin*. New York: Columbia University Press.

———. 1979. *Toward a Marxist Anthropology*. The Hague and New York: Mouton Publishers.

Dillingham, Beth, and Robert L. Carneiro, eds. 1987. *Ethnological Essays/Leslie A. White*. Albuquerque: University of New Mexico Press.

Dillon, Wilton S. 1980. "Margaret Mead and Government." *American Anthropologist* 82: 319–39.

Dole, Gertrude E., and Robert L. Carneiro, eds. 1960. *Essays in the Science of Culture in Honor of Leslie A. White*. New York: Crowell.

Eggan, Fred. 1954. "Social Anthropology and the Method of Controlled Comparison." *American Anthropologist* 56: 743–63.

Elmendorf, W. W., and Alfred L. Kroeber. 1960. *The Structure of Twana Culture, with Comparative Notes on the Structure of Yurok Culture*. Research Studies, A Quarterly Publication of Washington State University, vol. 28, no. 3. Monograph supplement No. 2. Pullman: Washington State University Press.

Étiemblé, René. 1961. *Le mythe de Rimbaud: Structure du mythe*. Paris: Gallimard.

Evans-Pritchard, E. E. 1965. *Theories of Primitive Religion*. Oxford: Clarendon Press.

Firth, Raymond. 1929. *Primitive Economics of the New Zealand Maori*. London: George Routledge & Sons.

———. 1936. *We, The Tikopia: A Sociological Study of Kinship in Primitive Polynesia*. London: Allen & Unwin.

———. 1946. *Malay Fishermen: Their Peasant Economy*. London: Kegan Paul, Trench, Trubner.

———. 1951. *Elements of Social Organization*. London: Watts & Co.

———. 1964. *Essays on Social Organization and Values*. London School of Economics Monographs on Social Anthropology No. 28. London: Athlone Press.

———. 1975. "An Appraisal of Modern Social Anthropology." *Annual Review of Anthropology* 4: 1–25.

Firth, Raymond, ed. 1957. *Man and Culture: An Evaluation of the Work of Bronislaw Malinowski*. London: Routledge & Kegan Paul.

———. 1967. *Themes in Economic Anthropology*. London: Tavistock.

Flugel, J. C. 1921. *The Psycho-Analytic Study of the Family*. International Psycho-Analytical Library No. 3. London: International Psycho-Analytical Press.

Freeman, Derek. 1983. *Margaret Mead: The Making and Unmaking of an Anthropological Myth*. Cambridge: Harvard University Press.

———. 1999. *The Fateful Hoaxing of Margaret Mead: A Historical Analysis of her Samoan Research.* Boulder, Colo.: Westview Press.

Fried, Morton H. 1976. "Energy and the Evolution of Leslie A. White." *Reviews in Anthropology* 3: 592–600.

Geertz, Clifford. 1962. "Studies in Peasant Life: Community and Society." In *Biennial Review of Anthropology, 1961*, edited by B. J. Siegel, 1–41. Stanford, Calif.: Stanford University Press.

———. 1973. *The Interpretation of Cultures.* New York: Basic Books.

Gluckman, Max. 1955. *Custom and Conflict in Africa.* Oxford: Blackwell.

———. 1963. *Order and Rebellion in Tribal Africa.* London: Cohen & West.

Goldfrank, Esther S. 1978. *Notes on an Undirected Life: As One Anthropologist Tells It.* Queens College Publications in Anthropology No. 3. Flushing, N.Y.: Queens College Press.

Goodman, Alan, Deborah Heath, and Susan Lindee, eds. 2003. *Genetic Nature/Culture: Anthropology and Science Beyond the Two Culture Divide.* Berkeley: University of California Press.

Gregg, Dorothy, and Elgin Williams. 1948. "The Dismal Science of Functionalism." *American Anthropologist* 50: 594–611.

Hanssen, B. 1953. "Fields of Activity and Their Dynamics." *Transactions of the Westermarck Society* 2: 99–133.

Harris, Marvin. 1968. *The Rise of Anthropological Theory.* New York: Crowell. (Reprinted 1999, AltaMira Press, Walnut Creek, Calif.)

———. 1979. *Cultural Materialism: The Struggle for a Science of Culture.* New York: Random House. (Reprinted 1999, AltaMira Press, Walnut Creek, Calif.)

Hart, C. W. M. 1950. Review of *The Science of Culture* by Leslie A. White. *American Journal of Sociology* 56: 88.

Hatch, Elvin. 1973. *Theories of Man and Culture.* New York: Columbia University Press.

Hymes, Dell. 1961. "Alfred Louis Kroeber." *Language* 37: 1–28.

———. 1965. "Some North Pacific Coast Poems: A Problem in Anthropological Philology." *American Anthropologist* 67: 316–41.

Hymes, Dell, ed. 1969. *Reinventing Anthropology.* New York: Random House.

Jacobs, Melville. 1964. *Pattern in Cultural Anthropology.* Homewood, Ill.: Dorsey Press.

Kluckhohn, Clyde and Olaf Prufer. 1959. "Influences during the Formative Years." In *The Anthropology of Franz Boas: Essays on the Centennial of His Birth*, edited by Walter Goldschmidt, 4–28. American Anthropological Association, Memoirs No. 89. *American Anthropologist* 61, no. 5, part 2.

Kroeber, Alfred L. 1917. "The Superorganic." *American Anthropologist* 19: 163–213.

———. 1923. *Anthropology.* New York: Harcourt Brace. (Revised edition, 1948, as *Anthropology: Race, Language, Culture, Psychology, Prehistory.*)

———. 1925. *Handbook of the Indians of California.* Smithsonian Institution, Bureau of American Ethnology, Bulletin 78. Washington, D.C.: Government Printing Office.

———. 1935. "History and Science in Anthropology." *American Anthropologist* 37: 539–69.

———. 1939. *Cultural and Natural Areas of Native North America.* University of California Publications in American Archaeology and Ethnology, vol. 38. Berkeley: University of California Press.

———. 1943. "Franz Boas: The Man." In *Franz Boas 1858–1942*, by A. L. Kroeber et al., 5–26. American Anthropological Association Memoirs No. 61. *American Anthropologist* 45, no. 3, part 2.

———. 1944. *Configurations of Culture Growth*. Berkeley: University of California Press.

———. 1949. "An Authoritarian Panacea." *American Anthropologist* 51: 318–20.

———. 1952. *The Nature of Culture*. Chicago: University of Chicago Press.

———. 1957. *Style and Civilizations*. Ithaca, N.Y.: Cornell University Press.

———. 1959. Preface to *The Anthropology of Franz Boas*, edited by Walter Goldschmidt, v–vii. American Anthropological Association Memoirs No. 89. *American Anthropologist* 61, no. 5, part 2.

———. 1960a. "Statistics, Indo-European and Taxonomy." *Language* 36: 1–21.

———. 1960b. "Evolution, History, and Culture." In *Evolution after Darwin*, edited by Sol Tax, vol. 2, 1–16. Chicago: University of Chicago Press.

———. 1962. *A Roster of Civilizations and Culture*. Chicago: Aldine.

———. 1963. *An Anthropologist Looks at History*. Berkeley and Los Angeles: University of California Press.

Kroeber, Alfred L., and Clyde Kluckhohn. 1952. *Culture: A Critical Review of Concepts and Definitions*. Papers of the Peabody Museum of American Archaeology and Ethnology, Harvard University, vol. 47, no. 1. Cambridge, Mass.

Kroeber, Alfred L., and Jane Richardson. 1940. "Three Centuries of Women's Dress Fashions: A Quantitative Analysis." *University of California Anthropological Records* 5: 111–54.

Kroeber, Theodora. 1970. *Alfred Kroeber: A Personal Configuration*. Berkeley: University of California Press.

Kuper, Adam. 1973. *Anthropologists and Anthropology: The British School 1922–1972*. London: Allen Lane.

Langendoen, D. T. 1968. *The London School of Linguistics*. Cambridge, Mass.: MIT Press.

Leach, E. R. 1957. "The Epistemological Background to Malinowski's Empiricism." In *Man and Culture: An Evaluation of the Work of Bronislaw Malinowski*, edited by Raymond Firth, 119–37. London: Routledge & Kegan Paul.

Leslie, Charles. 1968. "Robert Redfield." In *International Encyclopedia of the Social Sciences* 13: 350–53.

———. 1976. "The Hedgehog and the Fox in Robert Redfield's Work and Career." In *American Anthropology, The Early Years*, 146–66. Proceedings of the American Ethnological Society, 1974. St. Paul, Minn.: West.

Lesser, Alexander. 1933. *The Pawnee Ghost Dance Hand Game*. Columbia University Contributions to Anthropology, vol. 16. New York: Columbia University Press. (Reprinted, 1978, University of Wisconsin Press, Madison.)

———. 1939. "Research Procedures and Laws of Culture." *Philosophy of Science* 6: 345–55.

———. 1952. "Evolution in Social Anthropology." *Southwestern Journal of Anthropology* 8 :134–46.

———. 1961a. "Education and the Future of Tribalism in the United States: The Case of the American Indian." *Social Service Review* 35: 135–43. (Reprinted as "The Right Not to Assimilate," in *Readings in Anthropology*, edited by Morton H. Fried, vol. 2. New York: Crowell.)

———. 1961b. "Social Fields and the Evolution of Society." *Southwestern Journal of Anthropology* 17: 40–48.

———. 1968. "Franz Boas." In *International Encyclopedia of the Social Sciences* 2: 99–110.

Lévi-Strauss, Claude. 1950. "Introduction à l'oeuvre de Marcel Mauss." In *Sociologie et anthropologie*, edited by Marcel Mauss. Paris: Presses Universitaires de France.

———. 1962. *Le Totémisme aujourd'hui*. Paris: Presses Universitaires de France.

———. 1973. *Anthropologie structurale deux*. Paris: Plon.

Linton, Adelin, and Charles Wagley. 1971. *Ralph Linton*. New York and London: Columbia University Press.

Lombard, Jacques. 1972. *L'Anthropologie Britannique contemporaine*. Paris: Presses Universitaires de France.

Lowie, Robert H. 1917. *Culture and Ethnology*. New York: Douglas C. McMurtrie.

———. 1920. *Primitive Society*. New York: Boni & Liveright.

———. 1937. *The History of Ethnological Theory*. New York: Rinehart.

———. 1944. "Franz Boas, 1858–1942." *Journal of American Folklore* 57: 59–64.

———. 1946a. "Evolution in Cultural Anthropology: A Reply to Leslie White." *American Anthropologist* 48: 223–33.

———. 1946b. "Professor White and 'Anti-Evolutionist' Schools." *Southwestern Journal of Anthropology* 2: 240–41.

Mabee, Carleton. 1987. "Margaret Mead and Behavioral Scientists in World War II: Problems in Responsibility, Truth, and Effectiveness." *Journal of the History of the Behavioral Sciences* 23: 3–13.

Malinowski, Bronislaw. 1916. "Baloma: Spirits of the Dead in the Trobriand Islands." *Journal of the Royal Anthropological Institute* 46: 353–430.

———. 1922. *Argonauts of the Western Pacific*. London: Routledge.

———. 1923. "The Problem of Meaning in Primitive Languages." In *The Meaning of Meaning*, edited by C. K. Ogden and I. A. Richards, 451–510. London: K. Paul, Trench, Trubuer.

———. 1926a. "Address on Anthropology and Social Hygiene." In *Foundations of Social Hygiene*, 54–84. London: British Social Hygiene Council.

———. 1926b. *Crime and Custom in Savage Society*. London: Kegan Paul.

———. 1926c. *Myth in Primitive Psychology*. London: Kegan Paul.

———. 1927a. *Sex and Repression in Savage Society*. London: Kegan Paul.

———. 1927b. *The Father in Primitive Psychology*. London: Routledge.

———. 1929. *The Sexual Life of Savages in North-Western Melanesia*. London: Routledge.

———. 1935. *Coral Gardens and Their Magic*. 2 vols. London: Allen & Unwin.

———. 1936. Preface to *We, the Tikopia*, by Raymond Firth, vii–xi. London: Allen & Unwin.

———. 1939. "The Group and the Individual in Functional Analysis." *American Journal of Sociology* 44: 938–64.

———. 1944. *A Scientific Theory of Culture*. Chapel Hill: University of North Carolina Press.

———. 1945. *The Dynamics of Culture Change*, edited by Phyllis M. Kaberry. New Haven, Conn.: Yale University Press.

———. 1947. *Freedom and Civilization*. London: Allen & Unwin.

——. 1967. *A Diary in the Strict Sense of the Term.* New York: Harcourt, Brace & World.

Marcus, George E., and Michael Fischer. 1986. *Anthropology as Cultural Critique: An Experimental Moment in the Human Sciences.* Chicago: University of Chicago Press.

Marriott, McKim. 1955. "Little Communities in an Indigenous Civilization." In *Village India: Studies in the Little Community,* edited by McKim Marriott, 171–222. American Anthropological Association Memoirs No. 83.

Mauss, Marcel. 1923–24. "Essai sur le don: forme archaique de l'échange." *L'Année Sociologique,* n.s., 1: 30–186.

McDowell, Nancy. 1980. "The Oceanic Ethnography of Margaret Mead." *American Anthropologist* 82: 278–302.

Mead, Margaret. 1928a. *An Inquiry into the Question of Cultural Stability in Polynesia.* Columbia University Contributions to Anthropology, vol. 9. New York: Columbia University Press.

——. 1928b. *Coming of Age in Samoa: A Psychological Study of Youth for Western Civilization.* New York: New American Library.

——. 1930a. *Social Organization of Manua.* Bernice P. Bishop Museum Bulletin No. 76. Honolulu: Bernice P. Bishop Museum.

——. 1930b. *Growing Up in New Guinea: A Comparative Study of Primitive Education.* New York: William Morrow and Company.

——. 1934. "Kinship in the Admiralty Islands." Anthropological Papers of the American Museum of Natural History 34: 181–358.

——. 1935. *Sex and Temperament in Three Primitive Societies.* New York: William Morrow and Company.

——. 1949. *Male and Female: A Study of the Sexes in a Changing World.* New York: William Morrow and Company.

——. 1959. *An Anthropologist at Work: Writings of Ruth Benedict.* Boston: Houghton Mifflin.

——. 1964. *Anthropology: A Human Science.* Princeton, N.J.: Van Nostrand.

——. 1965 [orig. 1942]. *And Keep Your Powder Dry.* New York: William Morrow and Company.

——. 1966 [orig. 1956]. *New Lives for Old: Cultural Transformation—Manus, 1928–1953.* New York: Dell Publishing Company. (1956 edition by William Morrow, New York.)

——. 1972. *Blackberry Winter: My Earlier Years.* New York: Morrow.

——. 1974. *Ruth Benedict.* New York and London: Columbia University Press.

——. 1977. *Letters from the Field, 1925–1975.* Edited by Ruth Nanda Anshen. World Perspectives, vol. 52. New York: Harper and Row.

Mead, Margaret, and Rhoda Metraux, eds. 1953. *The Study of Culture at a Distance.* Chicago: University of Chicago Press.

Mead, Margaret, and Martha Wolfenstein, eds. 1955. *Childhood in Contemporary Cultures.* Chicago: University of Chicago Press.

Metraux, Rhoda. 1968. "Bronislaw Malinowski." In *International Encyclopedia of the Social Sciences,* 9: 541–49.

Metraux, Rhoda, and Margaret Mead. 1954. *Themes in French Culture: A Preface to a Study of French Community.* Stanford, Calif.: Stanford University Press.

Mintz, Sidney W. 1960. *Worker in the Cane: A Puerto Rican Life History.* Yale Caribbean Series, vol. 2. New Haven, Conn.: Yale University Press.

———. 1974. *Caribbean Transformations*. Chicago: Aldine.

———. 1985. *Sweetness and Power: The Place of Sugar in Modern History*. New York: Viking.

———. 1996. *Tasting Food, Tasting Freedom: Excursions into Eating, Culture, and the Past*. Boston: Beacon Press.

Mintz, Sidney W., ed. 1985. *History, Evolution and the Concept of Culture: Selected Essays of Alexander Lesser*. New York: Cambridge University Press.

Modell, Judith. 1975. "Ruth Benedict, Anthropologist: The Reconciliation of Science and Humanism." In *Toward a Science of Man*, edited by T. H. H. Thoreson, 183–203. The Hague: Mouton.

———. 1978. "A Biographical Study of Ruth Fulton Benedict." Ph.D. dissertation, University of Minnesota.

———. 1983. *Ruth Benedict: Patterns of a Life*. Philadelphia: University of Pennsylvania Press.

Morgan, Lewis H. 1851. *League of the Ho-de-no-sau-nee, or Iroquois*. Rochester, N.Y.: Sage and Broa.

———. 1877. *Ancient Society*. New York: World Publishing.

Murdock, George P. 1949. *Social Structure*. New York: Macmillan.

Murphy, Robert F. 1958. *Mundurucú Religion*. University of California Publications in American Archaeology and Ethnology, vol. 49, no. 1. Berkeley.

———. 1960. *Headhunter's Heritage: Social and Economic Change among the Mundurucú Indians*. Berkeley: University of California Press.

———. 1971. *The Dialectics of Social Life*. New York and London: Basic Books.

———. 1972. *Robert H. Lowie*. New York and London: Columbia University Press.

———. 1977. Introduction to *Evolution and Ecology*, by Julian Steward, edited by Jane C. Steward and Robert F. Murphy, 1–39. Urbana, Ill.: University of Illinois Press.

———. 1987. *The Body Silent: The Different World of the Disabled*. New York: H. Holt.

Murphy, Robert F., and Leonard Kasdan. 1959. "The Structure of Parallel Cousin Marriage." *American Anthropologist* 61: 17–29.

Murphy, Robert F., and Yolanda Murphy. 1960. *Shoshone-Bannock Economy and Society*. University of California Publications in Anthropological Records, vol. 21. Berkeley.

Murphy, Robert F., and Julian H. Steward. 1956. "Tappers and Trappers: Parallel Processes of Acculturation." *Economic Development and Cultural Change* 4: 335–55.

Opler, Morris E. 1961. "Cultural Evolution, Southern Athapaskans, and Chronology in Theory." *Southwestern Journal of Anthropology* 17: 1–20.

———. 1962. "Two Converging Lines of Influence in Cultural Evolutionary Theory." *American Anthropologist* 64: 524–47.

Panoff, Michel. 1972. *Bronislaw Malinowski*. Paris: Payot.

Parezo, Nancy J., Don D. Fowler, and Sydel Silverman. 2003. "Preserving the Anthropological Record: A Decade of CoPAR Initiatives." *Current Anthropology* 44: 111–16.

Powell, H. A. 1960. "Competitive Leadership in Trobriand Political Organization." *Journal of the Royal Anthropological Institute* 90: 118–45.

———. 1969. "Genealogy, Residence, and Kinship in Kiriwina." *Man* 4: 177–202.

Radin, Paul. 1913. "On Ojibwa Work, 1913." *Summary Reports*, Canada, Geological Survey, 374.

———. 1919. *The Genetic Relationship of the North American Indian Languages*. University of California Publications in American Archaeology and Ethnology, vol. 14, no. 5. Berkeley: University of California Press.

———. 1920. *The Autobiography of an American Indian*. University of California Publications in American Archaeology and Ethnology, vol. 16, no. 7. Berkeley: University of California Press.

———. 1923. *The Winnebago Tribe*. Bureau of American Ethnology, Annual Report No. 37, 1915–1916. Washington, D.C.: Government Printing Office.

———. 1924. *Wappo Texts*. University of California Publications in American Archaeology and Ethnology, vol. 19, no. 1. Berkeley: University of California Press.

———. 1927. *Primitive Man as Philosopher*. New York: Appleton.

———. 1929a. "Huave Texts." *International Journal of American Linguistics* 5: 1–56.

———. 1929b. *A Grammar of the Wappo Language*. University of California Publications in American Archaeology and Ethnology, vol. 27. Berkeley: University of California Press.

———. 1930. "A Preliminary Sketch of the Zapotec Language." *Language* 6: 64–85.

———. 1933a. *The Method and Theory of Ethnology: An Essay in Criticism*. New York: McGraw-Hill.

———. 1933b. "Mixe Texts." *Journal de la Société des Americanistes de Paris* 25: 41–64.

———. 1933c. "Notes on the Tlappanecan Language of Guerrero." *International Journal of American Linguistics* 8: 45–72.

———. 1934. *The Racial Myth*. New York: McGraw-Hill.

———. 1937. *Primitive Religion: Its Nature and Origin*. New York: Dover.

———. 1944. "The Classification of the Languages of Mexico." *Tlalocan* 1: 259–65.

———. 1945. *The Road of Life and Death: A Ritual Drama of the American Indians*. Bollingen Series No. 5. New York: Pantheon.

———. 1953. *The World of Primitive Man*. New York: Schuman.

Redfield, Robert. 1930. *Tepoztlán, A Mexican Village: A Study of Folk Life*. Chicago: University of Chicago Press.

———. 1941. *The Folk Culture of Yucatan*. Chicago: University of Chicago Press.

———. 1950. *A Village that Chose Progress: Chan Kom Revisited*. Chicago: University of Chicago Press.

———. 1953. *The Primitive World and Its Transformations*. Ithaca, N.Y.: Cornell University Press.

———. 1955. *The Little Community: Viewpoints for the Study of a Human Whole*. Chicago: University of Chicago Press.

———. 1956. *Peasant Society and Culture: An Anthropological Approach to Civilizations*. Chicago: University of Chicago Press.

———. 1960. "Thinker and Intellectual in Primitive Society." In *Culture in History: Essays in Honor of Paul Radin*, edited by Stanley Diamond, 3–18. New York: Columbia University Press.

———. 1962. *Human Nature and the Study of Society: The Papers of Robert Redfield*, vol. 1. Edited by Margaret Park Redfield. Chicago: University of Chicago Press.

———. 1963. *The Social Uses of Social Science: The Papers of Robert Redfield*, vol. 2, Edited by Margaret Park Redfield. Chicago: University of Chicago Press.

Redfield, Robert, and Milton B. Singer. 1954. "The Cultural Role of Cities " *Economic Development and Cultural Change* 3: 53–73.

Redfield, Robert, and Alfonso Villa Rojas. 1934. *Chan Kom: A Maya Village*. Carnegie Institution of Washington, Publication No. 448. Washington, D.C.

Richards, Audrey. 1943. "Bronislaw Kasper Malinowski: Born 1884–Died 1942." *Man* 43: 1–4.

Sahlins, Marshall D. 1958. *Social Stratification in Polynesia*. Seattle: University of Washington Press.

Sanday, Peggy Reeves. 1980. "Margaret Mead's View of Sex Roles in Her Own and Other Societies." *American Anthropologist* 82: 340–48.

Schorske, Carl E. 1962. "Schnitzler und Hofmannsthal." *Wort und Wahrheit* 17: 367–81.

Service, Elman R. 1976. "Leslie Alvin White, 1900–1975." *American Anthropologist* 78: 612–17.

Silverman, Sydel. 1975. *Three Bells of Civilization: The Life of an Italian Hill Town*. New York: Columbia University Press.

———. 1979. "On the Uses of History in Anthropology: The Palio of Siena." *American Ethnologist* 6: 413–46.

———. 2002. *The Beast on the Table: Conferencing with Anthropologists*. Walnut Creek, Calif.: AltaMira Press.

Silverman, Sydel, and Nancy Parezo, eds. 1995. *Preserving the Anthropological Record*. 2d ed. New York: Wenner-Gren Foundation.

Simpson, George Gaylord. 1949. *The Meaning of Evolution*. New Haven: Yale University Press.

Singer, Milton B. 1976. "Robert Redfield's Development of a Social Anthropology of Civilizations." In *American Anthropology, the Early Years*, 187–260. Proceedings of the American Ethnological Society, 1974. St. Paul, Minn.: West.

Smith, Carol. 1984. "Local History in Global Contexts: Social and Economic Transitions in Western Guatemala." *Comparative Studies in Society and History* 26: 193–228.

Smith, Marian W. 1959. "Boas' 'Natural History' Approach to Field Method." In *The Anthropology of Franz Boas*, edited by Walter Goldschmidt, 46–60. American Anthropological Association Memoirs No. 89. *American Anthropologist* 61, no. 5, part 2.

Spencer, Herbert. 1873. *The Study of Sociology*. New York: Appleton.

Starr, Betty. 1954. "Levels of Community Relations." *American Journal of Sociology* 60: 125–35.

Stern, Bernhard J. 1931. *Lewis Henry Morgan, Social Evolutionist*. Chicago: University of Chicago Press.

Steward, Julian H. 1936. "The Economic and Social Basis of Primitive Bands." In *Essays on Anthropology in Honor of Alfred Louis Kroeber*, edited by Robert H. Lowie, 311–50. Berkeley: University of California Press.

———. 1937. "Ecological Aspects of Southwestern Society." *Anthropos* 32: 87–104.

———. 1938. *Basin-Plateau Aboriginal Sociopolitical Groups*. Smithsonian Institution, Bureau of American Ethnology, Bulletin 120. Washington, D.C.: Government Printing Office.

———. 1941. "Determinism in Primitive Society?" *Scientific Monthly* 53: 491–501.

———. 1949. "Cultural Causality and Law: A Trial Formulation of the Development of Early Civilizations." *American Anthropologist* 51: 1–27.

———. 1950a. *Area Research: Theory and Practice*. Bulletin 63. New York: Social Science Research Council.

———. 1950b. Review of *The Science of Culture*, by Leslie A. White. *Scientific Monthly* 70: 208–9.

———. 1960. Review of *The Evolution of Culture*, by Leslie A. White. *American Anthropologist* 62: 144–48.

———. 1973. *Alfred Kroeber*. New York: Columbia University Press.

———. 1977. *Evolution and Ecology: Essays on Social Transformation*, edited by Jane C. Steward and Robert F. Murphy. Urbana: University of Illinois Press.

Steward, Julian H., ed. 1946–1959. *Handbook of South American Indians*. 7 vols. Smithsonian Institution, Bureau of American Ethnology, Bulletin 143. Washington, D.C.: Government Printing Office.

Stocking, George W., Jr. 1968a. "Franz Boas and the Culture Concept in Historical Perspective." In *Race, Culture, and Evolution: Essays in the History of Anthropology*, edited by George W. Stocking Jr., 195–233. New York: Free Press.

———. 1968b. "The Scientific Reaction against Cultural Anthropology, 1917–1920." In *Race, Culture, and Evolution: Essays in the History of Anthropology*, edited by George W. Stocking Jr., 270–307. New York: Free Press.

———. 1992. *The Ethnographer's Magic and Other Essays in the History of Anthropology*. Madison: University of Wisconsin Press.

———. 2000. "'Do Good, Young Man': Sol Tax and the World Mission of Liberal Democratic Anthropology." In *Excluded Ancestors, Inventible Traditions: Essays Toward a More Inclusive History of Anthropology*, edited by Richard Handler, 171–264. History of Anthropology, vol. 9. Madison: University of Wisconsin Press.

Symmons-Symonolewicz, Konstantin. 1958. "Bronislaw Malinowski: An Intellectual Profile." *Polish Review* 3: 1–22.

Tarn, Nathaniel. 1964. *Old Savage/Young City*. London: Cape.

———. 1976. "The Heraldic Vision: Some Cognitive Models for Ethnopoetics." *Alcheringa: Ethnopoetics*, n.s., 2: 23–41.

———. 2002. *Selected Poems: 1950–2000*. Middletown, Conn.: Wesleyan University Press.

Tarn, Nathaniel, and Martín Prechtel. 1998. *Scandals in the House of Birds: Shamans and Priests on Lake Atitlán*. New York: Marsilio.

Thomas, William I., and Florian Znaniecki. 1958 [orig. 1918–1920]. *The Polish Peasant in Europe and America*. 2 vols. New York: Dover.

Thurnwald, Richard. 1921. *Die Gemeinde der Banaro*. Stuttgart: F. Enke. (English translation: *Banaro Society*, published as American Anthropological Association Memoirs, vol. 3, no. 4, 1916).

Tylor, Edward. 1871. *Primitive Culture*. London: John Murray.

Uberoi, J. P. Singh. 1962. *Politics of the Kula Ring: An Analysis of the Findings of Bronislaw Malinowski*. Manchester: Manchester University Press.

Van Doren, Mark. 1945. Foreword to *The Road of Life and Death*, by Paul Radin. New York: Pantheon.

Vayda, Andrew P. 1965. "Anthropologists and Ecological Problems." In *Man, Culture, and Animals*, edited by Anthony Leeds and Andrew P. Vayda, 1–5. American Association for the Advancement of Science, Pub. no. 78. Washington, D.C.

Vayda, Andrew P., and Roy A. Rappaport. 1968. "Ecology: Cultural and Noncultural." In *Introduction to Cultural Anthropology*, edited by James A. Clifton, 476–97. Boston: Houghton Mifflin.

Wakin, Eric. 1992. *Anthropology Goes to War: Professional Ethics & Counterinsurgency in Thailand*. University of Wisconsin, Center for Southeast Asian Studies, Monograph 7. Madison.

Washburn, Sherwood L. 1963. "The Study of Race." *American Anthropologist* 65: 521–32.

Weber, Max. 1946 [orig. 1922–1923]. "The Social Psychology of the World Religions." In *From Max Weber: Essays in Sociology*, edited by H. H. Gerth and C. Wright Mills, 267–301. New York: Oxford University Press.

Weiner, Lynn. 1969. "Leslie White, Ecclesiastical Brimstone Scientist." *Michigan Daily* (Ann Arbor), March 23.

White, Leslie A. 1925. "Personality and Culture." *Open Court* 39: 145–49.

———. 1931. Review of *Lewis Henry Morgan, Social Evolutionist*, by Bernhard J. Stern. *American Journal of Sociology* 37: 483.

———. 1932a. "The Acoma Indians." U.S. Bureau of American Ethnology, 47th Annual Report, 1929–1930, 117–192.

———. 1932b. *The Pueblo of San Felipe*. American Anthropological Association Memoirs No. 38.

———. 1935. *The Pueblo of Santo Domingo, New Mexico*. American Anthropological Association Memoirs No. 43.

———. 1938. "Science is *Sciencing*." *Philosophy of Science* 5: 369–89.

———. 1939. "A Problem in Kinship Terminology." *American Anthropologist* 41: 566–73.

———. 1940a. "The Symbol: The Origin and Basis of Human Behavior." *Philosophy of Science* 7: 451–63.

———. 1942a. *The Pueblo of Santa Ana, New Mexico*. American Anthropological Association, Memoirs No. 60.

———. 1942b. "Lewis H. Morgan's Journal of a Trip to Southwestern Colorado and New Mexico, June 21 to August 7, 1878." *American Antiquity* 8: 1–26.

———. 1943. "Energy and the Evolution of Culture." *American Anthropologist* 45: 335–56.

———. 1944. "Morgan's Attitude Toward Religion and Science." *American Anthropologist* 46: 218–30.

———. 1945a. "History, Evolutionism, and Functionalism: Three Types of Interpretation of Culture." *Southwestern Journal of Anthropology* 1: 221–48.

———. 1945b. "Diffusion vs. Evolution: An Anti-Evolutionist Fallacy." *American Anthropologist* 47: 339–56.

———. 1946. "Kroeber's *Configurations of Culture Growth*." *American Anthropologist* 48: 78–93.

———. 1947a. "Evolutionary Stages, Progress, and the Evaluation of Cultures." *Southwestern Journal of Anthropology* 3: 165–92.

———. 1947b. "Evolutionism and Anti-Evolutionism in American Ethnological Theory." *Calcutta Review* 104: 147–59; 105: 29–40, 161–74.

———. 1947c. "Evolutionism in Cultural Anthropology: A Rejoinder." *American Anthropologist* 49: 400–413.

———. 1947d. "The Expansion of the Scope of Science." *Journal of the Washington Academy of Sciences* 37: 181–210.

———. 1948a. "Man's Control over Civilization: An Anthropocentric Illusion." *Scientific Monthly* 66: 235–47.

———. 1948b. "The Definition and Prohibition of Incest." *American Anthropologist* 50: 416–35.

———. 1949a. *The Science of Culture.* New York: Farrar, Straus.

———. 1949b. "Ethnological Theory." In *Philosophy for the Future; The Quest of Modern Materialism,* edited by Roy Wood Sellars, V. J. McGill, and Marvin Farber, 357–84. New York: Macmillan.

———. 1951. "Lewis H. Morgan's Western Field Trips." *American Anthropologist* 53: 11–18.

———. 1957. "How Morgan Came to Write *Systems of Consanguinity and Affinity.*" *Papers of the Michigan Academy of Sciences, Arts, and Letters* 42: 257–68.

———. 1959a. *The Evolution of Culture.* New York: McGraw-Hill.

———. 1959b. "The Concept of Evolution in Cultural Anthropology." In *Evolution and Anthropology: A Centennial Appraisal,* edited by Betty J. Meggers, 106–25. Washington D.C.: Anthropological Society of Washington.

———. 1959c. "The Concept of Culture." *American Anthropologist* 61: 227–51.

———. 1960a. Foreword to *Evolution and Culture,* by Marshall D. Sahlins and Elman R. Service, v–xii. Ann Arbor: University of Michigan Press.

———. 1960b. "Four Stages in the Evolution of Minding." In *Evolution after Darwin,* edited by Sol Tax. Vol 2, *The Evolution of Man,* 239–53. Chicago: University of Chicago Press.

———. 1962. *The Pueblo of Sia, New Mexico.* Smithsonian Institution, Bureau of American Ethnology, Bulletin 184. Washington, D.C.: Government Printing Office.

———. 1963. *The Ethnography and Ethnology of Franz Boas.* Texas Memorial Museum, Bulletin 6. Austin: Texas Memorial Museum, Museum of the University of Texas.

———. 1964. Introduction to *Ancient Society,* by Lewis H. Morgan, xiii–xlii. Cambridge: Belknap Press of Harvard University Press.

———. 1966. *The Social Organization of Ethnological Theory.* Rice University Studies, vol. 52, no. 4. Houston, Tex.: William Marsh Rice University.

———. 1969. *The Science of Culture.* 2d ed. New York: Farrar, Straus and Giroux.

———. 1973. *The Acoma Indians.* Forty-Seventh Annual Report of the Bureau of American Ethnology, 1929–1930, with a new publisher's preface and a new foreword by the author. Glorieta, N.Mex.: Rio Grande Press.

———. 1975. *The Concept of Cultural Systems.* New York: Columbia University Press.

———. 1987. Introductory Remarks to *Ethnological Essays/Leslie A. White,* edited by Beth Dillingham and Robert L. Carneiro. Albuquerque: University of New Mexico Press.

———. n.d. Unpublished manuscript by Leslie White about his boyhood in Kansas. Dated Elkland, Pa., October 3, 1952. On deposit in the Michigan Historical Collection, Bentley Historical Library, University of Michigan, Ann Arbor.

White, Leslie A., ed. 1937. "Extracts from the European Travel Journal of Lewis H. Morgan." *Rochester Historical Society Publications* 16 (2): 219–389.

———. 1940b. *Pioneers in American Anthropology, The Bandelier–Morgan Letters 1873–1883.* 2 vols. Albuquerque: University of New Mexico Press.

———. 1959d. *Lewis Henry Morgan: The Indian Journals, 1859–1862.* Ann Arbor: University of Michigan Press.

Willey, Gordon R., and Jeremy A. Sabloff. 1974. *A History of American Archaeology*. San Francisco: Freeman.

Wilson, Edward O. 1975. *Sociobiology: The New Synthesis*. Cambridge: Harvard University Press.

Wolf, Eric R. 1966. *Peasants*. Englewood Cliffs, N.J.: Prentice-Hall.

———. 1969a. *Peasant Wars of the Twentieth Century*. New York: Harper and Row.

———. 1969b. "American Anthropologists and American Society." In *Concepts and Assumptions in Contemporary Anthropology*, edited by Stephen A. Tyler, 3–11. Southern Anthropological Society Proceedings, no. 3. Athens: University of Georgia Press.

———. 1982. *Europe and the People without History*. Berkeley and Los Angeles: University of California Press.

———. 1999. *Envisioning Power: Ideologies of Dominance and Crisis*. Berkeley and Los Angeles: University of California Press.

———. 2001. *Pathways of Power: Building an Anthropology of the Modern World*. Berkeley and Los Angeles: University of California Press.

Yans-McLaughlin, Virginia. 1986. "Science, Democracy, and Ethics: Mobilizing Culture and Personality for World War II." In *Malinowski, Rivers, Benedict and Others: Essays on Culture and Personality*, edited by George W. Stocking Jr., 184–217. History of Anthropology, vol. 4. Madison: University of Wisconsin Press.

INDEX

acculturation, 145, 180–81, 193
adaptation, 38–39, 43, 138, 164, 165, 166
Adler, Alfred, 59
Algonkian Indians, 141, 149
Althwaite, Leonard, 55
Amahuaca, 175
American Anthropological Association
    (AAA), 3, 13–15, 24, 36, 44, 105,
    116–17, 145, 149, 158, 161, 167–68,
    199, 216, 217
American Ethnological Society, 1, 18
American Indians, 1, 2, 21, 24–25, 27, 35,
    43–44, 46, 63, 65, 103, 111, 125–26,
    130, 133–34, 137, 140, 145, 151; *see*
    also under specific groups
American Museum of Natural History, xv,
    xviii, 9, 22, 125, 175, 202, 204, 206,
    215
American school, *see under specific*
    individuals
Anaguta, 73
Année sociologique, L' (journal), 83, 90
Anthropological Society of Washington,
    1, 13–15, 162
anthropology, development of: in Britain,
    1, 75–76, 77, 88–89; in the United

States, xv–xvi, 1–3, 4–5, 27–28, 51, 76,
    103–4, 107, 125–26, 151–52, 177–78,
    198–200, 207–8, 215
applied anthropology, 87–88, 119, 205,
    216, 219
Arapaho, 29
archaeology, 3, 21–22, 126, 166, 181, 230
Arensberg, Conrad M., 222
Artanovskii, S. N., 229
Association on American Indian Affairs
    (AAIA), 24–25
Association for the Study of Negro Life
    and History, 16
Australian aborigines, 68, 75, 85, 87, 161
autobiography and life history, 51, 54, 62,
    65, 115–17, 122
Atkinson, J. J., 86

Bachofen, J. J., 1, 101
Baldwin, James, 72
Barnard College, 203, 208
Bames, Harry Elmer, 155, 172
Barotse, 94
Barrett, S. A., 44
Barth, Fredrik, 186
Bastian, Adolf, 2

SOAS LIBRARY